"Children, darkness reigns over the whole world. People are attracted by many things and they forget about the more important. Light won't reign in the world until people accept Jesus, until they live his words, which is the Word of the Gospel.

"Dear children, this is the reason for my presence among you for such a long time: to lead you on the path of Jesus. I want to save you and, through you, to save the whole world. Many people now live without faith; some don't even want to hear about Jesus, but they still want peace and satisfaction! Children, here is the reason why I need your prayer: prayer is the only way to save the human race."

The Blessed Virgin Mary to Visionaries at Medjugorje, Bosnia-Herzegovina, July 30, 1987

Our Lady of Medjugorje, Queen of Peace

Above is a photograph of a statue of the Blessed Virgin Mary, Our Lady of Medjugorje, Queen of Peace, overlooking the twin towers of St. James Church in Medjugorje, Bosnia-Herzegovina. It is a marvelous statue which faithfully reproduces Our Lady according to the descriptions of the visionaries of her apparitions in Medjugorje. The front cover shows a painting similar to the statue with the word *MIR*, that means peace in Croatian. May all who read my book find her peace.

On the next page, is a photograph of Richard Bingold, the faithful guardian of this statue from 1994 until 2019. Richard carried it on missionary journeys throughout the world to promote the messages of peace from the Queen of Peace. He made 85 pilgrimages to Medjugorje.

Dedication

This book is dedicated to Richard Bingold.
May he rest in peace!

In 2018, Richard Bingold carried the statue of Our Lady of Medjugorje, as shown on the opposite page, to South Africa on his last missionary journey. After an exhausting journey and return flight to Boston, Massachusetts, Richard packed the statue in his car and began his drive home to Vermont.

On his way home, on October 28, he fell asleep at the wheel and had a horrific accident. The statute survived, but Richard did not and, on June 24, 2019, the Feast of St. John the Baptist and the 38th anniversary of the first apparition of the Queen of Peace at Medjugorje, Richard died from complications arising from his injuries.

One day, while on a pilgrimage at Medjugorje, Richard and I sang a duet of the Lord's Prayer at the English Mass at St. James Church. Years later, I was the eulogist at his funeral. I closed my eulogy by asking Richard to join me as I sang a reprise of that duet which we had sung in Medjugorje.

Medjugorje visionary Mirjana Soldo and me displaying
my book, *The Ten Secrets of the Blessed Virgin Mary*,
after my interview at her home in Medjugorje

Mirjana told me, "It is good that you wrote the book not to scare people. This is important because a mother never scares her children or gives them reason to be afraid. She gives them hope and love.

"Blessed Mary of Medjugorje does not come to cause fear of the future, but for love and peace in the future with her.

"I will pray that the book gives people hope."

Mirjana was referring to the 2011 first edition of this book, *The Ten Secrets of the Blessed Virgin Mary*. This book, *Medjugorje's Ten Secrets*, is a completely revised and updated edition of that earlier book.

Mirjana told Father Petar, the designated recipient of Mirjana's First Secret, "I feel deeply sorry for [the unbelievers] and for the world. They have no idea what awaits them. If they can only take a tiny peek at these secrets, if they could see … they would convert in time. Still, Our Lady gave us God's ten secrets. They may still convert. Certainly, God always forgives all those who genuinely convert."

Testimony of Father Peter M. Damian Fehlner, OFM Conv., Author and Theologian

The late Father Peter M. Damian Fehlner, OFM Conv., was my spiritual director. He wrote,

"Once again Dan Lynch has given us a simple, clear presentation, this time on the much discussed and controverted apparitions of Our Lady at Medjugorje. His argumentation in favor of authenticity deserves a serious hearing. For the goals of Our Lady at Medjugorje touch not only local issues but also have worldwide implications and should be pondered in relation to previous apparitions of Mary, for instance, at Fatima, at Amsterdam (Our Lady of All Nations), and elsewhere."

On August 12, 1951, Father Peter entered the Franciscan Friars Conventual Novitiate in Middleburg, New York. He was ordained to the priesthood, on July 14, 1957, at the Basilica of St. Alessio in Rome, Italy. He was an avid scholar and received a Doctoral Degree in Sacred Theology (S.T.D.) from the Seraphicum in Rome in 1959. He was one of the world's leading experts on the writings and theology of St. Bonaventure.

Father Peter taught dogmatic theology at St. Anthony-on-Hudson Theological Seminary in Rensselaer, NY, for over 25 years. During his tenure, the theological library became a world-class collection. Through the years, he also held a position on the Pontifical Faculty of St. Bonaventure in the Seraphicum in Rome. In 1984, he moved to Casa Kolbe in Rome where he became the Assistant International Director of the Militia Immaculata and editor of its publication,

Miles Immaculatae. In this position, he became renowned worldwide as a speaker at conferences, retreats, symposia, and media events.

From 2008 to 2014, Father Peter served as Rector of the Shrine of Our Lady of Guadalupe in La Crosse, WI. In 2015, Father Peter's scholarly genius was recognized by academics at Notre Dame University at a symposium dedicated to his theological writings, including the 6-volume, critical edition of the *Collected Writings of Father Peter M. Damian Fehlner, OFM Conv*. In 2016, the Mariological Society of America bestowed upon Father Peter its highest accolade, *The Cardinal Wright Award*.

Father Peter's last months were full of suffering. Eventually, he lost his ability to communicate. For someone whose life was one of the mind, this was a tremendous trial. He died from a fall on his head on May 8, 2018.

Father James McCurry, Minister Provincial of the Order of Friars Minor Conventual, gave the homily at his funeral. He said that Father Peter was a "scholar, theologian, and...genuinely a true genius, one of the greatest scholars in the 800-year history of the Franciscan Order." Here are some links to his homily,

https://airmaria.com/2018/05/18/funeral-homily-for-fr-peter-damian-fehlner/ (Video)

https://www.olaprovince.org/2018/05/09/fr-peter-damian-fehlner-ofm-conv/ (Text)

Compliments for
Dan Lynch's Books

The Ten Secrets of the Blessed Virgin Mary, First Edition

"I praise Dan Lynch for his work at articulating an understanding of the Ten Secrets of Medjugorje. I also appreciate his use of favorable comments from persons of authority in the Church in assisting people to 'Not Be Afraid.'"

Father Charles Becker
Leader of pilgrimages to Medjugorje

"In the days of Fatima no one would have believed what has come of the world today. Our Lady's message in 1917 and 93 years later in Medjugorje has not changed. The message of Our Lady is the eternal message of the Gospels — prayer, fasting, conversion, penance, confession, Eucharist. Dan Lynch reminds us of the many apparitions of Our Lady and her heartfelt warning to 'turn away from sin and be faithful to the Gospel.' Only in embracing Our Lady's call will the world be saved from the road of self-destruction. In his book, Dan gives a concise presentation of Our Lady's messages and how we can practically respond in today's world. I pray that all who come in contact with this book will take seriously the warning of our Heavenly Mother, embrace her messages, and find true peace within their souls."

Father Jay Finelli
The iPadre Catholic Podcast & Videocast

"Dan Lynch has done a masterful job conveying the messages of the Queen of Peace in a simple and readable style for people of all ages.

"Medjugorje is the extension of the messages of Fatima, and what Dan has written are the keys to peace of mind and soul and will provide people answers in the midst of any storm."

Ted Flynn, Author

Saints of the States

"Too few of the faithful in our great country are aware of the lives and sacrifices of the American Saints. Thank you for your latest book, *Saints of the States*."

Most Reverend Robert J. Baker
Bishop of the Diocese of Birmingham
Co-author, *Cacique, A Novel of Florida's Heroic Mission History*

Our Lady of Guadalupe, Hope for the World

"This book will instruct, encourage, and inspire a wide variety of people in the Church and outside the Church. You may be a pro-life activist looking for signs of progress. You may be a priest seeking new ways to call your people to deeper faith. You may be a son or daughter of the Virgin Mary eager to find new ways to honor her. You may be someone considering abortion or wounded by it and looking for hope. You may be away from the Church looking for a way back, or someone without any background in Catholicism but interested in finding out more. Whoever you are, give this book some of your time and it will repay you abundantly."

Father Frank Pavone,
National Director Priests for Life

Our Lady of Guadalupe, Mother of Hope Video

"Stirring...gripping...comprehensive with moving testimonies!"

Reviews by producers, Ted Flynn, Dr. Tom Petrisko, Drew Mariani, and Ignatius Press

Our Lady of America, Our Hope for the States

"Are there sound grounds for hope about the immediate future of the USA? Without doubt the alleged messages of Our Lady of America to Sister Mary Ephrem certainly do offer such grounds. This simple, yet detailed sketch of the historical background and of the context of those messages makes perfectly clear why this is so and why Our Lady has chosen the States for a particular role in the salvation of souls, and what will be the consequences of not corresponding with her requests. Dan Lynch once again has succeeded in making crystal clear why the Immaculate Virgin is not simply a pious extra for us, but someone who must be at the very heart of our lives, socially as well as personally."

> Father Peter M. Damian Fehlner, OFM Conv.,
> Author and Theologian

The Gospel of Love

"You may have read fictional biographies of the Apostles. However, *The Gospel of Love* is the only historical fictional autobiography that I have read of any of them.

"Dan Lynch wrote this story of the life of the beloved disciple of Jesus, St. John the Evangelist, from John's personal point of view. Solidly based on the Bible, it is presented in such a way as to make it easy for the beginner to relate John's world to ours.

"You will experience John's life as if you were with him nearly 2000 years ago. You will experience John's innermost thoughts and doubts as he struggles to accept Jesus Christ as the Messiah, the Son of Man, and the Son of God, and his teachings that constitute the Gospel of Love. You will see John's transformation from tempestuousness to tranquility as he gradually comes to know and believe in the love that God has for all of us.

"More importantly, you will come away with a deeper understanding of how the Gospel of Love, taught by Jesus, affected John's character and growth in sanctity and how its reading can do the same for you.

"Nothing is so important in life as to grow in holiness by fulfilling the first and second laws of the Gospel: love of God who is love itself and love of neighbor as oneself made in the image and likeness of God. Nothing in life is so sad as not to have become a saint by loving God and neighbor as Jesus does.

"Our thanks to Dan Lynch for this inspiring work!"

> Father Peter M. Damian Fehlner, OFM Conv.,
> Author and Theologian

Teresita's Choices

"This book is a drama with many surprising twists and turns. While feminists claim that a key aspect of feminism is to 'listen to the voices of women,' ironically, those who support abortions fail to listen to the voices of those women who testify to the pain and devastation that it brings. Teresita is one of those voices."

> Father Frank Pavone
> National Director Priests for Life

"This book highlights the devastation of abortion yet gives hope that Our Lord can heal even the most devastating wounds. No doubt an inspiring book of hope. Thank you for this encouraging book."

> Judie Brown
> American Life League

The Call to Total Consecration

"I used Dan Lynch's book as a resource for my talk on the Total Consecration. Of the many books that I have received, this is one of the very few that I actually read and enjoyed!"

> Scott Hahn, Author and Professor of Theology
> and Scripture at Franciscan University of
> Steubenville

MEDJUGORJE'S TEN SECRETS

How to Prepare

Dan Lynch

Published by:
John Paul Press
144 Sheldon Road
St. Albans, VT 05478
www.JKMI.com

ISBN: 978-0-9884980-2-0

Printed in the United States

Contents

Preamble

During the height of the COVID-19 pandemic in 2020, Father Marinko Šakota, a parish priest at St. James Church in Medjugorje, Bosnia-Herzegovina, made a statement in Medjugorje. Father Marinko emphasized the five key points of the messages of Our Lady Queen of Peace at Medjugorje: conversion, faith, prayer, fasting, and peace.

He acknowledged that the pandemic was a cross for us, but that it is important for us to see it in its entirety. He said that we will always have problems, therefore it is very important to listen to what Our Lady said to us in a message during that time. She said, *"I would like to guide you on the way of salvation, return to my Son Jesus, return to prayer and fasting. Do not be afraid."*

Father Marinko said that Our Lady does not protect us from all of our problems and he explained her desires,

> Our Lady desires that we do something for all situations. That we are equipped through prayers and through fasting to strengthen our faith and to believe in the Lord; to strengthen our hope; to strengthen our love towards God and towards others; and to fast on Wednesdays and Fridays. She desires that we adore Jesus; that we pray before the Cross; that we read the Holy Scriptures; that we confess; that we convert; that we change; and that we love all people, regardless of their behavior.

> In this way, we draw closer to God's love and to grow in that love. We are then able to look into the eyes of Jesus, that we may love the way he desires us to love. We are called to love one another in the way that he has loved us. This is it, this is what Our Lady desires: that we work on our hearts; that we pray before the Cross and accept our crosses; that

we look towards Jesus, towards his love, to be inspired by him. All this Our Lady desires.

In this present situation of Coronavirus which we now find ourselves, doctors advise us that we cannot always protect ourselves from the virus, but we can do things to strengthen our protection, such as taking vitamin C, vitamin D, and so on. All these things will help our immune systems to protect against viruses.

Our Lady gives us the guidance and advice for spiritual protection, interior protection.

Foreword by Father Svetozar Kraljević OFM

Father Svetozar made the following remarks upon my presentation to him of my book, *The Ten Secrets of the Blessed Virgin Mary*, at his residence in Medjugorje,

"Dan, we met many years ago and from the beginning in Medjugorje, we have this most amazing phenomenon of people coming and investing their lives for the work of Our Lady. And this phenomenon continues on.

"So, when I see this book, I see really a life — life that is broken into the pieces of these sentences for all of us to receive this wonderful inspirational witness and the moving story of another human being who is willing to give so much for the work of the Lord and for the life of the Church.

"So, I see this book as the blood flowing in the body of the Church, as really the real life of the Church. I see it as the moment of outpouring of the Holy Spirit that will touch each reader. This is what we need now in this aggression of this secular thinking, in this aggression of godless logic.

"It is wonderful to have a testimony, to have a book, to have a word spoken to us, to our humanity, to our time, to our children, in the name of God. So, Dan, I really thank you for being such a powerful witness of Our Lady."

Author's Editorial Notes

This book contains many revelations from Jesus and the Blessed Virgin Mary through apparitions, visions, and locutions. "Apparitions" mean the interventions of a heavenly being, experienced by the external senses. "Visions" are perceived internally either as "imaginative" visions through the imagination, or "intellectual" visions through thoughts, or "external" visions through the eyes. "Locutions" are supernatural messages received internally in words; they are not heard audibly externally.

The Church calls revelations received through apparitions, visions, or locutions "private revelations." The *Catechism of the Catholic Church* says, "Throughout the ages, there have been so-called 'private' revelations, some of which have been recognized by the authority of the Church. They do not belong, however, to the deposit of faith. It is not their role to 'improve' or 'complete' Christ's definitive Revelation, but to help live more fully by it in a certain period of history....Christian faith cannot accept 'revelations' that claim to surpass or correct the Revelation of which Christ is the fulfilment, as is the case in certain non-Christian religions and also in certain recent sects which base themselves on such 'revelations.'" (*Catechism of the Catholic Church* 67). Hereinafter, citations to the *Catechism of the Catholic Church* will be abbreviated as *CCC*.

On May 13, 2000, Cardinal Joseph Ratzinger, later Pope Benedict XVI, said that private revelations help us to understand the signs of the times and to respond to them rightly in faith. He said, "The prophetic word is a warning or a consolation, or both together. In this sense, there is a link between the charism of prophecy and the category of 'the signs of the times,' which Vatican II brought to light anew: 'You know how to interpret the appearance of earth and sky; why then do you not know how to interpret the present time?' (Luke 12:56). In this saying of Jesus, the 'signs of the times' must be understood as the path he was taking; indeed, it must be understood as Jesus himself. To interpret the signs of the times in the light of faith means to recognize the presence of Christ in every age. In the private revelations approved by the Church — and therefore also in Fatima — this is the point: they help us to understand the signs of the times and to respond to them rightly in faith." (*Message of Fatima*, Theological Commentary, www.vatican.va).

The term "private revelations" is unfortunate and misleading. Perhaps a better term would be "prophetic revelations" since there is usually nothing private about them and many of them are revealed for the entire Church. They are prophetic just like the messages of the Old Testament prophets who spoke the Word of God, not to teach the people anything new but to remind them of teachings that they forgot. Nothing has changed since the full Revelation of Jesus Christ, but God has used his Mother since 1830 in a powerful way as the prophetess of chastisements, of the Triumph of Her Immaculate Heart, and of an Era of Peace.

However, her revelations were not only for the privacy of their recipients but were also for the general public. For example, in 1917, Our Lady of Fatima revealed a conditional chastisement that, if her requests were not heeded, a second world war would occur. This revelation was not only for the privacy of the three visionary children but was also for the whole world.

Her messages of so-called "private revelation" saved the whole world from nuclear war in 1984 when St. John Paul II consecrated the world to her Immaculate Heart, as she had requested at Fatima. Sister Lucia, one of the visionaries, said that the Holy Father's consecration satisfied Our Lady's request, saved us from this nuclear war, and led to the beginning of the conversion of Russia through the end of its Christian persecution.

Appearances of the Mother of God belong to the charism of prophecy in which the mysterious working of the Spirit of God comes to expression. St. Paul emphasizes, "Do not quench the Spirit! Do not despise prophetic utterances!" (1 Thessalonians 5:19-20). According to Thomas Aquinas, prophetic revelations after the Apostolic era are not given in order to spread a new teaching of faith but serve to guide human action. The *Catechism of the Catholic Church* calls them "private revelations" because the content conveyed does not belong to the public Revelation which closed with the Apostolic era.

The Church still stands by the rules set down in the eighteenth century by Pope Benedict XIV that "assent of human faith, according to the rules of prudence, is due [apparitions.]" We give *divine faith* to public Revelation, where the Church teaches infallibly. For private revelations, as in apparitions, visions, and locutions, only *human faith* is involved.

In a document of 1907, Pope Pius X reiterated the rules of Benedict XIV as they had also been renewed in statements from the Congregation of Rites in 1875 and 1877 with respect to Our Lady's apparitions in France at Lourdes and La Salette. Pius X said, "Such apparitions or revelations have neither been approved nor condemned by the Apostolic See, but it has been permitted piously to believe them merely with *human faith*, with due regard to the tradition they bear."

So, we are free to give human belief to any prophetic message so long as it does not contradict revealed faith or morals, has not been condemned by the Church, and there are good fruits from the mystics and the messages.

Such messages are not articles of faith but help to strengthen the faith that the Church authoritatively teaches. We don't have to wait for Church approval but are free to use our own discernment and to place *human faith* in such messages unless the Church discerns that they are not from God. "Guided by the Magisterium (Teaching Authority) of the Church, the *sensus fidelium* (sense of the faithful) knows how to discern and welcome in these revelations whatever constitutes an authentic call of Christ or his saints to the Church." (*CCC* 67).

The Fathers of Vatican II spoke about the prophetic office of the holy people of God,

> It is not only through the sacraments and the ministries of the Church that the Holy Spirit sanctifies and leads the people of God and enriches it with virtues, but, "allotting his gifts to everyone according as he wills, he also distributes special graces among the faithful of every rank." By these gifts he makes them fit and ready to undertake the various tasks and offices which contribute toward the renewal and building up of the Church, according to the

words of the Apostle: "The manifestation of the Spirit is given to everyone for profit." These charisms, whether they be the more outstanding or the simpler and more widely diffused, are to be received with thanksgiving and consolation for they are perfectly suited to and useful for the needs of the Church. Extraordinary gifts are not to be sought after, nor are the fruits of apostolic labor to be presumptuously expected from their use, but judgment as to their genuinity and proper use belongs to those who are appointed leaders in the Church, to whose special competence it belongs, not indeed to extinguish the Spirit, but to test all things and hold fast to that which is good. (Vatican II, *Dogmatic Constitution on the Church* 12).

Prophetic revelations can be counted among the charismatic gifts thus meant for the building up of the Church. So, we can be at peace about the revelations of Jesus and Mary in this book. They encourage us to convert, pray, fast, receive the sacraments, and have hope for the future. We don't have to be theologians to investigate and believe in these revelations. We also have to be patient and charitable with all those who don't believe them.

Pope Urban VIII said, to help doubters, "In cases which concern private revelations, it is better to believe than not to believe, for if you believe, and it is proven true, you will be happy that you have believed, because our Holy Mother asked it. If you believe, and it should be proven false, you will receive all blessings as if it had been true, because you believed it to be true."

None of the revelations contained in this book have been condemned by the Church and many of them have been approved. So, we may piously believe them merely with human faith.

There are various citations in this book to the book *I Will Sing of Mercy, the Journal of the Secretary of the Jesus King of All Nations Devotion*, such as this: (*Journal* 247). The number refers to the paragraph number in that book. That book may be obtained from,

John Paul Press
144 Sheldon Road
St. Albans, VT 05478
www.JKMI.com

These messages must always be interpreted in accordance with the teachings of the Catholic Church and never contrary to them. The *Journal* contains a *Nihil Obstat* that states that, as of August 15, 1993, "There is nothing contrary to faith or morals." Since that date, there have been other messages that have been submitted for approval to the appropriate bishops.

There are also various citations in this book to the book *To the Priests,* such as this: (*To the Priests* 47). The number refers to the message number in that book. That book may be obtained from,

The Marian Movement of Priests
PO Box 8
St. Francis, ME 04774
https://mmp-usa.net

To the Priests is a compilation of messages that Father Stefano Gobbi said that he had received from the Blessed Virgin Mary. Father Gobbi was the founder of the Marian Movement of Priests that tens of thousands of priests followed. He died on June 29, 2011.

He received his messages as interior locutions. These messages also must always be interpreted in accordance with the teachings of the Catholic Church and never contrary to them. *To the Priests* contains an *Imprimatur* that states, "There is nothing contrary to faith or morals in this manuscript."

The Jewish people have been known throughout history as the Hebrews, the Israelites, and the Jews. For consistency, I have used only the name "Jews," derived from the tribe of Judah.

Citations to Church documents refer to the name of the document and the paragraph number, if any, and look like this: (*That They May Be One,* 40).

Scriptural citations refer to the name of the document in the Bible and the chapter and verse and look like this: (John 3:17). The scriptural citations are from various translations. I selected from various translations the best that I thought fit the particular context in which the citation was quoted. However, because of the variety, none of the particular translations are added to the citation.

Some of my citations are to books and other sources which are not readily available and some of which are out-of-print. Some of them also have different editions with different page numbers. So, in the interest of simplicity, in most cases I have cited only the name of the source and the author.

Quotes from Mary, Jesus, and God are in italics, except in excerpts from the *Journal* and from Scripture. In the *Journal* excerpts, it is the supporting Scripture references that are italicized.

Here is a list of my other books available at my website http://www.JKMI.com/ or at my Amazon Author's Page (www.amazon.com/Dan-Lynch/e/B001KC7Q3G%3Fref=dbs_a_mng_rwt_scns_share),

- ° *I Will Sing of Mercy: The Journal of the Secretary of the Jesus King of All Nations Devotion (Editor)*
- ° *Our Lady of America, Our Hope for the States*
- ° *Our Lady of Guadalupe, Hope for the World*
- ° *Praying with Our Lady of Guadalupe*
- ° *Saints of the States*
- ° *Teresita's Choices*
- ° *The Gospel of Love*
- ° *The Call to Total Consecration*

Every precaution has been taken to verify the accuracy of the information contained in this book. However, the author and publisher assume no responsibility for any errors or omissions. No liability is assumed for damages that may result from the use of the information contained within. Some names have been changed to protect the privacy of individuals.

I gratefully acknowledge and thank my friends, Randy Pratt who edited my book and Lori Rainville who formatted it. Without their great help, the book would still be stored in my computer!

Thank you for reading my book.

Dan Lynch

Preface

The Blessed Virgin Mary, Mother of Jesus Christ, true God and true man, was assumed body and soul into Heaven after her life on earth in the first century. Since then, she has returned to earth many times in apparitions throughout the world. She comes to offer hope and consolation and especially, since the twentieth century, she requests conversion and prayer and warns of punishments or chastisements if people do not obey her requests.

On June 16, 1983, she came from Heaven and appeared to six child visionaries in Medjugorje, (pronounced Medge-you-gorey-ay), Bosnia-Herzegovina. She said, "*I have come to tell the world that God exists. He is the fullness of life, and to enjoy this fullness and peace, you must return to God.*"

Do you believe this? Will you return to God and accept his will for your life? This was the question that passenger Fred Beretta had to answer as US Airways flight 1549 approached the Hudson River in New York on January 15, 2009.

Seconds before the plane hit the river, God asked Fred, "*Where will you turn to now? Will you reconcile and trust? You must choose.*" As the plane hurtled towards the water and his expected death, the flight attendants kept screaming, "Brace for impact! Brace for impact!" A surge of adrenaline coursed through Fred's body and the world seemed to come to a sudden halt. The silent voice came again, "*Will you accept my will for your life?*"

Fred knew that he needed to reconcile to the fact that he was not in control. He had two choices, he later wrote, "Either in pride and anger turn away from God or in humility turn fully to him and accept his will, however inscrutable it was and regardless of the consequences. The river was coming for me and I had to decide."

Fred chose to accept God's will and he and all of the other passengers survived the airplane's crash landing on the Hudson River. This was called the "Miracle on the Hudson." (*Flight of Faith,*

Beretta, Frederick, Charlotte, North Carolina: St. Benedict Press, 2009, pp. 36-37).

The river of death and judgment is also coming for each of us, and each of us is called to answer *Yes* to the question that God put to Fred, *"Will you accept my will for your life?"* This book will tell you how to do so. Our Lady of Medjugorje revealed her five requests: peace, conversion, faith, prayer and fasting and Total Consecration to Jesus through Mary.

Mary's revelations at Medjugorje began in 1981. She gave Ten Secrets to several of the visionaries which contain warnings and prophesy chastisements for all mankind. The warnings will be events on earth that will be given for those who live as if God does not exist. After the first two secrets or warnings, Mary will leave a visible supernatural sign on the mountain where she first appeared. By that time, it will be too late to be converted, so she implored us, *"Hurry to be converted. I need your prayers and your penance."* (April 25, 1983).

Mirjana (pronounced Mere-yah-nah) Soldo, one of the Medjugorje visionaries, said that we should prepare ourselves for what will happen when the Ten Secrets revealed by Mary occur. She said, "Yes, prepare! The Madonna said people should prepare themselves spiritually, be ready, and not panic; be reconciled in their souls. They should be ready for the worst, to die tomorrow. They should accept God now so that they will not be afraid. They should accept God, and everything else. No one accepts death easily, but they can be at peace in their souls if they are believers. If they are committed to God, he will accept them."

Mary did not reveal the Ten Secrets to frighten us, but to give us a chance to prepare for them and to protect ourselves from them. The late Father Slavko Barbaric, former Medjugorje parish priest, said, "The Madonna did not come to announce catastrophes, but more to help us avoid them. We all know that a nuclear war is possible, even without apparitions. If the house burns, it doesn't burn because the mother cries 'fire.' On the contrary, the mother comes to save the house, which is burning. In that there is hope."

At Fatima, on May 11, 2010, Pope Benedict XVI said, "The Church must relearn conversion, prayer, penance....The Virgin Mary came from Heaven to remind us of the Gospel truths that constitute for humanity — so lacking in love and without any hope for salvation — the source of hope."

This book explains the revelations about the secrets, which include warnings and chastisements, prophesied by the Blessed Virgin Mary (sometimes referred to as "Our Lady") at Medjugorje since 1981 and how to prepare for them as she requested.

To those of you who have not as yet come to know the love of God, Our Lady of Medjugorje has a message for you. On June 2, 2011, she said,

> *As I call you to prayer for those who have not come to know the love of God, if you were to look into your hearts you would comprehend that I am speaking about many of you.*
>
> *With an open heart, sincerely ask yourselves if you want the living God or do you want to eliminate him and live as you want. Look around you, my children, and see where the world is going, the world that thinks of doing everything without the Father, and which wanders in the darkness of temptation.*
>
> *I am offering to you the light of the Truth and the Holy Spirit. According to God's plan I am with you to help you to have my Son, his Cross, and Resurrection, triumph in your hearts. As a mother, I desire and pray for your unity with my Son and his works. I am with you; you decide. Thank you.*

When Medjugorje visionary Mirjana Soldo was asked "Which is the dearest message to you, which you would share with readers?"

Mirjana replied, "Love: I'd like to share love with everybody. I'd like everybody to understand the essence of love, which is Jesus. When you love, when you have Jesus at the center of your life, you are happy. I'd like all people to be happy. Our Lady tells us that what happens here shows how much our Heavenly Father loves us. Then she speaks about her love, and of her Son's love. There's always this theme of love. I'd like everybody to feel this love."

I believe that Our Lady is preparing us for everything that is about to come in the world. She has trained us how to prepare for the Ten Secrets and the Triumph of Her Immaculate Heart. As she told us, we are now living in a time of grace, then will come the time of the secrets followed by the time of her triumph.

Sources

The basic sources for the information about the Ten Secrets in this book are exclusive interviews of the visionary Mirjana Soldo with the following people in chronological order: Father Tomislav Vlašić , Father Petar Ljubicic, Janice Connell, Padre Livio Fanzaga, and Dan Lynch, the author. The interviews by Father Vlašić, Father Ljubicic, and me are contained in Appendix B.

Mirjana is the only visionary used as a source for the Ten Secrets because she is the most educated and, as she told Father Vlašić, Mary told her that she was *"more mature than the others and therefore [she] must help them."*

Moreover, Mirjana has spoken more than any of the other visionaries about the Ten Secrets. Medjugorje priest, Father Svetozar Kraljević OFM wrote that Mirjana "has given the clearest and most descriptive accounts of the apparitions and messages."

Father Tomislav Vlašić OFM moved to Medjugorje in August of 1981, two months after the apparitions began. He was an associate pastor and spiritual advisor to the visionaries until September of 1984, after which he left.

Sadly, Father Vlašić was later reported to the Congregation for the Doctrine of the Faith for various alleged canonical infractions and sins. Father Vlašić did not respond to the reports. Because of those charges and his failure to respond to them, specific ecclesiastical sanctions and the censure of Interdict were imposed on him in 2008.

In 2009, Pope Benedict XVI accepted the request of Father Vlašić and granted him the favor of reduction to the lay state and of dismissal from the Franciscan Order. The Holy Father also granted him "the remission of the censure incurred as well as the favor of dispensation from religious vows and from all the responsibilities connected with sacred ordination, including celibacy."

The following precepts were imposed on the now *Mr.* Tomislav Vlašić, prohibition from the following: exercising any form of apostolate; releasing declarations on religious matters, especially regarding the "phenomenon of Medjugorje;" and residing in houses of the Order of Friars Minor.

The Decree against Mr. Vlašić did not find him guilty of the prior alleged reports, to which he had not responded. The Decree is simply a merciful response to his request to be laicized. The Decree does not sanction or discipline the Medjugorje visionaries, apparitions, or the parish. It only applies to Mr. Vlašić.

Notwithstanding this Decree, the writings and interviews of Father Vlašić before he left Medjugorje in 1984 are still authoritative. During the time he was in Medjugorje, he interviewed several visionaries on various occasions and, in 1983, he wrote a letter concerning the apparitions and messages to St. John Paul II.

Father Svetozar Kraljević OFM, who served in Medjugorje with Father Vlašić, printed the entire transcript of Father Vlašić's interview in his book, *The Apparitions of Our Lady at Medjugorje,* one of the first books about Medjugorje. Father Svetozar personally told me that this interview by Father Vlašić "is believable."

Father Svetozar studied philosophy and theology in Sarajevo and in Washington DC.

Father Svetozar arrived in the United States in 1975, was ordained a priest in Chicago in 1977, and did pastoral work in Chicago and New York. He returned to Medjugorje in 1983, two years after the apparitions began. He wrote books and articles and spoke about them at many conferences. He lived in Medjugorje where he gave many talks to the many pilgrims and administered the apostolate of Mother's Village, a community for orphans, abused women, and addicts.

Father Petar Ljubicic OFM is a Franciscan priest who served in Medjugorje. The Blessed Virgin Mary asked the visionary Mirjana Soldo, "*Choose a priest to whom you will tell the First Secret.*" Mirjana said, "Blessed Mary emphasized the singular. She did not tell me to tell him all the secrets. I chose Father Petar. I'll tell him the First Secret ten days before it occurs. We will fast and pray together for seven days and then he will announce the secret three days before it occurs. I don't know if each of the secrets will be announced."

Janice Connell founded the Pittsburgh Marian Center of Peace with her husband, Ed. She is the author of the following books: *The Visions of the Children: the Apparitions of the Blessed Mother at Medjugorje; Queen of the Cosmos;* and *Meetings with Mary.*

Padre Livio Fanzaga is the director of Radio Maria, an apostolate located in Medjugorje. He is the author of several books in Italian, including, *La Madonna Prepara per il Mondo un futuro di Pace* (The Madonna Prepares the World for a Future of Peace,) which also contains an interview with Mirjana.

Introduction

When the Blessed Virgin Mary came to earth in the past, she left supernatural signs in order to help people to believe in her apparitions and messages.

On December 12, 1531, in Mexico, God left her image on the cloak of St. Juan Diego, a miracle which has defied scientific explanation and still exists today for all to see in the Basilica of Our Lady of Guadalupe in Mexico City.

On October 13, 1917, at Fatima, Portugal, God manifested the so-called "Miracle of the Sun." Contrary to the laws of nature, the sun appeared as an opaque, spinning disc in the sky like a wheel of fire with all the colors of the rainbow. Similarly, the Miracle of the Sun has occurred many times at Medjugorje.

Miracle of the Sun at Medjugorje

In February 1988, I brought my wife and five of our nine children on a pilgrimage to Medjugorje. One evening, as we all approached St. James Church for Mass, we saw a large crowd of pilgrims outside next to the church. We joined them out of curiosity. The pilgrims were all excited and pointing at the sun. As I looked up, I saw the sun spinning with many colors radiating from it. Then I saw what looked like a protective translucent disk come over the sun so that I could view it directly without hurting my eyes. The sun then began to change colors.

The pilgrims appeared stupefied, as if they couldn't believe what they were seeing. Then a woman pilgrim pointed to my youngest son, John, who was then five years old, and yelled out to the pilgrims, "Ask the little boy what he sees. Children don't lie!" Then another woman pilgrim asked my son, "What color is the sun?" He responded, "Green!" She responded, "That's what I see!" Then another pilgrim asked my son, "What do you see now?" My son replied, "The sun has disappeared!" The man replied, "Yes, it has!"

Then the sun returned into view and the Miracle of the Sun phenomena continued, but ended in time for all of us pilgrims to enter the church in time for Mass.

On August 2, 2009, a congregation of 50,000 pilgrims gathered on Apparition Hill in Medjugorje to witness an apparition of the Blessed Virgin Mary to visionary Mirjana Soldo. By 5:00 a.m., the whole inner section surrounding the Blue Cross was filled with pilgrims. There were many youth who were sprawled out in sleeping bags, having spent the night on the mountain in anticipation of Mary's early morning apparition. According to an eyewitness, it was an incredible sight, with a sea of faces everywhere you looked.

Mirjana Soldo in ecstasy seeing the Blessed Virgin Mary
with a posture that shows her openness to her love

The apparition of Mary began at 8:45 a.m. and lasted approximately four minutes. Shortly after the apparition began, cries of surprise, shock, deep emotion, and awe were heard rippling through the crowd from different directions, growing in magnitude, while Mirjana was enraptured in her vision of Mary.

Pilgrims in awe viewing the Miracle of the Sun

The pilgrims began to point at the sun. Many witnessed the sun "dancing" or "spinning," while others saw what looked like a Cross illuminated in the sun; still others saw different colors spinning off the sun in many directions. Tears were streaming down many faces; others were watching in wonder; others in joy.

After the apparition, Mirjana said that she saw the sun behind the Blessed Virgin Mary during the entire apparition, which was a sign of the love of Jesus shining down upon the tens of thousands of pilgrims gathered there.

Mary told Mirjana, *"Dear children, I am coming, with my motherly love, to point out the way by which you are to set out, in order that you may be all the more like my Son, and by that, closer to and more pleasing to God. Do not refuse my love. Do not renounce salvation and eternal life for the sake of transience and frivolity of this life. I am coming to lead you and, as a mother, to caution you. Come with me."*

Regarding the Miracle of the Sun, a pilgrim said, "I have been here to Medjugorje about forty times but I have never seen such a miracle as I saw at Mirjana's apparition. After the apparition, I looked up at the sun and it became like a ball and was spinning very fast. People could look at the sun without sunglasses or protection over their eyes. There were many circular waves around

3

the sun like ripples from a stone thrown into the water, which were changing colors from blue to gray.

"At the end of this miracle," the pilgrim continued, "I looked at the Cross on Cross Mountain and around it there were like clouds rising up.

"They were green and yellow and they looked like columns and then some of the people began to cry; many were praying. It was very beautiful. Inside of me was a very strong and powerful feeling of God's love and peace. It was a great experience for my heart."

Medjugorje and St. John Paul II

St. John Paul II called Medjugorje "the confessional of the world" and said that, if he were not Pope, he "would be living in Medjugorje as a priest helping to hear confessions." On April 6, 1995, he made public his desire to go to Medjugorje and wrote to friends in Poland, "We every day return to Medjugorje in prayer." He concluded his daily private Rosary in the Vatican gardens with the prayer, "Our Lady of Medjugorje, pray for me."

He told visiting pilgrims in Rome, "Our Lady of Medjugorje will save America." He wrote to friends in his own hand, "I thank Sophia for everything concerning Medjugorje. I, too, go there every day as a pilgrim in my prayers. I unite in my prayers with all those who pray there or receive a calling from prayer from there. Today we have understood this call better. I rejoice that our time is not lacking in people of prayer and apostles. Medjugorje is better understood these days. I myself am very much attached to that place."

Mirjana spoke about St. John Paul II and Medjugorje. On October 3, 2009, she was asked whether she had ever met with St. John Paul II. Mirjana answered, "I am the only one of six visionaries who was lucky enough, had the honor, to encounter St. John Paul II. You can imagine how the other five are jealous of me," she said with a smile.

"I was in the Vatican," she continued, "St. Peter's Basilica, with an Italian priest. The Holy Father was walking by and he was blessing us. When he approached me, he blessed me and he just continued to walk. However, this Italian priest loudly said to him, 'Holy Father, this is Mirjana from Medjugorje.'

"The Pope came back and blessed me again. As he left, I said to the priest, 'He just thinks I need a double blessing.' But then, afterwards, the priest received a note, an invitation for both of us to Castel Gandolfo, close to Rome, in order to see the Pope. I couldn't sleep all night because I really loved him and I respected him and I could really feel his love for Our Lady.

"So, the next day when he and I met alone, I was just crying. I couldn't say a word because I was so excited. He noticed that I was excited. I think he tried to talk to me in Polish because he thought that in the Slavic languages there are things in common. I didn't understand a word!

"But, finally, I had enough strength and courage to ask him, 'What are you trying to tell me?' Then we talked. Among other things, he said to me, 'I know everything about Medjugorje. I've been following Medjugorje. Ask pilgrims to pray for my intentions, to keep, to take good care of Medjugorje, because Medjugorje is hope for the entire world. And if I were not Pope, I would have been in Medjugorje a long time ago.'

"A priest told me that from the very beginning," Mirjana continued, "the Pope was very fond of Medjugorje because two months before the apparitions in Medjugorje started, the Pope was praying to Our Lady to come again on earth. He said, 'I cannot do it all alone because Yugoslavia, Czechoslovakia, Poland, etc., are all Communist, I cannot do it on my own. I need you.' And later he heard that in Yugoslavia, a Communist country, in a little village, Our Lady appeared. Then he said, 'That is a response to my prayers.'

Mirjana concluded, "On the Mount of Apparitions, I saw a pair of shoes of the Pope in front of me. After the apparition, the gentleman who brought these shoes (he didn't introduce himself) said, 'It was the Pope's desire for a long time to come to Medjugorje.' So, I said to him, 'If you do not go, I will take your shoes.' And that is how I brought his shoes, so they may be present during the apparition.'"

And that is how the Pope's desire to come to Medjugorje was satisfied.

Good Fruits of Medjugorje

The Medjugorje revelations have not yet been officially approved or disapproved by the Catholic Church, which awaits future developments, such as the fulfillment of the prophesied secrets, warnings, and chastisements. Mary's requests at Medjugorje do not differ from other similar requests from God or Mary that are Church-approved, such as: at Fatima, Portugal, in 1917; at Akita, Japan, in 1973; and at Kibeho, Rwanda, in 1981; which was approved *after* the prophesied chastisement of a savage genocide occurred there.

Moreover, there are good fruits from Medjugorje that give us reason to believe in the prophecies of Mary. Austrian Cardinal Christoph Schönborn made a pilgrimage to Medjugorje from December 28, 2009 to January 2, 2010. Cardinal Schönborn is a former student and personal friend of Pope Emeritus Benedict XVI. He is well known for his work as editorial secretary of the *Catechism of the Catholic Church*, his contributions to the Pontifical Theological Commission, and his numerous scholarly publications.

During the Cardinal's pilgrimage, he celebrated New Year's Eve Midnight Mass in St. James Church, met with several Franciscan priests, and heard confessions. He also visited the hillside where the Blessed Virgin Mary appears.

While the Cardinal was in Medjugorje, he said, "[Medjugorje] is about faith in Christ, prayer, the Eucharist, about lived love of neighbor, about the essentials of Christianity, and the strengthening of Christian daily life. I always used to say what Jesus has said in the Gospel: '*You will recognize the tree by its fruits.*' When I see the fruits of Medjugorje back at home I can only say that the tree is surely good." He then gave examples of these good fruits,

> I will give you a couple of examples: vocation calls for the priesthood. Many of our young priests have received their vocation call here, but not strictly in Medjugorje, but because of Medjugorje.

> The second thing is conversions. I am impressed that conversions happen in every level of society, from noble families and industrialists down to the common little people. While I was flying from Vienna, via Zagreb to Split,

I was asked by a security guard where I was going and I told him I was going to Medjugorje. All of a sudden, his face started shining and he told me that he had his conversion in Medjugorje as well. A couple of weeks ago, on a small railway station, a worker told me his story. His wife died of cancer and he was desperate and his friends brought him to Medjugorje. He received a strong and living faith over here.

The third evidence is the healings. A young man who was addicted to drugs told me that he was almost forced by his friends to come over here. He told me that while the bus was entering Medjugorje, something happened with him. He was healed immediately.

The fourth evidence is the prayer groups. I've known a Medjugorje Prayer Group from Vienna since before I became a bishop. I've known them since the 1980s. To us Dominicans, it was very meaningful that these people pray for hours and their church is always full. The Dominican churches in Vienna are rarely so full; on Thursday nights, the church was always full. They have stayed faithful to the prayer until today. Jesus said that the bad tree doesn't bear any fruits. Which means that if the fruits are good, then the tree is good as well.

The Ruini Commission's Findings on Medjugorje

In 1987, Cardinal Joseph Ratzinger, later Pope Benedict XVI, entrusted the investigation of the apparitions and revelations from Medjugorje to the Yugoslavian Bishops' conference. On April 10, 1991, they ruled that, on the basis of the investigation to that day, "it cannot be affirmed that one is dealing with supernatural apparitions and revelations."

After that date, Serbia attacked Slovenia and a war broke out. The war resulted in the dissolution of the nation of Yugoslavia and the Bishops' Conference of Yugoslavia. The Holy See stated, "Since the division of Yugoslavia into different independent nations it would now pertain to the members of the Episcopal Conference of Bosnia-Herzegovina to eventually reopen the examination of this case, and to make any new pronouncements that might be called for."

However, the Episcopal Conference of Bosnia-Herzegovina never made any new pronouncements.

Bishop Ratko Perić was the Bishop of the Diocese of Mostar, in which Medjugorje is located. He did not believe in the apparitions and messages and it was his position that the apparitions or revelations were definitely not supernatural. However, this was only his personal opinion and was and is not binding on anyone. His negative comments about Medjugorje were addressed directly in 1998 by the Congregation for the Doctrine of the Faith, which sent a letter to Bishop Gilbert Aubry, Bishop of Saint-Denis de la Reunion, clarifying its position on Medjugorje.

At that time, the Congregation was presided over by Cardinal Joseph Ratzinger. Its letter said that Bishop Perić's opinion "should be considered the expression of the personal conviction of the Bishop of Mostar which he has the right to express as Ordinary of the place, but which is and remains his personal opinion."

Professor and Mariologist, Dr. Mark Miravalle, wrote in the book, *Are the Medjugorje Apparitions Authentic* (Hiawassee, Georgia, New Hope Press, 2008),

> The Medjugorje apparitions possess all the principal characteristics that the Church looks for in manifesting supernatural authenticity. The message contents are in complete conformity with the official doctrinal teachings of the Catholic Church. The phenomena that accompany the messages constitute scientifically validated ecstasy during the apparitions and numerous reports of healings. The visionaries manifest lives of moral integrity and psychological stability. The spiritual fruits from the apparitions have also had a monumental worldwide effect of conversions, returns to the Church and to proper states in life, as well as an extraordinary number of vocations to the priesthood and religious life.

> Further credibility is added by the fact that more than 200 bishops, archbishops, and cardinals have visited the site officially, in addition to the many unofficial visits by the shepherds of the Church. In addition, well over 100 bishops, archbishops, and cardinals have publicly expressed their belief in Our Lady's presence in Medjugorje. The spiritual

fruits of conversion and spiritual peace have been the ubiquitous testimony of the greater part of the forty-million pilgrims who have come to Medjugorje and have responded to the Queen of Peace's call for greater faith, prayer, fasting, conversion, and peace.

On March 17, 2010, the Vatican announced that it had formed a commission to investigate the phenomenon of Medjugorje. A short communiqué issued by the Vatican press office indicated that, "An international investigative commission on Medjugorje has been constituted, under the presidency of Cardinal Camillo Ruini and dependent upon the Congregation for the Doctrine of the Faith. Said commission—made up of cardinals, bishops, specialists, and experts—will work privately, submitting the results of its work to the authority of the Congregation." It came to be known as the Ruini Commission.

The press office explained, "it is not the Commission itself that makes the decisions, the definitive pronouncements, but it offers the result of its study, its 'vote,' as it is referred to in technical terms, to the Congregation, which will then decide on the case."

The Church has made few judgments on the many apparition claims in history. Father Salvatore Perrella, assistant dean at the Pontifical Theological Faculty Marianum said, "It's not always possible to ascertain if they are true or false because the phenomenon is much bigger than us."

Father Perrella is a theologian who also serves as an expert for the Congregation for the Doctrine of the Faith. He also is a member of the Ruini Commission. He said, "Although the visionaries have claimed to see apparitions of Mary at Medjugorje for the past 30 years, such an extended duration of alleged apparitions in one place is no longer something that generates suspicion." That's because there are similar precedents, such as the apparitions of Our Lady of Laus, France, which occurred during the 17th century and lasted for 54 years but did not receive formal Church recognition until 2008.

In 2014, the Ruini Commission submitted its report to Pope Francis who has not yet made a final decision regarding it.

In 2017, Pope Francis named Polish Archbishop Henryk Hoser to study the pastoral care given to Medjugorje's residents and visiting pilgrims. Hoser told Poland's KAI Catholic news agency in 2017 that "from a pastoral point of view, there is a very positive result." He said, "Every indication" is that the apparitions will be approved: "specifically, I think it's possible to recognize the authenticity of the first [seven] apparitions as proposed by the Ruini Commission."

In May 2018, Hoser was sent as "Apostolic Visitor" for an undetermined amount of time to the Saint James Parish in Medjugorje, Bosnia-Herzegovina. He said, "The devotion of Medjugorje is allowed. It's not prohibited and need not be done in secret....The decree of the former Episcopal Conference of what used to be Yugoslavia, which, before the Balkan War, advised against pilgrimages in Medjugorje organized by bishops, is no longer relevant."

On May 12, 2019, Pope Francis authorized pilgrimages to Medjugorje, which can now be officially organized by dioceses and parishes and need no longer take place only in a private capacity, as before.

The *"ad interim"* director of the Holy See Press Office, Alessandro Gisotti, said " Considering the considerable flow of people who go to Medjugorje and the abundant fruits of grace that have sprung from it, this authorization is part of the particular pastoral attention that the Holy Father intended to give to that reality, aimed at encouraging and promoting the fruits of good."

Finally, on February 25, 2020, the website *Aleteia* reported that the Ruini Commission reported that "it can affirm with reasonable certainty that the first seven apparitions [of the Medjugorje visionaries] are intrinsically credible. (See Appendix E.)

On August 1, 2020, Archbishop Hoser, Apostolic Visitor to the parish of Medjugorje, spoke during the opening press conference of the Medjugorje Youth Festival. He said,

"The Holy See's approach to Medjugorje is very good and positive, but the Church acts calmly and slowly. In his opinion, "the situation is getting better and better and a proof of this is also my presence."

1. The Role of the Blessed Virgin Mary in God's Plan of Salvation

The Blessed Virgin Mary appeared in Mexico on December 9, 1531. She identified herself as *"Our Lady of Guadalupe"* and told St. Juan Diego,

> *Know for certain, dearest of my sons, that I am the perfect and perpetual Virgin Mary, Mother of the one true God, through whom everything lives, the Lord of all things near and far, the Master of Heaven and earth. I ardently desire that a sacred house be built here for me where I will show him, I will exalt him and make him manifest, I will give him to the people and offer all my love, my compassion, my help, and my protection. I am your merciful mother, the merciful mother of all who live united in this land, and of all mankind, of all those who love me, of those who cry to me, of those who have confidence in me. Here I will hear their weeping and their sorrows, and I will remedy and alleviate their sufferings, necessities, and misfortunes.*

These words show that Mary's role in God's plan of salvation as our merciful mother is to manifest her Son Jesus to us and to bring us her help and protection as a mediatrix with her Son. God's plan of salvation is to bring all creation under the final rule of Christ. (See Ephesians 1:10). "In subjecting all things to him, God left nothing unsubjected. At present, we do not see all things thus subject, but we do see Jesus crowned with glory and honor because he suffered death." (Hebrews 2:8-9).

God the Father chose us in Christ to be his adopted sons and to be holy and blameless in his sight through Christ's redemption. His redemption bought back for us the gifts of the supernatural life of grace and Heaven which were lost by the Original Sin of Adam and

Eve. Our salvation is a fruit of this and, by his Passion and death, we have eternal salvation in Heaven through faith and the forgiveness of our sins. (See Ephesians 1:4-7; 2:8). The Father's creation is redeemed by the Son and is made holy by the Spirit's sanctification by which we have our salvation which is eternal life through the forgiveness of our sins.

St. Paul VI said that the Blessed Virgin Mary "has a most singular 'role in the mystery of the incarnate Word and of the mystical body,' that is to say, in the 'economy of salvation.'…" (*Signum Magnum* (The Great Sign), May 13, 1967).

St. Louis de Montfort said that "it was through Mary that the salvation of the world was begun, and it is through Mary that it must be consummated." (*True Devotion to Mary*, St. Louis de Montfort, 49).

St. Paul VI said, "…the Blessed Virgin Mary, after participating in the redeeming sacrifice of the Son…now continues to fulfill from Heaven her maternal function as the cooperator in the birth and development of divine life in the individual souls of redeemed men. This is a most consoling truth, which, by the free consent of God the All-Wise, is an integrating part of the mystery of human salvation; therefore, it must be held as faith by all Christians." (*Signum Magnum* (The Great Sign), May 13, 1967).

Mary's central role in the divine plan of our salvation is to cooperate in the redemption accomplished by her Son Jesus. On earth, she cooperated with him. In Heaven, she has cooperated with him from the time of her Assumption and Coronation. She will continue to cooperate with him as the Mediatrix of All Graces until God is all in all. (See 1 Corinthians 15:28). All graces that Jesus merited by his Passion and death are mediated to us by the intercession and dispensation of Mary.

As she was the Mother of Jesus in natural life (the order of nature), so, too, is she the mother of the baptized in supernatural life (the order of grace). As she brought forth Jesus at Bethlehem, so she brings him forth again in receptive human hearts through the mediation of her Immaculate Heart until he will reign in all hearts with her by the Triumph of Her Immaculate Heart in the world. This will be the fulfillment of de Montfort's prophecy that the consummation of the salvation of the world will be through Mary.

Her role is carried out throughout the history of the world amidst constant battle with Satan and his many followers, whose pride and disobedience will ultimately be defeated through her and her Son and the humility and obedience of their followers.

We can see this central role of Mary through the events of the Fall of the angels, the Fall of man, and the mysteries of her life.

The Fallen Angels

In the beginning of time, after God had created Heaven and earth, he created the angels as pure spirits. (See Colossians 1:16). They were created as immortal beings out of the goodness of God for his glorification. (See Hebrews 2:10). He endowed them with grace, but they were subjected to a moral testing. God gave them a one-time fundamental option to acknowledge him as their Lord and maker and to choose to serve him or not.

The good angels who passed the test were rewarded with the blessedness of Heaven. (See Matthew 18:10). Satan (meaning Adversary) and the other angels who did not pass the test through their own sin fell from Heaven and were eternally damned (see 2 Peter 2:4; Jude chapter 6), even though they knew that such would be the consequence of their disobedience! One unrepented mortal sin committed by us can have the same result.

On April 14, 1982, Medjugorje visionary Mirjana Soldo had a vision while she was waiting for Mary to appear. Satan arrived, disguised as Mary. Mirjana said, "He was ugly, horribly ugly. You cannot even imagine how ugly; he almost killed me with his gaze; I almost fainted. He then told me, 'You must leave God and Mary because they will make you suffer; come with me and I will make you happy in love and life.' My heart echoed — 'No! No! No!'

"Then Satan went away and Mary came and said to me,

I am sorry for this, but you must know that Satan exists. One day, he presented himself before the throne of God and asked permission to try the Church for a period of time. God permitted him to try it during one century but said, 'You will not destroy Her.' This century is under the power of the devil, but when the secrets which have been confided to you have been fulfilled, his power will be destroyed. Satan has become aggressive because he is losing his power. He is breaking up marriages, causing quarrels amongst priests, obsessing people, even killing them. Therefore, protect yourselves by prayer, fasting, and, above all, community prayer. Renew the use of holy water, wear blessed and holy objects, and put them in your homes."

We should also pray to our Guardian angels and pray the Prayer of St. Michael the Archangel. (See Appendix C). This was composed by Pope Leo XIII, in the late nineteenth century, when he saw in a vision the satanic evil to come. The angels protect us and help us towards our salvation.

The Fall of Man

God created Adam and Eve out of his goodness and for his glory with the gifts of immortality and grace. These gifts were not just for themselves, but for transmission to the whole human race. These gifts were lost by their Original Sin of disobedience to God's command through the temptation of Satan. (See Genesis 2:17; 3:1; and following). As a result of this, they, and all of us, became subject to suffering, sin, death, and the power of Satan. (See Genesis 3:15 and following).

The disobedience of the fallen angels and of Adam and Eve prompted the Protogospel (the first good news), whereby God set up an irreconcilable enmity and moral warfare between Satan and his followers on the one hand, and the Woman (Mary) and her children on the other hand. God promised to redeem fallen mankind through the Woman and her offspring (Jesus Christ and the baptized, as adopted children) who would achieve a complete and final victory over Satan and his offspring. St. John Paul II wrote,

"I will put enmity between you and the Woman, and between your offspring and hers; he will strike at your head, while you strike at his heel." (Genesis 3:15).

14

As we see from the words of the Protogospel, the victory of the Woman's Son will not take place without a hard struggle, a struggle that is to extend through the whole of human history.

The "enmity," foretold at the beginning, is confirmed in the Apocalypse (the book in the Bible of the final events of the Church and the world), in which there recurs the sign of the "Woman," this time "clothed with the sun." (Revelation 12:1).

Mary, Mother of the Incarnate Word, is placed at the very center of that enmity, that struggle which accompanies the history of salvation itself. (*Mother of the Redeemer*, 1987, 11).

The Protogospel is an implicit prophecy of Mary's role as the Immaculate Conqueror of Satan (Vatican II, *Dogmatic Constitution on the Church*, 55) and an explicit prophecy of her role as the Mother of our Redeemer and the Mother of the Church. We see, then, that Jesus and Mary are the new Adam and Eve whose humility and obedience will defeat the pride and disobedience of Satan by their cooperation in the divine plan of our salvation. Jesus is our brother, Mary is our mother, and we are the adopted children. St. John Paul II wrote,

The Mother of the Redeemer has a precise place in the plan of salvation, for, "when the time had fully come, God sent forth his Son, born of woman, born under the law, to redeem those who were under the law, so that we might receive adoption as sons, and because you are sons, God has sent the spirit of his Son into our hearts, crying 'Abba! Father!'" (Galatians 4:4-6). (*Mother of the Redeemer*, 1987, 1).

Mary's Prefigurement in the Old Testament

Mary is prefigured in the Book of Psalms and in the Wisdom books by many passages which refer to her in an implicit manner. The prophecy of the Protogospel also refers to her implicitly. (See Genesis 3:15). The prophecy of Isaiah, however, refers to her explicitly, "Therefore the Lord himself will give you this sign: the virgin shall be with child, and bear a Son, and shall name him

Immanuel." (Isaiah 7:14). This name means "God is with us" and was fulfilled in Mary's virgin birth of Jesus. (See Matthew 1:23).

As Jesus was prefigured by types in the Old Testament, such as Joseph, so, too, was Our Lady prefigured by the types of Judith and Esther. (See the Books of Judith and Esther). The stories of these two great women should be read in faith as referring to the Triumph of the Immaculate Heart of Mary. Judith cuts off her enemy's head. She is like Mary who strikes Satan's proud head. Esther is a Queen who saves her people from an evil scheme for their destruction. She is also like Mary who, ironically, reverses Satan's scheme to destroy her and her children. She delivers them from evil. The praise of Judith is applicable to Mary,

> You are the glory of Jerusalem, the surpassing joy of Israel; you are the splendid boast of our people. With your own hand you have done all this; You have done good to Israel, and God is pleased with what you have wrought. May you be blessed by the Lord Almighty forever and ever! And all the people answered, "Amen!" (Judith 15:9-10).

The Immaculate Conception

The "splendid boast of our people" (see Judith 15:9) is Mary, the Immaculate Conception, who, because of the great dignity of her role as the Mother of God, was the only creature preserved by God free from every stain of sin, even Original Sin, in the first moment of her conception. This great privilege was given to her by God in the consideration of the infinite merits obtained by Jesus. She is *tota pulchra* (all beautiful).

God willed that she be immaculate so that his wondrous plan in the creation of the universe would be reflected in her and Jesus might find in her a worthy gateway through which to come to us. She is the immaculate and virginal shoot from which the Divine Flower shall blossom. The doctrine of the Immaculate Conception is implicitly revealed in Sacred Scripture. (See Genesis 3:15; Luke 1:28; Luke 1:41).

This doctrine was infallibly defined by Pope Pius IX in 1854. The charism of infallibility means that there can be no error when the Pope alone as supreme teacher of the faithful, or the Pope and the

Bishops, in union with him, agree that a doctrine regarding faith or morals is to be held definitely and absolutely. Pope Pius IX said that the doctrine as follows was revealed by God and is, therefore, to be believed firmly and constantly by all the faithful, "The Most Holy Virgin Mary was, in the first moment of her conception, by a unique gift of grace and privilege of Almighty God, in view of the merits of Jesus Christ, the Redeemer of mankind, preserved free from all stain of Original Sin." (*Ineffabilis Deus*, 1854).

As the Immaculate Conception, Mary does not merely have the absence of sin, but also the presence of grace. She possesses the fullness of the grace obtained by her Son's redemption. The Eastern Church calls her the "All Holy One."

As such, her life was a pure reflection of the life of God. Her soul was completely filled with grace. Her mind was opened to seek and love the will of God. Her heart was completely filled with love and her body was clothed in the immaculate light of virginal purity. She completely reflected the original plan of the Eternal Father.

As a consequence of her Immaculate Conception, Mary was free from concupiscence (unruly passions) and every personal sin during her entire life. Also, unlike us, she had no moral ignorance, no weakness of the will, and no bodily infirmities. She voluntarily incurred sufferings out of her great love.

What Adam and Eve lost by Original Sin, God renewed in Mary, together with many other gifts which are beyond our comprehension. She is the new Eve, whose virgin birth brought forth Jesus, the new Adam. His obedience made up for the disobedience of Adam and Eve and merited our redemption in Baptism, when we receive the life of grace and become children of God. (See Romans 5:19).

God began his plan to destroy sin and death with the Immaculate Conception. His plan is to clothe us through Mary, in her own immaculateness, and to heal us from sin. Her mission in this plan is to mediate all his graces to us and to fight and defeat the prideful head of Satan who is still at work in the world, prowling like a roaring lion looking for someone to devour. (See 1 Peter 5:8). She is our leader in this battle and applies the graces merited by her Son to us, her children in her army, through our simple faith, trust, humility, and obedience. (See Genesis 3:15). She promised us at Fatima that *"in the end my Immaculate Heart will triumph."*

The Annunciation

As a young girl, Mary had prayerfully meditated on the Scriptures. She knew that the Messiah would be born of a Jewish virgin but, in her humility, she never expected that she would be the Mother of the Redeemer.

The angel Gabriel announced to this teenager that she was chosen to be the Mother of Jesus. Mary responded, "I am the servant of the Lord. Let it be done to me according to thy Word." (Luke 1:38). With this obedient response to the will of God, Mary contradicted both Satan's disobedience and the disobedience of Adam and Eve. Mary was the first human being to accept the Person of Jesus as her Lord and Savior.

The Eternal Word of the Father, the Second Person of the Most Holy Trinity, descended into Mary's pure womb in expectation of her maternal cooperation, to receive from her his human nature and to become, in the flesh, a true man in the Divine Person of Jesus. This was the Incarnation of Jesus and the beginning of his Redemption of humanity, which ended with his Crucifixion.

God established his plan for our salvation in Mary. "This union of the Mother with the Son in the work of salvation was manifested from the time of Christ's virginal conception up to his death." (Vatican II, *Dogmatic Constitution on the Church,* 57). Mary was called to be the virgin Mother of our Redeemer and she said, *"Yes!"* In her, the Divine Person and nature of Christ incarnated, shared, redeemed, and freed our fallen human nature from sin and death.

"The Word became flesh and made his dwelling among us." (John 1:14). "The Virgin Mary, who at the message of the angel received the Word of God in her heart and her body and gave Life to the world, is acknowledged and honored as being truly the Mother of God and of the Redeemer." (Vatican II, *Dogmatic Constitution on the Church,* 58).

God could have come into the world as he left it—as an adult on a cloud in the air. He had no need of Mary, but he chose to entrust himself completely to her as an infant because of her humility and her obedience by which she cooperated in his plan of our salvation. God chose her to reach men. Likewise, we should choose her to reach God by our consecration to her Immaculate Heart.

Mary's role as the Mother of God underlies the whole mystery of her identity as the Immaculate Conception and explains everything else about her. However, her role in the divine plan of our salvation continued to manifest itself in union with her Son until his Crucifixion.

The Visitation and Nativity

Mary was inspired by the angel Gabriel's message about her elderly cousin Elizabeth's pregnancy, and in charity she visited her. The Holy Spirit prophesied, through Elizabeth, "Blest are you among women and blest is the fruit of your womb." (Luke 1:42). Like Elizabeth, we should say, "But who am I that the Mother of my Lord should come to me?" (Luke 1:43).

Mary's Visitation to Elizabeth brought Our Lord to her and to her baby, John the Baptist. He was sanctified in his mother's womb, freed from Original Sin, and enriched by grace.

Mary's response in her Magnificat Canticle shows her profound humility by which she gives God all of the glory and acknowledges him as her Savior. (See Luke 1:46-55). She praises his greatness for pulling down the mighty and exalting the humble.

In this mystery of the Visitation, we see Mary's role in the divine plan of salvation as the instrument of our sanctification. Grace comes to us from Jesus through Mary as the Mediatrix of her Son.

Mary also gave birth to Our Lord for the whole world and brought forth the Light to a world in darkness, which neither expected nor welcomed him. (See John 1:5). She joyfully showed him to the shepherds and the Magi. (See Luke chapter 2). The people of Israel had awaited this arrival of the Messiah for hundreds of years. Their hope which had been maintained by the voices of the prophets was now rewarded.

In the fullness of time, the light of Heaven came to a dark, cold cave through Mary. As light passes through a crystal, so too in his birth, did Jesus pass through the veil of Mary's virginal womb while preserving her virginity.

In this mystery, Mary foreshadowed in natural life her role in the supernatural life for all time as a bearer of Jesus to unworthy humanity.

The Presentation and the Finding of Jesus in the Temple

Forty days after his birth, Mary and Joseph brought the baby Jesus to the Temple in obedience to the law which said that "every first born male shall be consecrated to the Lord." (Luke 2:23).

Mary presented Jesus in the Temple and offered him to the Lord. This was in remembrance of the day in Egypt on which God struck dead the first born of the Egyptians, but spared the Jews.

Simeon received the baby Jesus as the Messiah that was awaited for centuries and as a Savior of all peoples. Simeon prophesied to Mary that "you yourself shall be pierced with a sword." (Luke 2:35).

This mystery reveals Mary's universal maternal function of bringing Jesus to all peoples. It also reveals that her maternal mission was to be one of profound suffering in an intimate and personal participation in the sorrowful mission of her Son, Jesus.

When Jesus was 12 years old, Mary and Joseph lost him when they visited Jerusalem. Filled with anguish and sorrow, they searched for him for three days before finding him teaching the elders in the Temple. (See Luke 2:41-49).

In this mystery, Mary foreshadowed her role of seeking all of her lost children in the supernatural life for all time. In anguish and sorrow, she pities lost sinners and mediates graces for their conversion so that, like Jesus, they may come home with her in obedience and grow in wisdom, age, and grace. (See Luke 2:52).

The Crucifixion

Mary stood at the foot of the Cross and mournfully kept her station, with the apostle John, in union with Jesus to the end. (See John 19:25).

Here was fulfilled Simeon's prophecy that a sword of sorrow would pierce her heart. (See Luke 2:35). As the heart of Jesus was pierced by the soldier's lance, so too was the heart of his Mother pierced by this sword of sorrow. (See John 19:34). She voluntarily consented to her suffering and sacrifice, in union with her Son's, but her sacrifice was unbloody.

The soldier's lance released blood and water from the heart of Jesus. (See John 19:34). The blood and the water symbolize the graces of the sacraments of the Eucharist and Baptism (see 1 John 5:6) by which we are incorporated and nourished in the Church, the Mystical Body of Christ. The sword of sorrow that pierced Mary's heart cooperated in the release of these graces.

The Second Vatican Council says that this happened "not without a divine plan" but that by "suffering deeply with her only begotten Son and joining herself with her maternal spirit to his Sacrifice, lovingly consenting to the immolation of the Victim to whom she had given birth," Mary "faithfully preserved her union with her Son even to the Cross!" It is a union through faith—the same faith with which she had received the angel's revelation at the Annunciation. (*Mother of the Redeemer*, St. Pope John Paul II, 1987, 18, 62).

"Woman, there is your Son." (John 19:26). Jesus identified his Church with John and he identified his Mother with the Woman of Genesis (see Genesis 3:15) and with the Woman of Revelation (see Revelation 12:1). The expression "Woman" goes to the very heart of the mystery of Mary and indicates the unique role which she has in the divine plan of our salvation. (*Mother of the Redeemer*, St. Pope John Paul II, 1987, 24).

Jesus told John, and all of us, "there is your Mother." (John 19:27). In this mystery, Mary foreshadowed her role as the Mother of the Church. As Mother of the Church, she is there interceding for us at our Baptism and our Eucharistic receptions. As she was the Mother of the Redeemer in natural life, so is she the Mother of the Church in the supernatural life. (Vatican II, *Dogmatic Constitution on the Church*, 61). St. Louis de Montfort wrote, "God the Son wishes to form himself and so, to speak, to incarnate himself in his members every day by his dear Mother...." (*True Devotion to Mary*, 31). She cooperates in giving birth to us in the supernatural life and in sustaining us in it by the graces obtained through her maternal intercession. Mary's motherhood in the supernatural life will last without interruption until the eternal fulfillment of all the elect. (Vatican II, *Dogmatic Constitution on the Church*, 62).

Pentecost

After the Ascension of Jesus into Heaven, the Apostles stayed in the Upper Room in Jerusalem, where they devoted themselves to constant prayer. Mary was with them. (See Acts 1:1-4). As a result of this constant prayer, the Holy Spirit descended upon them on the day of Pentecost. (See Acts 2:1-4).

As the Holy Spirit had overshadowed Mary at the Annunciation (see Luke 1:35), he descended, by her intercession, on her and the Apostles at Pentecost.

In this mystery, Mary foreshadowed her role of bringing us the Holy Spirit, our Sanctifier, whose fruits and gifts we receive through her intercession by the merits obtained by Jesus Christ. The Holy Spirit constantly brings faith to completion by his gifts. His pathway is the Immaculate Heart of Mary through which he passes to us.

As Mary brought forth Jesus in natural life, so she now brings him forth in the supernatural life in the Church by her spouse, the Holy Spirit.

And so, in the redemptive economy of grace, brought about through the action of the Holy Spirit, there is a unique correspondence between the moment of the Incarnation of the Word and the moment of the birth of the Church. The person who links these two moments is Mary: Mary at Nazareth and Mary in the Upper Room at Jerusalem. In both cases her discreet yet essential presence indicates the path of birth from the Holy Spirit! Thus, she who is present in the mystery of Christ as Mother becomes — by the will of the Son and the power of the Holy Spirit—present in the mystery of the Church. In the Church, too, she continues to be a maternal presence, as is shown by the words spoken from the Cross, "*Woman, behold your Son! Behold your Mother.*" (*Mother of the Redeemer,* St. Pope John Paul II, 1987, 24).

The Assumption and Coronation

Mary's place is now at the right hand of her Son enjoying the fullness of his joys and delights after her Assumption into Heaven and Coronation by him as Queen of the Universe. (See Vatican II, *Dogmatic Constitution on the Church,* 59). She is Queen, both by her perfection and by the power given to her by the Son, "of bestowing upon us the fruits of the redemption." (*Ad Coeli Reginam,* Pope Pius XII, 1954).

Jesus had not suffered his "faithful one to undergo corruption" (see Psalm 16:10) but had assumed her body and soul into the glory of Heaven at the end of her earthly life.

This doctrine was infallibly declared by Pope Pius XII, on November 1, 1950, as follows: "By the authority of our Lord Jesus Christ, of the blessed Apostles Peter and Paul, and by our own authority, We pronounce, declare, and define it to be a divinely revealed dogma that the Immaculate Mother of God, Mary, ever Virgin, after her life on earth, was assumed, body and soul, into heavenly glory." (*Munificentissimus Deus,* Pope Pius XII, III, 44).

This doctrine is implicitly, although obscurely, revealed in Sacred Scripture (see Genesis 3:15; Psalm 16:10-11; Psalm 132:8; Revelation 11:19) as well as in Tradition. However, the living Teaching Authority of the Church, whose Spirit of truth is with her at all times, can infallibly discern and declare what has been divinely revealed, regardless of how cryptic the revelation may be.

As Mary had shared in Christ's struggle against Satan and in his victory over sin on Calvary and his victory over death by his Resurrection and Ascension, so now she, as the New Eve, shares the fruit of these victories by her Assumption. (See Pope Pius XII, *Acta Apostolicae Sedis* 42). On earth, Mary always associated with her Son through her role as his Mother. Now, in Heaven, she is associated in his glory, having a glorified body like his own with which she still loves us as our mother through her Immaculate Heart.

In this mystery, Mary's role in the divine plan of our salvation is culminated. As death is the consequence of Original Sin, her Assumption is the consequence of her Immaculate Conception. Jesus shared with his Mother his triumph over sin and death and assumed, glorified, and coronated her body and soul. She was "exalted by the Lord as Queen over all things...." (Vatican II, *Dogmatic Constitution on the Church*, 59). Her Queenship rests on her divine motherhood. She is the Mother of Jesus, who "will rule over the house of Jacob forever and his Reign will be without end." (Luke 1:32). However, she "is to be called Queen because she, by the will of God, had an outstanding part in the work of our eternal salvation." (*Ad Coeli Reginam*, Pope Pius XII, 1954).

Mary now stands at his right hand, interceding, mediating, and dispensing to us all of the graces that his redemption merited. "Taken up to Heaven, she did not lay aside this saving role, but by her manifold acts of intercession continues to win for us gifts of eternal salvation." (Vatican II, *Dogmatic Constitution on the Church*, 62).

In this role, she will lead us to the ultimate defeat of Satan and his followers through the Triumph of Her Immaculate Heart in the world.

Co-Redemptrix

Our redemption was merited solely by the Passion and death of Our Lord and Savior, Jesus Christ. (See Hebrews 9:15; 1 Timothy 2:5). By his redemption, he paid the full price to satisfy God's justice and to buy us back from the consequences of sin, death, and the loss of Heaven caused by the Original Sin of Adam and Eve. By his redemption, he merited for all humanity the supernatural life of grace and our salvation and the glory of Heaven. This is the *objective redemption*.

However, these graces must be applied to us through our following in Christ's footsteps on our earthly pilgrimage. Jesus said that "if a man wishes to come after me, he must deny his very self, take up his cross, and begin to follow in my footsteps." (Matthew 16:24). As the Cyrenean helped Jesus to carry his Cross, so we must join our efforts to his and participate in his redemptive work.

This is the *subjective redemption* by which, according to Christ's will, all members of the Church, his Mystical Body, follow in his footsteps in cooperation with his redemptive work, so that the graces merited by him may be applied to his greater glory. This is what Saint Paul meant when he said that "in my own flesh I fill up what is lacking in the sufferings of Christ for the sake of his body, the Church." (Colossians 1:24).

Jesus is the only Redeemer because he alone is the mediator between God and humanity. However, he has willed to take into partnership in his redemptive work all of those whom he redeemed in order that the merciful work of his love may shine forth through us.

This merciful work of love is shared by all of us who unite our sufferings with Christ and thereby "fill up what is lacking in the sufferings of Christ ...." (Colossians 1:24).

Mary encouraged this merciful work of love at Fatima when she said, "*Pray, pray very much, and make sacrifices for sinners; for many souls go to Hell, because there are none to sacrifice themselves and to pray for them.*" (*Fatima in Lucia's Own Words*, Cambridge, MA 02138: The Ravengate Press, 1976, p. 171).

Mary followed in her Son's footsteps and cooperated in the objective redemption (Vatican II, *Dogmatic Constitution on the Church*, 58) and still cooperates in the subjective redemption. Therefore, she can be called our Co-Redemptrix. Her role is as perfect leader and Mediatrix in the subjective redemption of humanity, applying the graces merited by her Son, with her cooperation, in the accomplished objective redemption.

Pope Benedict XV wrote in *Inter Sodalicia* (1918),

> With her suffering and dying Son, Mary endured suffering and almost death. She gave up her mother's rights over her Son to procure the salvation of mankind, and to appease the divine justice, she, as much as she could,

immolated her Son, so that one can truly affirm that together with Christ she has redeemed the human race.

As the Fall of man came about through the cooperation of Adam and Eve in the Original Sin, so did the restoration of man come about through the cooperation of Jesus and Mary in the Redemption.

Mediatrix of All Graces

Mary is the Mediatrix of All Graces. St. John Paul II said, "This role of Mary, totally grounded in that of Christ and radically subordinated to it, in no way obscures or diminishes the unique mediation of Christ, but rather shows its power." (*The Rosary of the Virgin Mary*, 2002, 1:15).

The sole mediator between God and humanity is Jesus Christ, who gave himself as a ransom for all. (See 1 Timothy 2:5-6). A mediator is a friendly third party who interposes between parties who are not united. Jesus is our mediator with God because he shared our human nature so that we could share his divine nature through the graces merited by his Passion and death.

Such mediation does not exclude a subordinate mediation by Mary between Jesus and us through her intercession and dispensation of the graces merited by him. It is in this sense that Vatican Council II probably used the title "Mediatrix." (Vatican II, *Dogmatic Constitution on the Church*, 62). However, neither this title nor that of "Co-Redemptrix" has been solemnly dogmatically defined. Nevertheless, "all theologians now agree in holding this most tender and salutary doctrine that Mary is the Mediatrix of All Graces." (Decree of the Congregation of Rites approved by Pope Pius XII, January 11, 1942, *Acta Apostolicae Sedis* 34:44). As Jesus is our mediator with God the Father of our redemption, Mary is our Mediatrix with God the Son of his graces.

It is the will of God to exercise the power of Christ's mediation by the application of his merited graces to us through his Mother, our Mediatrix in the subjective redemption. (Vatican II, *Dogmatic Constitution on the Church*, 60). Jesus is the source of Mary's mediation which makes available to us the richness of his mediation through her Immaculate Heart and the ministry of priests.

As Mary was our Co-Redemptrix while still on her earthly pilgrimage and gave us Jesus, the source of all graces, so now is she our Mediatrix in Heaven who distributes those graces to us. As Mother of the source of all graces, can she not be the mother of all graces from the source?

The title of Mediatrix befits Mary's dignity because she did such great things for our salvation as a participant with her Son in his objective redemption. She furnished him with a body with which she suffered in his Passion. Jesus makes her a continuing participant in the subjective redemption by placing her in charge of his merits to be distributed by her to the redeemed. In this way, she frees sinners, enriches the needy, elevates the just, and affords a universal refuge to all men.

Mary has demonstrated this role as Mediatrix very tenderly as a Mother, particularly at Medjugorje. There she has diffused graces which have converted sinners, healed the sick, and attracted millions to her as their refuge.

Pope Leo XIII quotes St. Bernardine of Siena as saying: "Every grace…has a threefold course. For, in accord with excellent order, it is dispensed from God to Christ, from Christ to the Virgin, and from the Virgin to us." (*Acta Apostolicae Sedis* 24:195-196, Pope Leo XIII, September 22, 1891).

St. Louis de Montfort says, "To go to Jesus, we must go to Mary; she is our mediatrix of intercession. To go to God the Father, we must go to Jesus; for he is our mediator of redemption." (*True Devotion to Mary*, 86).

As Jesus is the head of his Mystical Body, she is the heart, and all of the graces flow from the head through the heart to us as all of the other members of his Mystical Body. This is simply the will of God, which was decreed by Jesus on the Cross and carried out at Mary's Coronation. It was then that all of the graces which flow from the Father, merited for us by the Son and given by the Holy Spirit, were deposited with Mary as the treasurer for her distribution to the world according to her intercessory will, which is one with God's.

(*Mediator Dei*, Pope Pius XII, 1947). As the Father gave all to the Son (see John 3:35), so did the Son give all graces to his Mother for us.

The mediation of the Immaculate Heart of Mary is two-way. She mediates all graces to us from God and she also mediates to God from us all of our prayers, sacrifices, and good works, embellishing them with her own merits. She mediates the gratitude which we owe to God by which he is glorified.

Mary's role as Mediatrix was foreshadowed at the wedding feast of Cana where she interceded with Jesus and mediated his gift of new wine. (See John chapter 2). Similarly, Mary, as Mother of the Church, obtains the spiritual nourishment of all graces necessary for our eternal salvation. (*Mother of the Redeemer*, St. Pope John Paul II, 1987. 21:7). The mystery of her mystical maternity, first foreshadowed at the Annunciation, then at Cana, and finally at the Crucifixion, is now carried out in her role as Mediatrix.

At Medjugorje, on August 25, 1987, Mary said, *"Dear children, seek from God the graces which he is giving you through me. I am ready to intercede with God for all that you seek so your holiness may be complete. Therefore, dear children, do not forget to seek, because God has permitted me to obtain graces for you."*

As Queen of the Universe, Mary will exercise her role as Universal Mediatrix of All Graces "until the eternal fulfillment of the elect." (Vatican II, *Dogmatic Constitution on the Church*, 62), when the work of the redemption is completed and Jesus will subject himself and all created things to the Father, that God may be all in all. (See 1 Corinthians 15:27-28).

The Virtues of Mary

In her lifetime, Mary practiced all virtues to perfection. "However, Mary is not unapproachable to us because of her sublime privileges and virtues. She journeyed, as we do, in faith through the joys, sufferings, and trials of everyday life. The faithful still strive to conquer sin and increase in holiness. And so, they turn their eyes to Mary who shines forth to the whole community of the elect as the model of virtues." (Vatican II, *Dogmatic Constitution on the Church*, 65).

We have in Mary no other person more approachable, simpler, and more human. Mary is our model in the pilgrimage of faith. She is an attractive model since she practiced the virtues in ordinary, everyday life, like most of us, by fulfilling lowly daily duties and leading a hidden, retired life in joy and in sorrow.

She practiced obedient faith by believing the message of the angel Gabriel that she would be the Mother of God. She practiced ardent charity by visiting and caring for her elderly, pregnant cousin, Elizabeth. In maternal love, she gave birth to her Son. In obedience to the Law she presented him in the Temple. She docilely accepted God's will by receiving Simeon's prophecy of her suffering and by accepting her Son's mission to do the work of his Father.

A brief review of her pilgrimage of faith through the mysteries of her life exemplifies her practice of the virtues and should move us to imitate them. She practiced lively faith and the docile acceptance of the Word of God (see Luke 1:26-38; 1:45; 11:27-28; John 2:5); generous obedience (see Luke 1:38); genuine humility (see Luke 1:48); solicitous charity (see Luke 1:39-56); profound wisdom (see Luke 1:29, 34; 2:19; 33:51); and worship of God manifested in the fulfillment of religious duties (see Luke 2:21-41); gratitude for gifts received (see Luke 1:46-49); her offering in the Temple (see Luke 2:22-24); and her prayer in the midst of the Apostles (see Acts 1:12-14).

She practiced fortitude in exile (see Matthew 2:13-23) and in suffering (see Luke 2:34-35, 49; John 19:25); poverty reflecting dignity and trust in God (see Luke 1:48; 2:24); attentive care for her Son, from his humble birth to the ignominy of the Cross (see Luke 2:1-11); virginal purity (see Matthew 1:18-25; Luke 1:26-38); and strong and chaste married love.

St. Louis de Montfort lists the ten principal virtues of Mary: her profound humility; her lively faith; her blind obedience; her continual prayer; her universal mortification; her divine purity; her ardent charity; her heroic patience; her angelic sweetness; and her divine wisdom. (*True Devotion to Mary*, 108). These virtues will be ours if we study and follow her example. St. Louis tells us,

> The predestinate keep the way of our Blessed Lady; their good mother; that is to say, they imitate her. It is on this point that they are truly happy and truly devout, and bear

the infallible mark of their predestination, according to the words this good mother speaks to them: Blessed are they who practice my virtues (see Proverbs 8:32), and with the help of divine grace walk in the footsteps of my life. During life they are happy in this world through the abundance of grace and sweetness which I impart to them from my fullness, and more abundantly to them than to others who do not imitate me so closely. They are happy in their death, at which I am ordinarily present myself, that I may conduct them to the joys of eternity; for never has any one of my good servants been lost who imitated my virtues during life. (*True Devotion to Mary*, 200).

The Divine Mary

During the Liturgy of the Eucharist, when the priest pours wine and water into the chalice, he says, "By the mystery of this water and wine, may we come to share in the divinity of Christ who humbled himself to share in our humanity."

As Christ shared in our humanity, so, too, by grace, do we share in his divinity. A soul in the state of grace is divinized. That is, it shares the very divine nature of God. (See 2 Peter 1:4). Mary shares in the divine nature to the highest degree.

"All glorious is the king's daughter as she enters; her raiment is threaded with spun gold." (Psalm 45:14). As the daughter of an earthly king partakes of his royalty, so too does Mary, the daughter of Our Father, the Heavenly King, partake of his divinity.

"Consequently, through the power of the Holy Spirit, in the order of grace, which is a participation in the divine nature, Mary receives life from him to whom she herself, in the order of earthly generation, gave life as a mother." (*Mother of the Redeemer*, St. Pope John Paul II, 1987, 10).

So it is that St. Louis calls her "the divine Mary." (*True Devotion to Mary*, 6, 217). By this, he meant that she is so transformed into Christ by grace that she lives no more, and is as though she were not, Christ living and reigning in her more perfectly than in all the angels and the blessed. (*True Devotion to Mary*, 63).

Likewise, St. Maximilian Kolbe stated that Mary was "the creature most elevated among creatures, the most perfect creature, divine." (Conference July 26, 1939 as quoted in *The Immaculate Conception,* Piacentini, Ernest, Kenosha, Wisconsin: Franciscan Marytown Press, 1975, p. 164).

Mary's human nature was overshadowed by the divine nature at the Annunciation. (See Luke 1:35). She continued to merit grace through her earthly pilgrimage, so that her human nature could be said to have been completely divinized by grace because of her cooperation in the objective and subjective redemptions.

In God's plan of salvation, the role of the Blessed Virgin Mary also includes her as a Prophetess of Chastisements.

2. Warnings and Chastisements

God has a *perfect will* that we should love him and one another. He also has a *permissive will*, whereby he permits us to exercise our own free will, which is a gift from him, to hate him and one another.

This is a simple explanation of how a God of love can chastise us himself or allow others to do so and can allow human suffering, hate, and violence. However, in his mysterious providence, all of these work for the good. (See Romans 8:28).

The Book of Judith tells us how the God of love allowed his Chosen People, the Jews, to suffer at the hands of the Assyrians and their general Holofernes who cut off their water supply and laid siege against them for 34 days.

The Jews were prostrate from thirst and exhaustion and saw this as God's vengeance for their sins and the sins of their forefathers. But Judith, a holy widow, did not see this as God's vengeance against them, but as a warning for them to turn to him.

Judith said, "Not for vengeance did the Lord put [their forefathers] in the crucible to try their hearts, nor has he done so with us. It is by way of admonition that he chastises those who are close to him." (Judith 8:27).

In his providence, God delivered the Jews through the hands of Judith, who cut off the head of Holofernes in his tent with his own sword. This led to the panic and retreat of the Assyrian army whom the Jews pursued and defeated.

The terms "justice," "judgment," and "chastisement" are often used interchangeably. A chastisement is an act of God's love, justice, and mercy to correct our consciences and to bring us to repentance, reconciliation, and peace with him.

It is not vengeance that God exacts, but a just punishment either by God directly through his perfect will, such as the Great Flood, or indirectly through his permissive will and the hands of others, such as the two destructions of Jerusalem by the Babylonians and by the Romans, or through nature, such as "from the Lord of hosts you will be punished with thunder and earthquake and loud noise, with whirlwind and tempest, and the flame of a consuming fire." (Isaiah 29:6).

God's justice is not vengeful and mean-spirited. His chastisements are not for destruction, but for *reconstruction* — to bring us to repentance and conversion and back to him and to his divine mercy through the forgiveness of our sins. Divine judgments are not to consume us, but to purify us. They are not to condemn us, but to redeem us. They are not an end, but a chance for a new beginning. We can bring about this new beginning through prayer, fasting, and the sacraments of Confession and Eucharist.

Through chastisements, we can participate in Christ's redemptive act by sharing in his sufferings. Moreover, it is better to suffer from God's justice and chastisements and to repent and receive his mercy in our lifetime than to possibly suffer from the justice of his particular judgment of damnation to Hell for unrepented sins upon our death.

God does judge. Hell is eternal punishment for unrepented sin. It is a real consequence of wrongdoing and is deservedly suffered. But to save us from Hell, God chooses to impose chastisements. These are intended to discourage us from self-injury by wrongdoing and to encourage us to rectify our lives. Sin is separation from God and violation of his loving plan. Punishment shows sinners what they are doing to themselves. So, God permits humankind to experience the consequences of sin.

Sister Lucia, the Fatima, Portugal visionary, wrote with respect to chastisements, "And let us not say that it is God who is punishing us in this way; on the contrary it is people themselves who are preparing their own punishment. In his kindness, God warns us and calls us to the right path, while respecting the freedom he has given us; hence people are responsible."

Chastisements hang over the nations of the world because of the enormity of sin and the outright denial of and hatred of the one true God. If we do not convert and return to him, he punishes us because he loves us and wants to correct us.

God will not be ridiculed forever. As St. Paul tells us, "Make no mistake: God is not mocked." (Galatians 6:7). Again and again, God has appealed to mankind to turn from their evil and sinful ways. He longs to forgive us and to pour out his great mercy upon us rather than his perfect justice.

As the prophet Micah tells us, "Who is there like you, the God who removes guilt and pardons sin for the remnant of his inheritance; who does not persist in anger forever, but delights rather in clemency, and will again have compassion on us, treading underfoot our guilt? You will cast into the depths of the sea all our sins." (Micah 7:16-19).

In his first encyclical, *Deus Caritas Est,* (God is Love), Pope Benedict XVI invited us to recall that "even in their bewilderment and failure to understand the world around them, Christians continue to believe in the 'goodness and loving kindness of God.' (Titus 3:4)." (*Deus Caritas Est,* 38).

Nevertheless, what good and loving father would not correct his children?

St. Paul tells us that "with flaming power he will inflict punishment on those who do not know God nor heed the good news of Our Lord Jesus." (2 Thessalonians 1:8).

Our Lady of Fatima prophesied an Era of Peace and St. John Paul II announced a New Era of Peace. However, these eras will not come without warnings and chastisements.

A "warning" is a call either to change through conversion and repentance or to suffer from a chastisement or punishment. Mary's Ten Secrets at Medjugorje contain both warnings and chastisements.

The prophets warned us to stop sinning or be punished. God never inflicts chastisements without warning us through his servants, the prophets. God's love for his sinful children is shown through the prophets who issue warnings either to turn back to God with faith, prayer, and fasting or to suffer chastisements.

Jesus gave the same warning that the prophet John the Baptist gave. They both gave the same call, "Repent, for the Kingdom of Heaven is at hand." (Matthew 3:2; 4:17). After the Tower of Siloam fell and killed eighteen people, Jesus was asked if they were guiltier than all of the others in Jerusalem. He replied, in a statement that still applies today, "Certainly not! But I tell you, unless you repent, you will all perish as they did." (Luke 13:5).

Chastisements and God's Love

Scripture says that God chastises those he loves. "Whoever is dear to me I reprove and chastise. Be honest about it, therefore, and repent!" (Revelation 3:19). God allows chastisements to serve his divine plan of love, to help awaken the consciences of our souls and thereby to turn our hearts and minds to him, our God and Savior.

The Bible assures us of God's love. St. John the Evangelist wrote, "For God so loved the world that he gave his only Son, that whoever believes in him should not perish but have eternal life. For God sent the Son into the world, not to condemn the world, but that the world might be saved through him." (John 3:16-17).

In the Letter to the Hebrews, it says, "My son, do not regard lightly the discipline of the Lord nor lose courage when you are punished by him. For the Lord disciplines him whom he loves and chastises every son whom he receives." (Hebrews 12:5-6). The Letter to the Hebrews says that chastisements are to make the righteous holy, just as an earthly father disciplines his children to teach them to be good. (See Hebrews 12:5-13).

God passed before Moses and proclaimed, "The Lord, the Lord, a merciful and gracious God, slow to anger and rich in kindness and fidelity, continuing his kindness for a thousand generations, and forgiving wickedness and crime and sin; yet not declaring the guilty guiltless, but punishing children and grandchildren to the third and fourth generation for their fathers' wickedness!" (Exodus 34:6-7).

However, fear of chastisements is useless; what is needed is trust. "We should have confidence on the day of judgment...." (1 John 4:17). "Be sincere of heart, be steadfast, and do not be alarmed when disaster comes. Trust him and he will uphold you, follow a straight path and hope in him." (Sirach 2:2-6).

St. John wrote, "So we know and believe the love God has for us. God is love, and he who abides in love abides in God, and God abides in him. In this is love perfected with us, that we may have confidence for the day of judgment, because as he is so are we in this world. There is no fear in love, but perfect love casts out fear. For fear has to do with punishment, and he who fears is not perfected in love." (1 John 9-10, 16-18).

Chastisements of the Innocent

God's chastisements can result in the death of innocent people. The death of Jesus himself is the prime example. God allows this for a greater good. God's chastisements bring suffering, which is mysteriously meritorious to those who accept it, abandon themselves, and offer it to him. Suffering brings people to repentance that brings God's merciful forgiveness, healing, and union with him.

The greatest act of God's justice was upon Jesus himself, the God-Man, who was a totally innocent victim. He took upon himself the punishment for all of our sins in order to save us and grant us the gift of eternal life through the forgiveness of our sins. This is one way that we can begin to understand how so merciful a work as our salvation could require so cruel a form of justice or satisfaction in the form of death by crucifixion. God willed to save us, not in just any way but in the best way by fulfilling all justice and so attracting us most powerfully to love his mercy.

The innocent also suffer from chastisements, as shown by the trials of Job.

God allowed the chastisements of the innocent Job for God's greater glory. Job's story is told in the Book of Job. He was an innocent man who was "blameless and upright who feared God and avoided evil." (Job 1:1). He had many children, animals, and much property and was "greater than any of the men of the East." (Job 1:3). God allowed that he suffer chastisements and lose it all.

The Book of Job shows that God allowed him to be chastised through Satan by means that still happen today: enemy raiders (like today's terrorists); forces of nature, such as lightning and a great wind (like today's hurricanes and tornadoes); a loathsome disease causing boils and scabs (like today's AIDS); and the death and loss of property, animals, employees, and children.

Job is a model of a good attitude towards the chastisements of innocent people. He was humble and realized that God allows the chastisements of innocent people like himself. He recognized that God does not have to justify his actions to men, that he is almighty and omnipotent, and that one must humbly accept suffering and must trust in God that "all things work for good for those who love God." (Romans 8:28).

We should say with Job, "Happy is the man whom God reproves! The Almighty's chastening do not reject. For he wounds, but he binds up; he smites, but his hands give healing." (Job 5:17-18).

We should imitate him and his acceptance of chastisements. Job said, "Naked I came forth from my mother's womb, and naked shall I go back again. The Lord gave and the Lord has taken away; blessed be the name of the Lord!" (Job 1:21). "We accept good things from God; and should we not accept bad?" (Job 2:10). And all was restored to Job with more than he had before the chastisements.

Finally, we should stop questioning God and trust in his ways of divine providence. Job said, "I know that you can do all things and that no purpose of yours can be hindered. I have dealt with great things that I do not understand; things too wonderful for me, which I cannot know. I had heard of you by word of mouth, but now my eye has seen you. Therefore, I disown what I have said, and repent in dust and ashes." (Job 42:2-6).

Jesus Christ was the totally innocent one that suffered from chastisement. Isaiah prophesied, "But he was wounded for our transgressions, he was bruised for our iniquities; upon him was the chastisement that made us whole, and with his stripes we were healed....But the Lord laid upon him the guilt of us all." (Isaiah 53:5-6).

Chastisements in the Bible

There are many examples of chastisements in the Bible: the Great Flood (Genesis 6:5); the destruction of Sodom and Gomorrah (Genesis 28:20); the earthquake that swallowed up Korah and his followers (Numbers 16:32); and the plagues of Egypt (Exodus 6:6; 12:12).

King David sinned grievously by counting the number of his army, rather than trusting in the strength of God. He was punished and God sent a pestilence that killed 70,000 people. (2 Samuel 24:15). Later, God allowed the Babylonian Captivity and the destruction of Jerusalem.

The prophets warned of biblical chastisements. Isaiah, Jeremiah, Ezekiel, and Jesus all prophesied the destruction of Jerusalem for its sins. (See Isaiah chapter 1; Jeremiah chapter 1; Ezekiel chapter 23; Luke 21:5-6, 20-24). These were prophecies of divine chastisements that were fulfilled. Jesus' prophecy of the destruction of Jerusalem was fulfilled with the killings of almost one million people by the Roman General Titus in the year 70 A. D. (See Luke 19:41-44; 21:5-6, 20-24).

God creates everything good. Evil comes from creatures' abuses of their freedom, and punishment for sin is not arbitrarily imposed by God.

Human punishment often has the character of a more or less vengeful reaction, but God's punishment has nothing of this character. It comes from his love and his desire to save us.

Without excluding our free will, God "desires all men to be saved and to come to the knowledge of the truth." (1 Timothy 2-4). Jesus comes to save, not to condemn. (See John 3:17; 12:7).

God's justice ultimately consists in being faithful to his gifts of life and freedom. God simply cannot be unfaithful. (See 2 Timothy 2:12-13). God tries every means to win the love of sinners who initially reject him, but still might repent. In the death of our Lord Jesus, we see how far he goes, "God so loved the world that he gave his only Son." (John 3:16).

≈≈≈

This book teaches us how to prepare for the secrets and chastisements prophesied by the Blessed Virgin Mary at Medjugorje. Prophesied secrets, warnings, and chastisements from Mary are nothing new. She gave secrets and warned of chastisements before she came to Medjugorje. Mary has warned of chastisements in modern times, since 1917, beginning in Fatima, Portugal.

Mary, Prophetess of Chastisements

God's chastisements are his secrets which he reveals to his prophets. They speak his word and reveal them to us so that by repentance and conversion we can mitigate or avoid them. "For the Lord God does nothing without revealing his secrets to his servants, the prophets." (Amos 3:7).

God revealed chastisements to his prophets so that those whom they warned could mitigate or avoid them. He revealed to Noah the Great Flood; to Abraham and Lot the destruction of Sodom and Gomorrah; to Joseph the seven years' famine in Egypt; to Moses the plagues of Egypt; and to Jonah the destruction of Nineveh. These were prophets sent by God in the Old Testament. In modern times, he has sent his Mother as the prophetess of chastisements.

As such, Mary has warned the world in modern times to repent and convert or to suffer chastisements, long before her apparitions at Medjugorje. In 1917, at Fatima, Portugal, during World War I, she prophesied destruction as a divine chastisement and punishment for sins. She said, "*War is a punishment for sins*" and that God was "*about to punish the world for its crimes by means of war, famine, and persecutions of the Church and of the Holy Father.*" She also warned that if her messages were not obeyed, "*nations will be annihilated.*"

On July 13, 1917, she revealed the vision of the Third Secret of Fatima. On June 26, 2000, Cardinal Joseph Ratzinger, later Pope Benedict XVI, interpreted this vision and said, "This represents the threat of judgment [chastisements] which looms over the world. Today the prospect that the world might be reduced to ashes by a sea of fire [as Mary prophesied at Akita, Japan in 1973] no longer seems pure fantasy: man himself, with his inventions, has forged the flaming sword. The vision then shows the power which stands opposed to the force of destruction — the splendor of the Mother of God and…the summons to penance.…The vision speaks of dangers and how we might be saved from them."

We have been saved from these dangers or they have been mitigated by Mary's intercession. However, the threat of judgment still looms over the world. Mary is the prophetess of coming chastisements. She comes in love for all of her earthly children to warn us so that we might be able to do something about it.

On October 13, 1973, at Akita, Japan, Mary said, "*If men do not repent and better themselves, the Father will inflict a terrible punishment on all humanity. It will be a punishment greater than the deluge, such as one will never have seen before. Fire will fall from the sky and will wipe out a great part of humanity, the good as well as the bad, sparing neither priests nor faithful. The survivors will find themselves so desolate that they will envy the dead.*"

In 1981, at Kibeho, Rwanda, Mary said, "*I am concerned with and turning to the whole world to repent because otherwise the world is on the edge of catastrophe.*"

Mary still appears throughout the world pleading for prayer and fasting to bring conversions and peace. The alternative, she warns, is to suffer chastisements.

As these calamities approach, we should prepare for them and protect ourselves against them. Jesus told us to "*be prepared.*" He said,

> For as it was in the days of Noah, so it will be at the coming of the Son of Man. In those days before the flood, they were eating and drinking, marrying and giving in marriage, up to the day that Noah entered the ark.
>
> They did not know until the flood came and carried them all away. So, will it also be at the coming of the Son of Man.
>
> Two men will be out in the field; one will be taken, and one will be left. Two women will be grinding at the mill; one

will be taken, and one will be left. Therefore, stay awake! For you do not know on which day your Lord will come. Be sure of this: if the master of the house had known the hour of night when the thief was coming, he would have stayed awake and not let his house be broken into. So too, you also must be prepared, for at an hour you do not expect, the Son of Man will come. (Matthew 24:37-44).

In his great mercy, Jesus King of All Nations has provided a means for protection from chastisements for us.

Protection from Chastisements through The Jesus King of All Nations Devotion

Chastisements can be averted (turned away or avoided) or mitigated (lessened in severity) if people respond to the warning of the chastisement. For example, the prophet Jonah warned Nineveh (ancient Iraq) that it would be destroyed in forty days. But the people repented, prayed, and fasted and the chastisement was averted. (See Jonah chapter 3).

History shows that heeding the call to repentance is critical. At the preaching of Jonah, Nineveh repented and was spared its chastisement. At the preaching of Jesus, Jerusalem did not repent and was chastised by its utter destruction by the Romans.

Mary told Sister Agnes of Akita, "*Pray very much the prayers of the Rosary. I alone am able still to save you from the calamities which approach. Those who place their confidence in me will be saved.*"

At Medjugorje, Mirjana said that the Tenth Secret's chastisement is "unconditional." However, chastisements can be mitigated by prayer and penance. According to visionary Mirjana, we are close to chastisement and so she says to "convert yourselves as quickly as possible. Open your hearts to God."

Our attitude towards chastisements should be as Mary told Jelena, another visionary at Medjugorje, "*Don't think about wars,*" *chastisements, evil. It is when you concentrate on these things that you are on the way to enter into them. Your responsibility is to accept divine peace, to live it."*

Excessive curiosity regarding the prophesied chastisements should be replaced by confidence and obedience to Mary's requests for conversion, faith, prayer, fasting, and consecration to her Immaculate Heart.

Beginning in 1988, two American women received apparitions from Jesus. He revealed his title as "Jesus King of All Nations" in apparitions to them in the State of Virginia in the United States. Most of the revelations were made to the younger woman who called herself "his servant." Jesus called her "his Secretary." The older woman called herself his Secretary's "Spiritual Mother." After the death of her Spiritual Mother, his Secretary has continued to receive the revelations of Jesus King of All Nations.

Jesus revealed that he wants his Reign to be *recognized* on earth. He also revealed his image and an ejaculation to help us to recognize his Reign, "*O Jesus King of All Nations, may your Reign be recognized on earth!*" These words are engraved on a medal that Jesus requested be struck for us to keep in reverence for our protection from chastisements.

The revelations of Jesus King of All Nations are recorded in his Secretary's journal, *I Will Sing of Mercy, The Journal of the Secretary of the Jesus King of All Nations Devotion*, edited by Dan Lynch, hereinafter referred to as *Journal.* A citation to the *Journal* is followed by its paragraph number.

The Devotion is consistent with Scripture, Tradition, and the Teaching Authority of the Church. It was granted the *Nihil Obstat*, which is a declaration that the Devotion contains nothing contrary to faith or morals.

In his great love for us, Jesus revealed images of himself; of Mary Mediatrix of All Graces; and of St. Michael the Archangel. He requested that a medal be struck of himself and St. Michael. He also revealed prayers and promises of healings, conversions, protection, and the peace, love, and joy of his Kingdom so that we may be one in him with unity in one flock with one shepherd in the one holy apostolic Catholic Church.

Jesus called these revelations the Jesus King of All Nations Devotion. He wants to reign in all hearts and nations and he wants his Reign to be recognized on earth. He wants us to practice his revealed Devotion: to enthrone and venerate his revealed image; to wear his revealed medal; to pray the Rosary and his revealed prayers; to receive the sacraments of Penance and the Eucharist; to recognize Saint Michael the Archangel as the Protector of the Blessed Sacrament; and to recognize his Mother as the Mediatrix of All Graces.

Jesus also wants his Church to proclaim the dogma and title that his Mother is "Mary Mediatrix of All Graces." He wants to grant us graces of forgiveness, conversion, healing, protection, and peace through the mediation of his Mother.

In his mercy, Jesus gives us an opportunity to recognize his Reign now, before he reclaims it in his justice. We should accept this opportunity and "approach the throne of grace to receive mercy...." (Hebrews 4:16).

Jesus told his Secretary with his scriptural citation in italics, "I have come to entrust to you a message of great importance for the world. I tell you, my very little one, the days are coming when mankind will cry out to me for mercy. I tell you, my child, that in these times only one thing will be given as a remedy. I myself am that remedy! *"...for the healing of the nations."* (Revelation 22:2). Let souls give devotion to me, through my Most Holy Mother, as 'Jesus King of All Nations.'" (*Journal* 159-160).

Jesus said, "I want to reign in all hearts!" (*Journal* 233). "...my throne on this earth remains in the hearts of all men. *"...in your hearts...by his grace."* (Colossians 3:16). I most particularly reign in the most holy Eucharist, *"Take and eat; this is my body."* (Matthew 26:26) and in loving hearts *"Welcome him, then, with all joy..."* (Philippians 2:29) that believe in me, that speak with me, and I tell you, my daughter, that I do speak in the hearts of all men." (*Journal* 197).

The Reign of Jesus King of All Nations is recognized by our acceptance of his sovereignty and submission to his Reign, authority, rule, and law through faith and conversion. His Reign is established in our hearts by our consecration to Mary Mediatrix of All Graces in which we pray, "I give and consecrate myself to you,

Mary Mediatrix of All Graces, that Jesus, our one true mediator, who is the King of All Nations, may reign in every heart."

The Jesus King of All Nations Devotion contains prayers and promises for protection from chastisements. The promises to those who embrace the Devotion include protection from harm and mitigation of chastisements and all forms of God's justice.

To mitigate (lessen) chastisements and to help us save souls, Jesus asked us to pray the Novena in Honor of Jesus as True King and made us a promise. He asked us to pray, "Forgive us, O Sovereign King, our sins against you. *"Father, I have sinned against heaven and before thee."* (Luke 15:18). Jesus, you are a king of mercy. *"...who giveth us the early and the latter rain in due season..."* (Jeremiah 5:24). We have deserved your just judgment. *"...to what then shall I liken the men of this generation?"* (Luke 7:31). Have mercy on us, Lord, and forgive us. We trust in your Great Mercy! *"The Lord is gracious and merciful, slow to anger and full of kindness."* (Psalms 144:8). O most awe-inspiring King, we bow before you and pray; May your Reign, your Kingdom, be recognized on earth! Amen." *(Journal* 29). He promised us, "...each time you say these prayers,...I will mitigate the severity of the chastisements upon your country." *(Journal* 41).

Jesus also revealed his only medal to the world and promised us protection if we wore it. (See Appendix B).

In his will, God can rescue the devout from chastisements. St. Peter writes, "For if God did not spare the angels when they sinned, but condemned them to the chains of Tartarus and handed them over to be kept for judgment; and if he did not spare the ancient world, even though he preserved Noah, a herald of righteousness, together with seven others, when he brought a flood upon the godless world; and if he condemned the cities of Sodom and Gomorrah to destruction, reducing them to ashes, making them an example for the godless people of what is coming; and if he rescued Lot, a righteous man oppressed by the licentious conduct of unprincipled people, then the Lord knows how to rescue the devout from trial and to keep the unrighteous under punishment for the day of judgment. " (2 Peter 2:4-9).

COVID-19, The Beginning of the Chastisements to Correct the Conscience of Mankind

On March 18, 2020, Jesus King of All Nations revealed a message to his Secretary, the mystic of the Jesus King of All Nations Devotion. He said that what we were then seeing happen around us was the beginning of the chastisements that he has prophesied to correct the conscience of mankind. In my opinion, he was referring to the COVID-19 pandemic.

Monsignor Nicola Bux, former theologian for the Vatican Congregations for the Doctrine of the Faith, for Divine Worship, and for the Pontifical Celebrations Office, confirmed the March 18 message of Jesus King of All Nations that the COVID-19 virus pandemic was a chastisement.

Six days later, on March 24, Monsignor. Bux gave a YouTube Address, *COVID-19 Caso o Castigo?* (A Chance Event or a Chastisement?). He said, "Today, the word 'chastisement' arouses scandal even among churchmen, because they have forgotten that, at the beginning of world history, after love, there is sin, anger, and judgment."

Monsignor Bux's implication is that the "sin" is idolatry and the "judgment" is the chastisement of the COVID–19 pandemic. He warned us about idolatry and referred to the worship of the Pachamama idols at the Amazon Synod in October, 2019, at the Vatican in Rome. He said that idolatry is the "...gravest sin....We gave in to idolatry...by kneeling before heaps of earth and worshiping idolatrous statues, even in St. Peter's Basilica."

Before the idols were placed in the Santa Maria Church at the Amazon Synod, they were exhibited as part of a pagan ritual before the very eyes of Pope Francis. As he looked on, an Amazonian woman chanted to the idols. Several people carried the idols in procession to Pope Francis who then made the Sign of the Cross over them. After that they were placed in the Santa Maria Church.

Moreover, on March 18, 2020, the same day that Jesus King of All Nations revealed his message about the COVID-19 pandemic chastisement, Medjugorje visionary Mirjana Soldo announced that Our Lady had told her that she will no longer appear to her on the second day of every month.

Beginning on April 2, 2020, Mirjana's so-called "extraordinary apparitions" on the second of each month ended. They had previously occurred regularly on the second, in addition to Mirjana's annual apparitions which occurred every year on March 18, her birthday.

Although Mirjana will continue to have the annual apparitions on March 18 for the rest of her life, the end of the second of the month apparitions means that she will only see Our Lady once each year instead of 13 times as in previous years.

Our Lady's stated intention for the second of the month apparitions was to pray for all those who do not yet know God's love. The "extraordinary apparitions" ceased at virtually the same time that the public celebration of Masses were being canceled in many countries because of the COVID-19 pandemic. Is the time getting late for us to respond to Our Lady's requests?

On April 8, 2020, visionary Luz de Maria de Bonilla received a message from Our Lady. Her messages to Luz from 2009 and thereafter were approved by her Bishop, Juan Abelardo Mata, of Nicaragua, on March 19, 2017.

Our Lady told Luz, "Be cautious regarding those who call you to view this virus [COVID-19] as something else, when you know that it has emerged from human hands with the aim of reducing the world's population."

So, what is the remedy for what Jesus King of All Nations described in his March 18 message as "the ills of the world?"

He pleaded with us to practice his Devotion in order that he may, as he said in his message, "pour out abundant blessings upon poor, aching mankind." He said, "This shall call down my mercy and my healing upon the world."

Jesus concluded with a Call to Action, "Take heed of my words. Take action now."

The following is his complete message with his scriptural citations in italics.

> My children, pray my devotion, enthrone my image of Jesus King of All Nations.

What you see happening around you [the COVID-19 pandemic] is the beginning of the chastisements foretold by me to correct the conscience of mankind.

"Be watchful! I have told it all to you beforehand." (Mark 13:23).

Once more I appeal to my holy Church to rapidly approve my Jesus King of All Nations Devotion and allow the public practice of my devotion and the enthronement of my image.

As I have said before, this is the remedy for the ills of the world: the re-acclamation of my Sovereign Kingship over all of mankind, over all nations.

"Great and wonderful are your works, Lord God Almighty. Just and true are your ways, O king of the nations. Who will not fear you, Lord, or glorify your name? For you alone are holy. All the nations will come and worship before you, for your righteous acts have been revealed." (Revelation 15:3-4).

This shall call down my mercy and my healing upon the world.

"But for you who fear my name, there will arise the sun of justice with its healing rays;…" (Malachi 3:20).

Take heed of my Words. Take action now.

"Turn to me and be safe, all you ends of the earth, for I am God, there is no other!" (Isaiah 45:22).

I wait to pour out abundant blessings upon poor, aching mankind.

"If you wish to return, O Israel, says the Lord, return to me." (Jeremiah 4:1).

Jesus previously revealed in the message below that the Jesus King of All Nations Devotion is the "crowning glory" of all of the devotions to him.

This work is eternal for it is the proclamation of my Sovereign and Divine Kingship; the acknowledgment of my supreme authority over all creation; it is the song of praise sung by the Heavenly Court, by the angels who continually cry, 'Holy! Holy! Holy!' as they claim my divine sovereignty. (*Journal* 706).

Contained within it is the totality of all of the devotions to my Sacred and Divine Person for it is the crowning glory of all others: the absolute and supreme authority granted me by my Father. This authority which must be recognized by all and re-acclaimed by my Holy Church. (*Journal* 708).

Father Peter M. Damian Fehlner, OFM Conv., was the spiritual director of the Jesus King of All Nations Devotion. He believed, without any doubt, all of the revelations of the Devotion.

He studied all of the revelations of the Devotion and wrote that he believed in "the authenticity of these revelations as revelations directly dictated by Jesus to his Secretary and the truth of their content as a remedy for the imminent chastisement under way."

Summary Explanation of the Jesus King of All Nations Devotion by Father Peter M. Damian Fehlner, OFM Conv.

(The following is the Summary Explanation of the Devotion by Father Peter M. Damian Fehlner, OFM Conv., in his own words.)

The Jesus King of All Nations Devotion is one of recent origin, given by Jesus himself via interior locutions to two American women, mainly between 1988 and 1993, and described in great detail in a book with the title *I Will Sing of Mercy, The Journal of the Secretary of the Jesus King of All Nations Devotion*, edited by Dan Lynch.

What follows here is a summary explanation of the Devotion in outline form, intended to help first readers of the texts above to recognize the profoundly theological character of the Devotion and its roots in Sacred Scripture, both Old and New Testaments. The Devotion, as such, may be of recent origin but the mystery at its core, to be enthroned in the hearts of its practitioners by its practice, is nothing less than the acceptance of and living the kingship of Jesus everywhere in the world.

The image central to the Jesus King of All Nations Devotion, one drawing heavily on the Book of Esther, but adapted to the conditions of the Church in our times, is precisely the kingship of Jesus dwelling in our hearts, adored and worshiped, the foundation of that unity and communion of the faithful for which Jesus prayed before his crucifixion. (See John 17:22).

From this arises the importance of prominent public enthronement of this image in cathedrals and churches throughout the world and in all nations and the exercise of the Devotion not only by individuals, but by the entire Church and the desire of Our Lord for public approval for the practice of this Devotion publicly as well as privately. He has made this the condition for dispensing a stupendous number of blessings as fruits of the practice of this Devotion at a moment when the world is threatened by catastrophic disasters because the kingship of Jesus has been rejected by so many.

The principle exercise of this Devotion is the practice of virtue and loving obedience to the commandments of Jesus, precisely because we love him as our King and law-giver, where the central commandment is love of God the Father and love of neighbor as ourselves as Jesus does in the sacrifice of the Cross and Eucharist. Tributary prayers designed by Jesus provide a way of linking this exercise to specific needs of our neighbors and to the comfort of God. Among these prayers are *The Novena in Honor of Jesus as True King*; *The Chaplet of Unity*; *The Novena of Holy Communions*; *The Litany in Honor of Jesus King of All Nations*; and *The Consecration to Mary Mediatrix of All Grace,* in view of the Triumph of Her Immaculate Heart as the final realization of the Kingdom of God in the Church.

Finally, there is the medal (see *Journal* 75-76, 163-164), to be carried in one way or another by those exercising the Devotion, as a reminder of the great mercy our King has shown us in forgiving our indifference to and rejection of his kingship that otherwise would have ended in our just condemnation.

This contempt for the enthronement of Jesus as King in our hearts is the root of that catastrophic future looming over the world today and particularly over the United States. And it is this contempt for the kingship of Jesus that the practice of the Jesus King of All Nations Devotion strives to replace with that humble fear of the Lord as preface for obtaining the mercy of the King. Like the publican in the parable of the publican and the Pharisee (see Luke 18:9-14), we can begin to enjoy peace which only the kingship of Jesus can provide.

In this context, Jesus tells us (with his confirming scriptural references in italics,)

> This Devotion to me as Jesus King of All Nations is to be a companion devotion to that of my mercy as given to my beloved daughter Faustina, and to that of my Sacred Heart as given to my beloved daughter Margaret Mary. *"the saints"* (2 Corinthians 9:12). (*Journal* 165).

Precisely, in view of the terrorism of the times looming everywhere, Jesus says that this Devotion is necessary because the recognition of Christ's kingship, publicly by all, is the indispensable condition for dealing successfully with these evils which are not willed by Jesus but are a fruit of our refusal of his merciful kingship. He said,

> Let souls give devotion to me, through my Most Holy Mother, as Jesus King of All Nations. Mankind must recognize my Divine Kingship, my divine rights over them! *"The Lord is reigning, he is arrayed in majesty...Firm is thy throne from of old, from eternity thou art."* (Psalm 92:1-2). It is only in me, my child, that mankind will find peace. *"...but he will give you true peace..."* (Jeremiah 14:13). They senselessly strive after the things of this world. *"...for after all these things the nations of the world seek..."* (Luke 12:30). What of their death? What of the account they will have to render to me? *"The time is fulfilled, and*

the Kingdom of God is at hand. Repent and believe in the Gospel." (Mark 1:15). (*Journal* 160).

According to Jesus, the decline of the world then explains the need for the Devotion. He said, "Let it be known clearly and without question; the poor state of the world shall decline yet further, indeed from day to day, so long as my image and Devotion of Jesus King of All Nations remain hidden from the eyes of my Church and of the world." (*Journal* 380).

It provides, as well, the context for correctly understanding references to chastisements as instruments of Jesus to awaken in the nations the need to welcome in the lives of all the King of All Nations and to rejoice in his presence via the enthronement and so avoid a definitive catastrophe.

Jesus exhorts us, "Take up my Devotion of Jesus King of All Nations for in its practice you shall find for yourselves a haven of grace, mercy and protection. Enthrone this my image everywhere for I shall be powerfully present there and the power of my Sovereign Kingship shall surely shield you from my just judgment." (*Journal* 418).

In light of the above, lack of approval withholds the marvelous gifts and graces Jesus has guaranteed if the Devotion is practiced only privately, but not publicly, throughout the Church. Jesus himself said, "The promised graces and mercy stand at the ready, waiting to be poured out upon my Church, individual souls, religious communities, all nations and indeed truly upon the entirety of creation and yet are being withheld due to the absence of recognition and approval by my Holy Church." (*Journal* 381).

In conclusion, let us entrust ourselves to Jesus' Mother and ours. As Jesus himself said, "All is coming to fulfillment. Be at peace. Trust in my mercy and love. Pray to my Holy Mother. Entrust your lives to her. Receive the sacraments worthily and frequently. Obey my Holy Spouse, the Church. Remain faithful. I love you. I bless you." *"For I did not receive it from a human being, nor was I taught it, but it came through a revelation of Jesus Christ."* (Galatians 1:12). (*Journal* 321; see also 319, 320).

Jesus asked us to "Pray to My Holy Mother" because in her great love for us she has prophesied chastisements in order to bring us to conversion. Some of these chastisements have been fulfilled and some have not been fulfilled.

3. Chastisement Prophesies of the Blessed Virgin Mary - Fulfilled

We are living in an era of moral darkness and a Culture of Death. Secularism, atheism, paganism, relativism, materialism, sexual deviations including contraception, sodomy, same-sex false marriage and false transgenderism, abortions, no-fault divorce, and the weakening of the family are rampant throughout the world. These sins of humanity cry out to God for vengeance and his chastisements.

Jesus King of All Nations appealed to the world for conversion, a world, he said, "…which has forgotten its God!" (*Journal* 212). He said, "My holy and dear Mother has instructed you many times in many places how to bring down my mercy upon the world. This Woman of Hope still pleads for you all, her children. *"Blessed are you daughter, by the Most High God, above all the women on earth; and blessed be the Lord God, the creator of heaven and earth who guided your blow at the head of the chief of our enemies. Your deed of hope will never be forgotten by those who tell of the might of God. May God make this redound to your everlasting honor, rewarding you with blessings,…you averted our disaster, walking uprightly before our God."* (Judith 13:18-20). Souls underestimate the power of Mary's prayers. One glance from my dear Mother is enough to disarm my perfect justice. She is the channel of my mercy. Through her flows my life to mankind. Trust your Mother. Honor your Mother. Beseech your Mother to pray for the world. She gathers your prayers and sacrifices and presents them to me perfumed with the fragrant incense of her love." (*Journal* 319).

"Yes, the times are so grave that I desire this great prayer of the holy Rosary to rise from the faithful as a sacrifice of propitiation. Only through the Immaculate Heart of Mary will I have mercy on this sinful world. I have entrusted it to her. Therefore, you must come to me through her. Hurry, my children. Run to Mary!" (*Journal* 342).

"My most holy Mother has appealed to you time and time again! She still pleads. Will you not listen to her? Children, listen to your Heavenly Mother. Is there a more tender or loving ambassadress then my own Mother?" (*Journal* 212).

In the Old Testament, God sent his prophets to warn of chastisements. Since the 17th century, he has sent his Mother "time and time again," as Jesus said, as his ambassadress and as the prophetess of the chastisements of the modern world. Some of Mary's prophecies have been fulfilled and some of them are not yet fulfilled. The next chapter contains those that have not yet been fulfilled. Prophecies of Mary that have been fulfilled occurred in her apparitions at: Quito, Ecuador; Paris, France;

La Salette, France; Champion, Wisconsin, United States; Fatima, Portugal and Kibeho, Rwanda.

Quito, Ecuador

In the early 17th century, the Blessed Virgin Mary, under the title of Our Lady of Good Success, appeared to Mother Mariana de Jesus Torres of the Convent of the Immaculate Conception in Quito, Ecuador.

The apparitions were approved by the local bishop. Mother Mariana was named a Servant of God, and the cause for her canonization is on-going. The convent church was named an archdiocesan Marian sanctuary in 1991, making it an official place of pilgrimage.

Our Lady prophesied a worldwide crisis of faith and morals in the Church and society that would begin in the 19th century and extend throughout the 20th century that suffered from Nazism, Communism, and Secularism.

She promised that precisely when it seems that evil has triumphed, *"This will mark the arrival of my hour, when I, in a marvelous way, will dethrone the proud and cursed Satan, trampling him under my feet."* (See Genesis 3:15).

Our Lady of Good Success promised a complete restoration precisely when *"all would seem lost and paralyzed."* Here is a portion of the message of Our Lady to Mother Mariana on January 21st, 1610,

> *As for the Sacrament of Matrimony, which symbolizes the union of Christ with his Church, it will be attacked and deeply profaned. Freemasonry, which will then be in power, will enact iniquitous laws with the aim of doing away with this Sacrament, making it easy for everyone to live in and encouraging the procreation of illegitimate children born without the blessing of the Church.*

> *The Catholic spirit will rapidly decay; the precious light of faith will gradually be extinguished until there will be an almost total and general corruption of customs. Tied to this will be the effects of secular education, which will be one reason for the death of priestly and religious vocations. The Devil will try to persecute the ministers of the Lord in every possible way; he will labor with cruel and subtle astuteness to deviate them from the spirit of their vocation and will corrupt many of them. These depraved priests, who will scandalize the Christian people, will make the hatred of bad Catholics and the enemies of the Roman Catholic and apostolic Church fall upon all priests.*

> *During that epoch, [the twentieth century,] the Church will find herself attacked by terrible hordes of the Masonic sect, and this poor Ecuadorian land will be agonizing because of the corruption of customs, unbridled luxury, the impious press, and secular education. The vices of impurity, blasphemy, and sacrilege will dominate in this time of depraved desolation, and that one who should speak out will be silent.*

In February 1634, Mary said,

> *In order to free men from bondage to these heresies, those whom the merciful love of my Most Holy Son has designated to effect the restoration will need great strength of will, constancy, valor, and confidence in God. To test this faith and confidence of the just,*

there will be occasions in which everything will seem to be lost and paralyzed. This will be, then, the happy beginning of the complete restoration.

The spirit of impurity will saturate the atmosphere in those times. Like a filthy ocean, it will inundate the streets, squares, and public places with an astonishing liberty. There will be almost no virgin souls in the world.

Pray insistently without tiring and weep with bitter tears in the secrecy of your heart, imploring our celestial Father that for love of the Eucharistic Heart of my Most Holy Son and his Precious Blood, shed with such generosity and by the profound bitterness and sufferings of his cruel Passion and death, he might take pity on his ministers and quickly bring to an end those ominous times, sending to this Church the prelate that will restore the spirit of its priests.

The postulator for the cause of Mother Mariana has pointed out that all of the prophecies of Our Lady of Good Success have already been fulfilled, with the exception of the promised restoration.

Paris, France

On July 18, 1830, the Blessed Virgin Mary appeared in Paris, France, to St. Catherine Labouré. She appeared at the Motherhouse of the Daughters of Charity located on a street named Rue du Bac.

Catherine was a twenty-four-year-old novice sister when she was privileged to see Mary, late on that night in the chapel at the convent. She was escorted by a figure she later took to be her guardian angel and saw Mary descend the altar steps and sit in the spiritual director's chair.

In her first apparition, Our Lady described in tears the great trials that would come upon France and the world. She said,

The moment will come when the danger will be enormous; it will seem that all is lost; at that moment, I will be with you; have confidence....There will be victims....There will be victims among the clergy of Paris. Monsignor, the archbishop...my child, the Cross will be treated with contempt. They will hurl it to the ground. Blood will flow. They will open up again the side of Our

Lord. The streets will stream with blood. Monsignor, the archbishop will be stripped of his garments....My child, the whole world will be in sadness.

Sister Catherine asked herself, "When will this be?" Interiorly, she was immediately granted the understanding of forty years.

Sister Catherine Labouré was declared a saint by the Church on July 27, 1947, and, after 57 years of interment, her body was exhumed and found incorrupt.

Only nine days following these prophecies, on July 27, 1830, the July Revolution erupted in Paris. It was also called the "Glorious Three Days." Charles X was toppled from his throne. The trappings of royalty fell from him as they had fallen from Our Lord in one of St. Catherine's visions.

Charles was toppled by constitutional monarchists, middle-class merchants, and radical anarchists, all of whom united in a mob which committed countless murders throughout Paris. The Church, which Charles had supported, was attacked with a particular vengeance, with bishops, priests, and religious imprisoned, beaten, and murdered; churches desecrated; crosses and statues pulled down and trampled underfoot; and Archbishop de Quélen was forced to flee for his life, all in specific fulfillment of Our Lady's prophecy.

In 1848, another revolution followed in France, after which Prince Louis Napoléon, nephew of Napoléon Bonaparte, was chosen President of the Second French Republic. This was followed by the Communist Commune Revolution of 1871.

During the revolution in 1871, churches were desecrated, sacred things were profaned, many clergy were arrested, and thirty priests, including the Archbishop, were killed. These deaths marked the end of the Communist Commune and the Third French Republic was proclaimed, with Marshal MacMahon elected as its first President.

La Salette, France

In 1846, at La Salette in the French Alps, the effects of the French Revolution and the rampant actions of Secularism were manifest.

As in Paris, more and more people worked on Sundays and less and less people attended Mass on the Lord's Day. Licentiousness, cursing, and blasphemy were common.

On September 19, two children, Maximin Guiraud and Melanie Calvate, were tending sheep there when they saw a light brighter than the sun. As they approached it, they noticed a "Beautiful Lady" seated on a rock and crying, with her face in her hands. In tears, she stood and spoke to them in their local French dialect. She said,

> Come to me, my children. Do not be afraid. I am here to tell something of the greatest importance. If my people will not obey, I shall be compelled to loosen my Son's arm. It is so heavy, so pressing that I can no longer restrain it. How long I have suffered for you! So that my Son will not cast you off, I am obliged to entreat him without ceasing. But you don't take the least notice of that. No matter how well you pray in the future, no matter how well you act, you will never be able to make up to me what I have endured for your sake.

> I have appointed you six days for working. The seventh I have reserved for myself. And no one will give it to me. This is what causes the weight of my Son's arm to be crushing. The cart drivers cannot swear without bringing in my Son's name. These are the two things which make my Son's arms so burdensome.

> If the harvest is spoiled, it is your own fault. I warned you last year by means of the potatoes. You paid no heed. Quite the reverse, when you discovered that the potatoes had rotted, you swore, you abused my Son's name. They will continue to rot, and by Christmas this year there will be none left.

> If you have grain, it will do no good to sow it, for what you sow the beasts will devour, and any part of it that springs up will crumble into dust when you thresh it.

> A great famine is coming. But before that happens, the children under seven years of age will be seized with trembling and die in their parent's arms. The grownups will pay for their sins by hunger. The grapes will rot, and the walnuts will turn bad.

> Only a few old women go to Mass in the summer. All the rest work every Sunday throughout the summer. And in winter, when they don't know what to do with themselves, they go to Mass only

to make fun of religion. During Lent, they flock to the butcher shops, like dogs.

Mary concluded, "*My children, you will make this known to all my people.*" She then walked away up a steep path and disappeared in a bright light.

Mary's prophecies were soon fulfilled because her warnings were not heeded. In December 1846, most of the popular crops died from disease and the famine followed. Europe, especially France and Ireland, suffered terribly. The famine caused the deaths of approximately 1 million people, including at least 100,000 in France. Also, as prophesied, the lives of many children were claimed by the cholera that became prevalent in various parts of France.

On September 19, 1851, Bishop de Bruillard determined that the apparition "bore in itself all the marks of truth and that the faithful are justified in believing it to be certain and indubitable."

Champion, Wisconsin, United States

In the only Church-approved apparition of the Blessed Virgin Mary in the United States, Mary made a request and gave a warning if it was not fulfilled. In October of 1859, at Robinsonville (now Champion), Wisconsin, 18 miles northeast of Green Bay, she appeared to Adele Brise, a devout 28-year-old Belgian farm woman.

According to Sister Pauline LaPlant, to whom Adele often told her story, Mary told Adele,

> *I am the Queen of Heaven, who prays for the conversion of sinners, and I wish you to do the same. You received Holy Communion this morning, and that is well. But you must do more. Make a general confession and offer Communion for the conversion of sinners. If they do not convert and do penance, my Son will be obliged to punish them....Gather the children in this wild country and teach them what they should know for salvation. Teach them their catechism, how to sign themselves with the sign of the Cross, and how to approach the sacraments; that is what I wish you to do. Go and fear nothing. I will help you.*

Adele obediently began to catechize the children and admonish the sinners of the Bay Settlement. Her father erected a chapel near the spot where Mary had appeared.

Apparently, the response to Mary's request was not sufficient and on October 8, 1871, almost the 12th anniversary of Mary's apparition, a tremendous fire destroyed 1.2 million acres of Wisconsin and Michigan.

The Great Peshtigo Fire of 1871 is the worst fire in American history. It was described as "a wall of flame, a mile high, five miles wide, traveling 90 to 100 miles an hour, hotter than a crematorium, turning sand into glass." It killed almost 2000 people.

A report stated, "Balls of fire were observed to fall like meteors in different parts of the town [of Peshtigo], igniting whatever they came in contact with. By this time the whole population was thoroughly aroused and alarmed, panic-stricken. A brilliant and fearful glare grew suddenly into sight. Men and women snatched their children and ran for the river. Inhaling the burning air, hundreds dropped within sight of the river while many fell within a few feet of the river. Those who reached the river threw water and wet cloths on their heads, and even kept under water as much as they could, and yet were burned to death."

Adele and others sought refuge in the chapel built by her father. There they prayed in terror, begging Mary's intercession for God to save them. The early history reported, "Filled with confidence, they entered the chapel, reverently raised the statue of Mary, and, kneeling, bore it in procession around their beloved sanctuary. When wind and fire exposed them to suffocation, they turned in another direction and continued to hope and pray, saying the Rosary."

Several hours later, their prayers were answered when a rainfall extinguished the fire. There was devastation for miles around, but the chapel and its five acres of land, which had been consecrated to Mary, were spared. Tongues of fire had reached the chapel fence but the fire had not entered the chapel ground.

On December 8, 2010, Feast of the Immaculate Conception, Bishop David L. Ricken of Green Bay, Wisconsin, issued a formal decree and approved "the events, apparitions, and locutions given to Adele Brise in October of 1859." These apparitions are the first in the United States to receive approval of a diocesan bishop.

Fatima, Portugal

In 1917, during World War I, Mary appeared at Fatima, Portugal, to three shepherd children. In 2010, Pope Benedict XVI said, "At a time when the human family was ready to sacrifice all that was most sacred on the altar of the petty and selfish interests of nations, races, ideologies, groups, and individuals, our Blessed Mother came from Heaven, offering to implant in the hearts of all those who trust in her the love of God burning in her own heart...." (*Homily at Fatima*, May 13, 2010).

Mary said, *"War is a punishment for sins."* She said that if people did not change and pray, a war worse than World War I would come. On July 13, 1917, she said,

> God wishes to establish in the world devotion to my Immaculate Heart. If what I say to you is done, many souls will be saved and there will be peace. The war is going to end [World War I,] but if people do not cease offending God, a worse one will break out during the pontificate of Pius XI [World War II.] When you see a night illumined by an unknown light [which later hovered over Europe,] know that this is the great sign given you by God that he is about to punish the world for its crimes by means of war, famine, and persecutions of the Church and of the Holy Father. To prevent this, I shall come to ask for the consecration of Russia to my Immaculate Heart and a Communion of reparation on the first Saturday of each month.

> If my requests are heeded, Russia will be converted, and there will be peace. If not, she will spread her errors throughout the world, causing wars and persecutions of the Church. The good will be martyred, the Holy Father will have much to suffer, and various nations will be annihilated. In the end, my Immaculate Heart will triumph. The Holy Father will consecrate Russia to me, and she will be converted, and a period of peace will be granted to the world.

The prophesied "night illuminated by an unknown light" occurred on January 25, 1938. On that night a bright red light, likened to the blaze of a gigantic fire, filled the evening sky and was seen across Europe and even in parts of North America and Northern Africa.

Sister Lucia, one of the Fatima visionaries, immediately recognized the blazing light as the prophesied sign and later wrote to her bishop and confirmed it. Sister Lucia maintained that World War II really began during the reign of Pius XI. "The annexation of Austria was the occasion for it," she explained. The invasion of Austria and its annexation in March 1938 was the beginning of the war, although not formally declared, and it occurred during the pontificate of Pope Pius XI, as Our Lady had prophesied.

In spite of Mary's prophesied warnings, World War II still occurred because of a lack of response to her requests for prayer, especially the daily Rosary.

Sister Lucia later said in a letter to St. John Paul II on May 12, 1982, "And let us not say that it is God who is punishing us in this way; on the contrary, it is people themselves who are preparing their own punishment. In his kindness, God warns us and calls us to the right path, while respecting the freedom he has given us; hence people are responsible."

As Our Lady had prophesied, a worse war than World War I came. The total number of casualties in World War I was more than 41 million. The casualties included over 18 million deaths and 23 million wounded.

World War II was the deadliest military conflict in world history. Approximately 80 million people were killed. Civilians killed totaled approximately 50 million, including approximately 20 million from war-related disease and famine. Military deaths from all causes totaled approximately 30 million.

Mary's prophecy that Russia's "errors [would] spread about the world, promoting wars and the persecution of the Church" was fulfilled by atheistic Communism's persecution of the Church through the destruction of its churches, the prohibition of worship, and the killings of priests and believers.

The madness of Russia's "errors" was the promotion of atheistic Communism's ideology that attempted the abolition of God, the family, and the State through a totalitarian dictatorship that denied the fundamental dignity, freedom, and rights of human beings. It resulted in the imprisonment of millions behind the Iron Curtain of the United Soviet Socialist Republics and the killings of millions of innocent human beings.

Pope Pius XI called Communism a "satanic scourge." This scourge through Communist and socialist demagogues killed over 100 million innocent people through dictators from Russia's Lenin and Stalin, China's Mao, Cuba's Castro, Cambodia's Pol Pot, to North Korea's Kim Jung-il and Kim Jong-un.

A part of Mary's revelations of July 13, 1917 came to be known as The Third Secret of Fatima.

The Third Secret of Fatima

The Third Secret of Fatima is a text that the visionary, Sister Lucia, wrote describing a vision that the three children had on July 13, 1917. A painting of this vision is shown on the next page. The Third Secret vision summarized Mary's message of prayer and penance as the remedies against her prophesied chastisements from God, which would occur if the world did not respond to her requests. The world did not respond and her prophecies were fulfilled.

The text of the Third Secret of Fatima was released to the world from Vatican City on June 26, 2000 by the Congregation of the Doctrine of the Faith. Sister Lucia committed the Third Secret vision to paper on January 3, 1944, and wrote,

> At the left of Our Lady and a little above, we saw an angel with a flaming sword in his left hand; flashing, it gave out flames that looked as though they would set the world on fire; but they died out in contact with the splendor that Our Lady radiated towards him from her right hand.

> Pointing to the earth with his right hand, the angel cried out in a loud voice: "Penance! Penance! Penance!"

> And we saw in an immense light that is God: (something similar to how people appear in a mirror when they pass in front of it) a Bishop dressed in white (we had the impression that it was the Holy Father.) Other bishops, priests, men and women religious going up a steep mountain, at the top of which there was a big Cross of rough-hewn trunks as of a cork-tree with the bark. Before reaching there the Holy Father passed through a big city half in ruins and half trembling with halting step, afflicted with pain and sorrow, he prayed for the souls of the corpses he met on his way.

Having reached the top of the mountain, on his knees at the foot of the big Cross, he was killed by a group of soldiers who fired bullets and arrows at him. In the same way, there died one after another the other bishops, priests, men and women religious, and various lay people of different ranks and positions. Beneath the two arms of the Cross there were two angels each with a crystal aspersorium [a sprinkler container] in his hand, in which they gathered up the blood of the Martyrs and with it sprinkled the souls that were making their way to God.

This vision was interpreted by Cardinal Joseph Ratzinger, later Pope Benedict XVI, Prefect of the Congregation for the Doctrine of the Faith, on June 26, 2000. He wrote that the "key word" of the Third Secret of Fatima "is the triple cry, 'Penance! Penance! Penance!'..." This cry of the angel is still relevant today and should be heeded.

Cardinal Ratzinger also considered the "images" of the Secret and wrote, "The angel with the flaming sword on the left of the Mother of God recalls similar images in the Book of Revelation. This represents the threat of judgment which looms over the world. Today the prospect that the world might be reduced to ashes by a sea of fire no longer seems pure fantasy: man himself, with his inventions, has forged the flaming sword.

"The vision," he continued, "then shows the power which stands opposed to the force of destruction — the splendor of the Mother of God and, stemming from this in a certain way, the summons to penance. In this way, the importance of human freedom is underlined: the future is not in fact unchangeably set, and the image which the children saw is in no way a film preview of a future in which nothing can be changed. Indeed, the whole point of the vision is to bring freedom onto the scene and to steer freedom in a positive direction....Its meaning is to mobilize the forces of change in the right direction. Therefore we must totally discount fatalistic explanations of the 'secret,' such as, for example, the claim that the would-be assassin [of St. John Paul II] of May 13 1981 was merely an instrument of the divine plan guided by Providence....Rather, the vision speaks of dangers and how we might be saved from them."

Cardinal Ratzinger explained that "the place of the action is described in three symbols: a steep mountain, a great city reduced to ruins, and finally a large rough-hewn Cross. The mountain and city symbolize the arena of human history: history as an arduous ascent to the summit, history as the arena of human creativity and social harmony, but at the same time a place of destruction, where man actually destroys the fruits of his own work....On the mountain stands the Cross—the goal and guide of history. The Cross transforms destruction into salvation; it stands as a sign of history's misery but also as a promise for history.

"At this point," the Cardinal continued, "human persons appear: the bishop dressed in white [apparently the Pope]...other bishops, priests, men and women religious, and men and women of different ranks and social positions. The Pope seems to precede the others, trembling and suffering because of all the horrors around him. Not only do the houses of the city lie half in ruins, but he makes his way among the corpses of the dead. The Church's path is thus described as a Via Crucis [Way of the Cross], as a journey through a time of violence, destruction, and persecution. The history of an entire century can be seen represented in this image. Just as the places of the earth are synthetically described in the two images of the mountain and the city, and are directed towards the Cross, so, too, time is presented in a compressed way.

"In the vision, we can recognize the last century [the 20th century] as a century of martyrs, a century of suffering and persecution for the Church, a century of World Wars, and the many local wars which filled the last fifty years and have inflicted unprecedented forms of cruelty. In the 'mirror' of this vision we see passing before us the witnesses of the faith decade by decade."

The Cardinal also stated that "in the Via Crucis of an entire century, the figure of the Pope has a special role. In his arduous ascent of the mountain we can undoubtedly see a convergence of different popes. Beginning from Pius X up to the present Pope [St. John Paul II,] they all shared the sufferings of the century and strove to go forward through all the anguish along the path which leads to the Cross. In the vision, the Pope, too, is killed along with the martyrs. When, after the attempted assassination on May 13, 1981, the Holy Father had the text of the third part of the 'secret' brought to him, was it not inevitable that he should see in it his own fate?

He had been very close to death, and he himself explained his survival in the following words: '...it was a mother's hand that guided the bullet's path and in his throes the Pope halted at the threshold of death.' (May 13, 1994). That here 'a mother's hand' had deflected the fateful bullet only shows once more that there is no immutable destiny, that faith and prayer are forces which can influence history and that, in the end, prayer is more powerful than bullets and faith more powerful than armies.

"The conclusion of the secret," continued the Cardinal, "uses images which Lucia may have seen in devotional books and which draw their inspiration from long-standing intuitions of faith. It is a consoling vision, which seeks to open a history of blood and tears to the healing power of God. Beneath the arms of the Cross, angels gather up the blood of the martyrs and, with it, they give life to the souls making their way to God. Here, the blood of Christ and the blood of the martyrs are considered as one: the blood of the martyrs runs down from the arms of the Cross. The martyrs die in communion with the Passion of Christ, and their death becomes one with his.

"The vision of the third part of the 'secret,' so distressing at first, concludes with an image of hope: no suffering is in vain, and it is a suffering Church, a Church of martyrs, which becomes a sign-post for man in his search for God....From the suffering of the witnesses there comes a purifying and renewing power, because their suffering is the actualization of the suffering of Christ himself and a communication in the here and now of its saving effect....

"What remains was already evident when we began our reflections on the text of the 'secret:' the exhortation to prayer as the path of 'salvation for souls' and, likewise, the summons to penance and conversion."

This "summons to penance and conversion" announced by the angel in the vision for sins committed is the essence of the Third Secret. If we respond to this summons, our hope is that Our Lady's hands will avert any chastisement, as symbolized in the vision from the fiery sword of the angel, and mediate rays of mercy through her hands.

Many cynics believe that the totality of the Third Secret was not released. The Church, through Cardinal Ratzinger and in the presence of St. John Paul II, said that it was. To believe otherwise is to make Cardinal Ratzinger a liar and St. John Paul II an accomplice to the supposed lie.

Regarding the Third Secret, in his introductory remarks at Fatima on May 13, 2000, Archbishop Tarcisio Bertone, SDB, Secretary of the Congregation for the Doctrine of the Faith, said, "There is only one manuscript, which is here reproduced photostatically. The sealed envelope was initially in the custody of the Bishop of Leiria. To ensure better protection for the 'secret' the envelope was placed in the Secret Archives of the Holy Office on 4 April 1957." (*The Message of Fatima*, The Congregation for the Doctrine of the Faith, May 13, 2000).

At the end of the Mass presided over by St. John Paul II at Fatima on May 13, 2000, Cardinal Angelo Sodano, the Secretary of State, announced regarding the Third Secret,

> That text contains a prophetic vision similar to those found in Sacred Scripture, which do not describe photographically the details of future events but synthesize and compress against a single background facts which extend through time in an unspecified succession and duration. As a result, the text must be interpreted *in a symbolic key.*

> The vision of Fatima concerns above all the war waged by atheistic systems against the Church and Christians, and it describes the immense suffering endured by the witnesses of the faith in the last century of the second millennium. It is an interminable Way of the Cross led by the Popes of the twentieth century.

> In order that the faithful may better receive the message of Our Lady of Fatima, the Pope has charged the Congregation for the Doctrine of the Faith with making public the third part of the "secret," after the preparation of an appropriate commentary.

> Cardinal Ratzinger then began his commentary and said, "A careful reading of the text of the so-called third "secret" of Fatima, published here in its entirety long after the fact and by decision of the Holy Father, will probably prove disappointing or surprising after all the speculation it has stirred. No great mystery is revealed; nor is the future

unveiled. (*The Message of Fatima, T*he Congregation for the Doctrine of the Faith, May 13, 2000).

Later, Pope Benedict XVI said, "The tragedies foretold in Fatima did not come to an end with the demise of Communism. The crisis has not been resolved. From a certain point of view, it is still as serious as it ever was, as it is primarily a crisis of faith, hence a moral and social crisis." (*Fatima Mysteries*, Grzegorz Górny and Janusz Rosikón, Ignatius Press, 2017).

Fatima expert Father Andrew Apostoli wrote, "Our Lady had warned that these wars and persecutions would result if people did not change their sinful ways. Her warning is still relevant for us now because sin continues to cause social upheaval and violence. The struggle against evil in the world is still going on." (*Fatima for Today*, Father Andrew Apostoli, Ignatius Press, 2012).

Kibeho, Rwanda

In 1981, only four months after the beginning of her apparitions at Medjugorje, Mary began appearing at Kibeho, Rwanda. She emphasized the call to pray the Rosary and asked for penance and fasting, similar to her requests at Fatima and Medjugorje.

Mary showed the visionaries images of savage murders, machetes, a "river of blood," people brutally killing each other, decapitated bodies, abandoned corpses with no one to bury them, and the putrefying remains of hundreds of thousands. These visions are now considered a prophecy of the ethnic genocide of almost 1 million people that later took place in their country in 1994 and 1995.

On August 19, 1982, Mary appeared and, according to Father Gabriel Maindron, author of *Kibeho*, "The visionaries sometimes cried, their teeth chattered, they trembled. They collapsed several times with the full weight of their bodies during the apparitions, which lasted nearly eight hours without interruption. The crowd of about 20,000 present on that day was given an impression of fear — indeed, panic and sadness." Apparently, Mary herself was sad.

Immaculée Ilibagiza, Rwandan genocide survivor and author of *Our Lady of Kibeho*, wrote that Mary had the visionary, Alphonsine

Mumureke, repeat three times into the microphone an apparent lament for the failure to respond to her requests, "You opened the door and they refused to come in. You opened the door and they refused to come in. You opened the door and they refused to come in."

Then Immaculée reported, "Suddenly Alphonsine let out a gut-wrenching scream that cut through the startled crowd like a razor. 'I see a river of blood! What does that mean? No, please! Why did you show me so much blood? Show me a clear stream of water, not this river of blood!' the seer cried out, as the Holy Mother revealed one horrifying vision after another. The young woman was subjected to so many images of destruction, torture, and savage human carnage that she pleaded, 'Stop, stop, please stop! Why are those people killing each other? Why do they chop each other?'"

Alphonsine was next shown "a growing pile of severed human heads, which were still gushing blood. The grotesque sight worsened still as Our Lady expanded Alphonsine's vision until she beheld a panoramic view of a vast valley piled high with the remains of a million rotting, headless corpses, and not a single soul left to bury the dead."

Mary gave a clear warning. She said, *"My children, it does not have to happen if people would listen and come back to God."* She told them to warn government leaders, who belonged to the Hutu tribe, not to battle with the minority Tutsis.

Unfortunately, the warning was not heeded and, 12 years after the first apparitions, the two tribes entered a horrible civil war. One of the slaughters took place on the very spot where Mary had appeared. Twenty-five thousand people were killed in the place where pilgrims once knelt. The hands of a statue of Mary were shot off during the war and a bullet was embedded in her heart. Three of the eight visionaries were slaughtered in the mayhem.

Many of the deceased were chopped up and thrown in a river. As prophesied, machete-wielding soldiers killed almost a million Rwandans in the span of a few short months. This was the highest killing-rate in recorded history.

The Kibeho warnings were not just for Rwanda but for the whole world. Mary said, *"When I tell you this, I am not addressing myself strictly to you, child, but I am making this appeal to the world which is in revolt against God. I am concerned with and turning to the whole world to repent because otherwise the world is on the edge of catastrophe."*

On June 29, 2001, the Church approved the Kibeho apparitions in the "Declaration on the Definitive Judgment on the Apparitions of Kibeho." This declaration, written by Rwandan Bishop Augustine Misago and released by the Vatican, proclaimed, "Yes, the Virgin Mary did appear in Kibeho on Nov. 28, 1981," and then over "the course of the following six months. There are more reasons to believe this than to deny it." This approval came *after* Mary's warnings for Rwanda were fulfilled.

The *Catechism of the Catholic Church* teaches us, "Throughout the ages, there have been so-called 'private' revelations, some of which have been recognized by the authority of the Church. They do not belong, however, to the deposit of faith. It is not their role to improve or complete Christ's definitive Revelation, but to help live more fully by it in a certain period of history. Guided by the Magisterium [Teaching Authority] of the Church, the *sensus fidelium* [the sense of the faithful] knows how to discern and welcome in these revelations whatever constitutes an authentic call of Christ or his saints to the Church." (CCC 67).

So, to help us to live more fully by Christ's Revelation in this period of history, let us discern and welcome, in the revelations from Medjugorje, the authentic call of the Blessed Virgin Mary to the Church today. As she told one of the visionaries at Rwanda, *"The world is on the edge of catastrophe. Cleanse your hearts through prayer. The only way is God. If you don't take refuge in God, where will you go to hide when the fire has spread everywhere?"*

The Rwandan people did not listen to Mary's motherly guidance and were unable to escape the tragic consequences of the genocide. When the terrifying scenes shown to the visionaries became reality, and the Church approval came, it was simply too late.

Mary still appears throughout the world pleading for prayer and fasting to bring conversions and peace. The alternative, she warns, is to suffer chastisements. However, some of her chastisement prophecies remain unfulfilled.

4. Chastisement Prophecies of the Blessed Virgin Mary - Unfulfilled

Rome City, Indiana and Fostoria, Ohio, USA

Sister Mildred Neuzil (1916-2000) reported in her *Diary* that the Blessed Virgin Mary appeared to her and gave her messages and that she had visions and received locutions at the Kneipp Springs Sanitarium in Rome City, Indiana and in Fostoria, Ohio from 1956 until her death in 2000 at the age of 83. These came to be known as the Our Lady of America Devotion.

On May 7, 2020, six bishops, led by Most Reverend Kevin C. Rhoades, Bishop of Fort Wayne-South Bend, approved the Our Lady of America Devotion as a private devotion. These were the bishops of the dioceses where the alleged visions, locutions, and private revelations to Sister Mildred Neuzil (1916-2000) were said to have occurred in relation to the Our Lady of America Devotion.

In their Statement, the bishops stated, "Given this history of prayers and religious articles being given approval by competent ecclesiastical authority, the use of such prayers [and] religious articles may continue as a matter of private devotion, but not as a public devotion of the Church. Indeed, such private devotion would be consistent with the history of the United States of America being dedicated to Our Lady."

Although the bishops did not approve the Devotion "as a public devotion of the Church", they did not condemn or prohibit anything in the Devotion, especially the prayers, *The Diary* of Sister Mildred, or the medal of Our Lady of America. However, they did note that St. Joseph's title of "Co-redeemer" was an "error" although they did not condemn it as contrary to the faith or as heretical.

The Diary contained prayers and descriptions of the image and the medal of Our Lady of America. On January 25, 1963, Archbishop Paul Leibold, Sister Mildred's spiritual director, and Father Daniel Pilarczyk, granted *The Diary* the *Imprimtur* and the *Nihil Obstat* and declared them to contain nothing contrary to faith or morals.

In a letter to the United States Bishops dated May 31, 2007, Cardinal Raymond L. Burke, D.D., J.C.D., while Archbishop of the Archdiocese of St. Louis, reviewed the prior history and the state of the Devotion, as well as the earlier actions of Archbishop Leibold approving the devotion. Archbishop Burke wrote, "What can be concluded canonically is that the devotion was both approved by Archbishop Leibold and, what is more, was actively promoted by him."

Bishop Rhoades' Commission stated, "Looking at the nature and quality of the experiences [of Sister Mildred] themselves, we find that they are more to be described as subjective inner religious experiences rather than objective external visions and revelations." The Commission also stated, "It seems that these were authentically graced moments, even perhaps of a spiritual quality beyond what most people experience, but subjective ones in which her own imagination and intellect were constitutively engaged, putting form to inner spiritual movements."

Based on these findings, Bishop Rhoades came to the conclusion that "the visions and revelations themselves cannot be said to be of supernatural origin in the sense of objective occurrences *(non constat de supernaturalitate)*; thus further, I cannot approve or support public devotion or cult." The bishops of the other five dioceses accepted these findings and conclusions. Therefore, the Devotion may not be practiced "as a public devotion of the Church." However, the Devotion, as it has been practiced, may still be practiced privately.

So, the statements below by Sister Mildred cannot be considered as supernatural revelations to her, but they may be considered, as Bishop Rhoades wrote, "as subjective inner religious experiences....

[and] that these were authentically graced moments, even perhaps of a spiritual quality beyond what most people experience, but subjective ones in which her own imagination and intellect were constitutively engaged, putting form to inner spiritual movements."

Sister Mildred wrote that the Blessed Virgin Mary appeared to her in 1956 and revealed her titles as *"Our Lady of America, the Immaculate Virgin"* and *"I am the Immaculate One, Patroness of your land."*

In April of 1957, Sister Mildred wrote that Our Lady of America said, *"Unless my children reform their lives, they will suffer great persecution. If man himself will not take upon himself the penance necessary to atone for his sins and those of others, God in his justice will have to send upon him the punishment necessary to atone for his transgressions."*

On November 22, 1980, Sister Mildred wrote that Our Lady said,

> *Beloved daughter, the United States is a small one among nations, yet has it not been said that 'a little child shall lead them'? It is the United States that is to lead the world to peace, the peace of Christ, the peace that he brought with him from heaven in his birth as man in the little town of Bethlehem. Dear child, unless the United States accepts and carries out faithfully the mandate given to it by heaven to lead the world to peace, there will come upon it and all nations a great havoc of war and incredible suffering. If, however, the United States is faithful to this mandate from heaven and yet fails in the pursuit of peace because the rest of the world will not accept or co-operate, then the United States will not be burdened with the punishment about to fall. (Diary 28).*

Today, with wars, international terrorism, nuclear threats, natural disasters, and pandemics, Our Lady of America's alleged messages for purity, peace, and prayer are more urgent than ever.

Sister Mildred wrote that Our Lady of America gave her final message to on January 3, 1984 and that she asked her, "Dear Mother, will there be a nuclear war? Everyone is so afraid." She wrote that Our Lady answered,

My faithful one, if my warnings are taken seriously and enough of my children strive constantly and faithfully to renew and reform themselves in their inward and outward lives, then there will be no nuclear war.

What happens to the world depends upon those who are living in it. There must be much more good than evil prevailing in order to prevent the holocaust that is so near approaching. Yet I tell you, my daughter, that even should such a destruction happen because there were not enough souls who took my warnings seriously, there will remain a remnant untouched by the chaos who, having been faithful in following me and spreading my warnings, will gradually inhabit the earth again with their dedicated and holy lives.

These souls will renew the earth in the power and light of the Holy Spirit, and these faithful children of mine will be under my protection, and that of the holy angels, and they will partake of the life of the Divine Trinity in a most remarkable way. Let my dear children know this, precious daughter, so that they will have no excuse if they fail to heed my warnings. Be at peace, dear one, I will never leave you. (Diary 34).

Sister Mildred wrote, "From this final message, I received the very strong impression that Our Lady was telling us that she had done everything she could do to help and warn us. Now it was up to us. Whatever happens we will have brought on ourselves so whatever we decide and do now is our responsibility. Our Lady, however, will not forsake us because we are her children and she loves us." (*Diary* 34-35).

Akita, Japan

In 1973, the Blessed Virgin Mary appeared to Sister Agnes Sasagawa in Akita, Japan. God left a sign to help us to believe in her messages. A statue of Mary miraculously wept on 101 occasions over the next six years.

On October 13, 1973, at Akita, Mary said,

If men do not repent and better themselves, the Father will inflict a terrible punishment on all humanity. It will be a punishment greater than the deluge [the Great Flood] such as one will never have seen before. Fire will fall from the sky and will wipe out a great part of humanity, the good as well as the bad, sparing neither priests nor faithful. The survivors will find themselves so desolate that they will envy the dead. The only arms which will remain for you will be the Rosary and the Sign left by my Son. Each day recite the prayers of the Rosary. With the Rosary, pray for the Pope, the bishops, and the priests.

Bishop Ito of Akita declared that the apparitions were authentic. In June of 1988, Cardinal Joseph Ratzinger, later Pope Benedict XVI, Prefect of the Congregation for the Doctrine of the Faith, gave a definitive judgment on the Akita events and messages as reliable and worthy of belief.

Bishop Ito affirmed that the warnings of Fatima and Akita are essentially the same. He noted the following similarities: at Fatima, Our Lady prophesied that God *"is going to punish the world for its crimes;"* at Akita, she prophesied, *"The Father will inflict a terrible punishment on all humanity;"* at Fatima, Our Lady made an unfulfilled prophesy that *"various nations will be annihilated;"* and at Akita, she prophesied, *"Fire will fall from the sky and will wipe out a great part of humanity."*

Similar to the Akita warning of fire, St. Peter wrote that the godless "deliberately ignore the fact that the heavens existed of old and earth was formed out of water and through water by the Word of God, and that it was through these same factors that the world of those days was destroyed by the floodwaters. It is the same Word which is reserving the present heavens and earth for fire, keeping them until the Day of Judgment and of the destruction of sinners." (2 Peter 3:5-7).

On September 28, 2012, Jesus King of All Nations said "I promised by holy covenant never to flood the earth in totality again; no, this time my all-holy justice shall come through fire. *"I will send fire upon Magog and upon those who live securely in the coastlands; thus, they shall know that I am the Lord. I will make my holy name known among my people Israel; I will no longer allow my holy name to be profaned. Thus, the nations shall know that I am the Lord, the Holy One in Israel. Yes, it is coming and shall be fulfilled, says the Lord God. This is the day I have decreed."* (Ezekiel 39:6-8). So greatly does this world require divine cleansing that only by means of the purifying power of fire shall it be renewed..." (*Journal* 453-455). A great catastrophe is about to descend on the world. *"…fire, sent from on high…"* (Baruch 6:63). *"…the time of trial that is going to come to the whole world to test the inhabitants of the earth."* (Revelation 3:10). *(Journal* 341).

On October 6, 2019, at 3:30 a.m., at Akita, Sister Agnes received a new warning message from an angel. The message was similar to the prophet Jonah's message of warning to the idol-worshiping Ninevites to repent or be destroyed. Jonah's message was, "Forty more days and Nineveh will be overthrown." (Jonah 3:4).

"The Ninevites believed God. A fast was proclaimed, and all of them, from the greatest to the least, put on sackcloth." (Jonah 3:5). When the King of Nineveh heard about the message, he got up from his throne, removed his robe, covered himself with sackcloth, and sat in ashes. "When God saw what they did and how they turned from their evil ways, he relented and did not bring on them the destruction he had threatened." (Jonah 3:10). May we imitate the good example of the pagan Ninevites who had also worshiped idols!

Sister Agnes received the new warning message on October 6, the same day that Pope Francis inaugurated the Amazon Synod in the Vatican. He allowed the display of idols that some people venerated, like the Ninevites did in the past, in St. Peter's Basilica, Santa Maria Church, and in the Vatican Gardens.

This was the first public message that Sister Agnes had received in 46 years. This is the *Now* Warning message that Sister Agnes received on October 6, 2019, "Cover in ashes and please pray a penitential Rosary every day. You [Sister Agnes] become like a child and every day please give sacrifice."

The warning was short and to the point, as was the warning to the Ninevites. May we respond to it *Now* as they did!

I believe that the phrase, "Cover in ashes," is metaphorical and does not mean that God wants us to literally cover ourselves in ashes, as did the Ninevites, but rather it means that we should assume a penitential attitude, as we should also do during Lent.

A penitential Rosary is a Rosary that is prayed with contrition and in sorrow for one's own sins or for the sins of others and their conversion. It is offered in atonement and reparation to our merciful God who is so horribly offended by the sins of the modern world. Let us fervently pray the Rosary daily for the conversion of all people who are lost in sin and have not come to know the love of the one true God.

The courier, who brought the message of Sister Agnes to America, wrote that after the angel appeared to her, Sister Agnes said, "I felt the time is near." The courier wrote that it "means the time of the message of Our Lady of Akita", referring not to the angel's message of October 6, 2019, but to Our Lady's chastisement warning of October 13, 1973 that fire will "*wipe out a great part of humanity.*"

The time of that warning is NOW!

San Nicolas, Argentina

The Blessed Virgin Mary appeared in San Nicolas, Argentina, to Gladys Quiroga de Motta, a middle-aged housewife and mother, on September 25, 1983. Thereafter she had apparitions of Mary and Jesus almost daily until 1991.

The messages of Mary and Jesus to Gladys are some of the sternest ever approved by the Church. Mary warned of "*chastisements, the loss of two thirds of the world to evil [as was also revealed at Akita, Japan,] the great danger to the earth, and that humanity is hanging by a thread. The devil wants to have full dominion of the earth and wants to destroy it.*"

Mary said, "*You must be warned, children, the plague is big. At these moments all humanity is hanging by a thread. My children, the senseless person is dead, even if alive, because he does not fear the justice of God, nor fears not fulfilling of his commandments. He wants to ignore the fact that the Lord's Day and his judgment will arrive. Blessed are those who fear God's judgment.*

"*God's warning is over the world. Those who stay in the Lord have nothing to fear, but those who deny what comes from him do. Two-thirds of the world is lost and the other part must pray and make reparation for the Lord to take pity. The devil wants to have full domination over the earth. He wants to destroy. The earth is in great danger.*"

Mary also said, "*The majority of mankind has allowed itself to become contaminated and as a result the world is under a warning....The young* find themselves facing a corrupt, horrifying world. Do not allow yourselves to be taken in by the calamities which you have before your eyes. At these moments all humanity is hanging by a thread. If the thread breaks, many will be those who do not reach salvation. That is why I call you to reflection. Hurry, because time is running out; there will be no room for those who delay in coming!"

Mary tells everyone, "*The weapon that has the greatest influence on evil is to say the Rosary.*" She described pride as a "*giant evil*" in the world of today. To fight this, she said that there should be special devotion to the holy Rosary and perpetual novenas, "*never interrupted.*"

Our Lady told Gladys, "*The Prince of Evil spills today his poison with all the forces because he sees that he is concluding his sad reign. He has little time left and his end is near....Make known what I am saying to you. Atheism is flooding the nations, and the absence of God is everywhere....The Redeemer is offering to the world a way to face Satan. He is offering, as he did on the Cross, his Mother, Mediatrix of All Graces....The holy Rosary is the most feared weapon of the enemy. It is also the refuge for those seeking relief and is the door to enter my heart....God gives complete freedom and he allows each one to make his own choice: to purify oneself or to live in sin, grow in Christ or be annihilated.*"

Jesus told Gladys, "*If this generation will not listen to my Mother, it will perish. I ask everyone to listen to her....In the past, the world was saved by Noah's Ark. Today, my Mother is the Ark. Through her, souls will be saved because she will lead them to me. He who rejects my Mother rejects me!*"

Mary gave us hope and said, "*A new time has begun. A new hope has born; attach yourselves to this hope. The very intense light of Christ is going to be reborn, for just as on Calvary, after Crucifixion and death, the Resurrection took place, the Church too will be born again through the strength of love.*"

On May 22, 2016, Bishop Hector Sabatino Cardelli approved the apparitions and revelations of the Blessed Virgin Mary at San Nicolas, Argentina. He acknowledged them as of "supernatural origin" and "worthy of belief." This is the highest form of Church approval.

Itapiranga, Brazil

Edson Glauber, from Brazil, has been receiving daily apparitions of the Blessed Virgin Mary since 1994. The apparitions began in the city of Manaus but, eventually, Our Lady asked Edson and his mother to pray for the city of Itapiranga, (pronounced EE-tap-ee-rang-ah,) a city in the Amazon where his father owned a large piece of property. Our Lady told Edson that the property belonged to her and that she would show her concern for the poor in the Amazon. She asked that a small chapel be built in her honor, initially out of straw, to signify the simplicity, the poverty, and the suffering of all her children of the Amazon, who had been mistreated, exploited, and killed by the more powerful of the land.

On October 29, 1994, Our Lady told Edson, "*A great chastisement is coming for the whole world, and it is already at hand! Many will suffer if there is no conversion; so, pray the Rosary every day for Brazil and for the peace of the whole world.*"

On October 4, 1996, Our Lady said at Itapiranga that she would leave a visible sign on the Cross located there. Later, she said, "*When the moment arrives for the sign left on the Cross, the time for the conversion of the world will end. All of humanity will suffer great calamities and will be devastated by punishments as has never happened from the creation of the world. Let us open our hearts to God and make a sincere commitment to convert, and he will have mercy on us.*" Some of the chastisement prophecies revealed by Our Lady to Edson have already taken place, such as the Asian tsunami that killed over 200,000 people in 2004.

However, Our Lady told him, "*I put all of my children in my heart. My love is big, my love embraces the whole world. On the day of chastisement, I will cover all of my children with my mantle; all those who heard my calling and lived my messages; only those who listened and were obedient. Those who did not believe, who said the messages were false, who did not convert and did nothing for families, Jesus said, by his order 'he will throw into Hell for dry wood, good for nothing.'*"

In 1994, Edson's Bishop, Carillo Gritti, wrote, "We are appreciating the probable supernatural nature of the events and of the messages."

In order not to be thrown *"into Hell for dry wood, good for nothing"*, as Jesus warned, we should respond now to Our Lady's requests to live her messages!

5. Respond Now!

People did not respond to Mary's requests at Champion, Fatima, and Kibeho and they suffered from the prophesied chastisements.

We don't have to wait for the Church's approvals of the messages, secrets, warnings, and chastisements of Medjugorje before we respond to Mary's requests. If we do, it may be too late, like it was for Champion, Fatima, and Kibeho, and they may happen before any approvals. We don't even have to believe that Mary appeared or gave any messages at Medjugorje, but we still should respond to her requests.

All of her requests that are listed and explained in this book are consistent with the teachings of the Catholic Church.

Immaculée Ilibagiza said, "I only share messages not yet approved because, like the title of my fourth book, *If Only We Had Listened* to Our Lady and Our Lord who warned us to what was going to happen to Rwanda and told us what to do to avoid it, long before the Church could approve those apparitions, the genocide would not have happened, so it is up to you to discern."

When Pope Benedict XVI visited Fatima on May 11, 2010, he said,

> The Lord told us that the Church would constantly be suffering, in different ways, until the end of the world....We need to relearn precisely these essentials: conversion, prayer, penance, and the theological virtues.

> This is our response, we are realists in expecting that evil always attacks, attacks from within and without, yet that the forces of good are also ever present and that, in the end, the Lord is more powerful than evil and Our Lady is for us the

visible, motherly guarantee of God's goodness, which is always the last word in history.

During the Mass at Fatima on May 13, in the presence of half a million people, the Pope reaffirmed that "the demanding but consoling message the Virgin left us at Fatima is full of hope. It is a message that focuses on prayer, penance, and conversion, a message projected beyond the threats, dangers, and horrors of history, inviting humankind to have faith in the action of God, to cultivate great hope, and to experience the grace of the Lord in order to love him, the source of love and peace...

"In Fatima, the Blessed Virgin Mary invites us to walk with hope," the Pope continued, "letting ourselves be guided by the 'wisdom from on high' which was manifested in Jesus, the wisdom of love, to bring the light and joy of Christ into the world."

Let us not be caught unprepared. The time to convert, pray (especially the Rosary), fast, and receive the sacraments of Penance and Eucharist is NOW! Let it not be for us as it was in the days of Noah. Jesus said, "For as it was in the days of Noah, so it will be at the coming of the Son of Man. In those days before the flood, they were eating and drinking, marrying and giving in marriage, up to the day that Noah entered the ark. They did not know until the flood came and carried them all away." (Matthew 24:37-39).

Let us pray, "Blessed be God who lives forever, whose Kingdom is eternal. For he both punishes and then has mercy." (Tobit 13:1-2).

Let us pray for his merciful protection from any punishments of the Ten Secrets.

6. The Ten Secrets and a Sign

The Blessed Virgin Mary came from Heaven to Medjugorje and revealed Ten Secrets. She prophesied that she would leave a permanent supernatural sign on the hill where she had first appeared. These will all come to light, for as the Gospel says, "Nothing is secret except to come to light." (Mark 4:22).

The Beginning of the Apparitions

Medjugorje (Croatian for "between the hills") is a remote village located in Bosnia-Herzegovina, surrounded by rocky hills and centered on St. James Church. Millions of pilgrims of all faiths, races, and nationalities have traveled there because of the apparitions of the Blessed Virgin Mary. They began on June 24, 1981, the feast of St. John the Baptist, the first herald of Jesus. Now she comes as his modern herald. Like John the Baptist, she goes "before the Lord to prepare his ways, to give his people knowledge of salvation through the forgiveness of their sins." (Luke 1:76-77).

On the afternoon of June 24, Mirjana Soldo, then 16 and her friend, Ivanka Ivanković, then 15, went out for a walk. Mirjana said, in an interview with Sabrina Čović-Radojičić, "When we got tired, we sat just below the hill. In the middle of that quite ordinary conversation, she said, 'I think that Our Lady is on the hill!' She looked at the hill, while I was turned away from it. It never occurred to me to turn. I just responded to her, 'Yes, surely Our Lady! She has nothing else to do so she came to see what the two of us are doing.'

"Ivanka said to me, 'Look now, please!' Shocked by her appearance, I looked towards the hill and that is when I saw a woman in a long gray dress with a child in her arms in the midst of the rocks. It was Our Lady.

"I felt all emotions that exist, from misunderstanding and fear to the unreal feeling of beauty and amazement. From that intensity that poured from me, I felt that the way out was to escape. I thought, *Pinch yourself, perhaps you're dead! Run, Mirjana!* In the end, I said to myself, 'Run, Mirjana, I don't know what it is!' And I escaped. It was inglorious, that first day."

On the next day, Mirjana, Ivanka, and four other children returned to the hill and climbed it with amazing speed. Mirjana said, "I felt like I was flying to the place of the apparition, as if something was carrying me. That is how readily and easily we reached her. Then she presented herself and said, *'My children, do not be afraid, I am the Queen of Peace!'"*

From then until June 29, Our Lady appeared to them, responded to their questions, and gave them messages. The summary of her messages are that peace can come only from God through conversion and faith, maintained by the sacraments, prayer and fasting, reading Scripture, and the use of sacramentals.

In those first days, all the children told the same story about seeing Our Lady. She also showed signs, including the disappearance of the large Cross from the top of Mount Križevac; the appearance of the word *MIR* (peace) written in the sky, and two miraculous healings. Knowing the children and seeing all of that, led the locals to believe in the children immediately.

The apparitions have continued since 1981. The six visionaries experience the apparitions with their senses and not their imaginations. They see and hear the Blessed Virgin Mary who appears to them as a young lady of about twenty with a beauty that is beyond human description.

Mary identified herself as the Queen of Peace. She said that she came to Medjugorje *"because there are many true believers here."* (June 26, 1981). She asked, *"that those who do not see, believe as those who see."* (June 28, 1981).

Janice Connell, author of several books about Medjugorje, reported that visionary Mirjana Soldo described Mary's appearance as, "Dressed in a gray dress, a white veil, [with] that beautiful face [and] those incredibly beautiful eyes of love. Her whole demeanor is filled with God's love."

Mary told the visionaries that God sent her to the world to help us convert our hearts and lives back to her Son, Jesus, true God and true man. In her motherly love for us, she promised to leave a visible sign on the hill where she first appeared so that the whole world would believe.

Father Tomislav Vlašić OFM wrote St. John Paul II a letter, dated December 2, 1983, based upon his interviews with some of the visionaries. He wrote, "All of the youngsters basically agree that:

> We see the Blessed Virgin just as we see anyone else. We pray with her, we speak to her, and we can touch her.

> The Blessed Virgin says that world peace is at a critical stage. She repeatedly calls for reconciliation and conversion.

> She has promised to leave a visible sign for all humanity at the site of the apparitions of Medjugorje.

> The period preceding this visible sign is a time of grace for conversion and deepening the faith."

Mary told the visionaries,

> *Children, darkness reigns over the whole world. People are attracted by many things and they forget about the more important. Light won't reign in the world until people accept Jesus, until they live his words, which is the Word of the Gospel.*

> *Dear children, this is the reason for my presence among you for such a long time: to lead you on the path of Jesus. I want to save you and, through you, to save the whole world. Many people now live without faith; some don't even want to hear about Jesus, but they still want peace and satisfaction! Children, here is the reason why I need your prayer: prayer is the only way to save the human race.* (July 30, 1987).

Mary showed Hell to some of the visionaries. She explained why she did this and said, "*Do not be afraid! I have shown you Hell so that you may know the state of those who are there.*" (November 6, 1981).

Mary gave several of the visionaries Ten Secrets each. It is not known if they all have the same secrets. As the prophet Amos tells us, "The Lord God does nothing without revealing his secrets to his servants, the prophets." (Amos 3:7).

Visionary Mirjana Soldo, like the prophet Amos, has her Ten Secrets. She will reveal them and they will come to light in the fullness of the time of God's sovereign love and providence.

Mirjana told me in my interview with her, on October 23, 2010, that she was born on March 18, 1965, in Sarajevo, in what was then Yugoslavia and is now Bosnia-Herzegovina. She attended the University of Sarajevo for three years. However, it was impossible for her to continue her education because she could not receive permission from the Communist government. They knew her as a "visionary" and she said that she was an enemy of the state and that, "God does not exist in Yugoslavia."

Both of her parents were born in Medjugorje and she used to travel there to visit her grandparents when she lived in Sarajevo. The apparitions of Our Lady began there in 1981, while she was on a visit. Later, she married her husband, Marco, and they moved to Medjugorje in 1989. She has two adult daughters, Maria and Veronica.

In his 1983 letter to St. John Paul II, Father Vlašić summarized the substance of his interview with Mirjana about the secrets. He wrote,

> Mirjana said that before the visible sign is given to humanity, there will be three warnings to the world. The warnings will be in the form of events on earth. Mirjana will be a witness to them. Three days before one of the admonitions, Mirjana will notify a priest of her choice. The witness of Mirjana will be a confirmation of the apparitions and a stimulus for the conversion of the world.
>
> The Ninth and Tenth Secrets are serious. They concern chastisement for the sins of the world. Punishment is inevitable, for we cannot expect the whole world to be converted. The punishment can be diminished by prayer and penance, but it cannot be eliminated. Mirjana says that

one of the evils that threatened the world, the one contained in the Eighth Secret has been averted, thanks to prayer and fasting. [Mirjana told me that this was a mistake and that it was the Seventh Secret and not the Eighth Secret that had been averted.] That is why the Blessed Virgin continues to encourage prayer and fasting and said, "*You have forgotten that through prayer and fasting you can avert war and suspend the laws of nature.*"

After the first admonition, the others will follow in a rather short time. Thus, people will have some time for conversion.

That interval will be a period of grace and conversion. After the visible sign appears, those who are still alive will have little time for conversion. For that reason, the Blessed Virgin invites us to urgent conversion and reconciliation.

The invitation to prayer and penance is meant to avert evil and war, but most of all to save souls.

According to Mirjana, the events predicted by the Blessed Virgin are near. By virtue of this experience, Mirjana proclaims to the world: "Hurry, be converted; open your hearts to God."

Mirjana told author Janice Connell that she knows the date of each of the secrets and that all of them will occur during her lifetime. She said, "The first two secrets will be warnings to the world — events on the earth as warnings to the world that will occur before the visible sign is given to humanity. These will happen in my lifetime. That is why Mary's call to conversion is so urgent. She is our mother, and she would like all of us to heed the message she is giving us. She wishes this so that later, when the secrets are to be revealed, there will not be any unbelievers."

Mirjana told Mrs. Connell that we should not be frightened because we are God's children and if people only realized how much he loves us and what he has prepared for us, they would be filled with such peace! She added that those who use their freedom to choose things that are not of God will suffer the tortures of the children of Satan. God gives his children Heaven, but Satan brings his children to Hell.

Mirjana concluded the interview with Mrs. Connell and said, "My witness will be an affirmation to the world of the authenticity of the apparitions at Medjugorje and a stimulus for the conversion of the world. After the visible sign, those still alive will have little time for conversion. God is not cruel! God is love, only love. Cruelty and evil come from Satan. But with our free will we choose God or Satan every moment. Those who freely choose Satan, who disobey God's commandments, will perish."

Mother Mary said, "*Dear Children! God gives me this time as a gift to you, so that I may instruct and lead you on the path of salvation. You do not comprehend this grace, but soon a time will come when you will lament for these messages.*" (August 25, 1997).

In an interview at Medjugorje on October 3, 2009, Mirjana said,

I never think about the secrets. I don't even think about it, because it is dear God who keeps the secrets and his will be done. For example, this morning, I spoke to Italians, maybe you saw there were thousands of them! Any and every question they asked started with, "Why, why, why, why this, why that, waving their hands."

Then I said to them, "You know why Our Lady did not appear in Italy but in Croatia?" And they said again, "Why?" I said if she appeared in Italy she would run away after the third day because it would always be, "Why, why, why?" Whatever she said, we just accepted it the way it is. I never said, "Why?" because whatever Our Lady says that is for our good and it is not up to me to ask "Why?"

Mirjana told Sabrina Čović-Radojičić,

As I said, I never think of the secrets. I pray and good God helps me to carry them. I always recommend to all pilgrims: "Don't speak of the secrets! Don't waste your time, because you don't know when the time of the secrets will be. It may be this evening. You should be ready at any moment to present yourselves before God." Our Lady tells us to think of our lives and to ask ourselves if we will dare raise our head or keep it low because of our sins. This is what we should think of....

I already explained to you that it's not me who keeps secrets, but dear God. I do not think about the secrets. If pilgrims did not ask me, the days and months would pass, and I would never think of them. This may be a gift from God or my prayer that helps me in this; prayer which leads me and shows me what Our Lady wants from me. In fact, it is Jesus through our Mother.

On another occasion, Padre Livio, director of Radio Maria in Medjugorje, pressed Mirjana about details of the secrets. She told him, "Look, Father, if we want to continue the interview on important things, about Our Lady and her messages, I'll respond willingly. But I won't speak about the secrets because secrets are secrets! We [visionaries] have been asked about them by everyone from priests to the Communists, particularly, who questioned Jakov when he was only nine and a half years old, but we have never revealed the secrets. We always avoided this topic."

Mirjana also told me, "We visionaries do not talk to each other about the secrets, so we don't know if we have the same secrets or not."

Of course, everyone is curious to know more about the secrets; Mirjana told Padre Livio that even Father Petar, whom Mirjana chose as the recipient of her First Secret, is curious. She said that when he came to Medjugorje from Germany, he joked with her and said, "Tell me at least one secret."

Mirjana told Padre Livio, "What is really important is to be ready to meet the Lord at any time. Everything that happens will be the will of the Lord, and we can't change that, we can only change ourselves."

The First Secret

Mirjana is the only visionary who has revealed details of the First Secret. She told me, "I never ask Blessed Mary questions. I just listen to what she tells me. She told me, *'Choose a priest to whom you will tell the First Secret.'* She emphasized the singular. She did not tell him to tell *all* of the secrets. I chose Father Petar Ljubicic. I'll tell him the First Secret ten days before it occurs. We will fast and pray together for seven days and then he will announce the secret three days before it occurs. I don't know if each of the secrets will be announced."

Mirjana said, "On Christmas Day, 1982, I received the last of my Ten Secrets. Then Blessed Mary gave me all of the Ten Secrets. I received these Ten Secrets at the same time on one thing. It was like...[Mirjana paused and looked up searching for words] what the Queens wrote on 150 years ago—a scroll! Blessed Mary presented it to me and it contained all Ten Secrets and I could immediately read it. It was in my house in Sarajevo during the war and it was brought from there to here in Medjugorje for safekeeping.

"Others have seen it and can see something, but they see it differently. I showed it to one of my cousins who saw it as a letter asking for help. I also showed it to a friend who saw it as a prayer. Since then, I have not shown it to anyone else because different people see it in different ways, and only I can see it as containing the Ten Secrets.

"Regarding my release of the First Secret, I will not *give* the scroll to Father Petar," Mirjana continued. "Blessed Mary told me, '*You will* tell *the priest 10 days in advance.*' [Mirjana emphasized the word 'tell' in contrast to the word 'give.'] Blessed Mary never told me to give him the scroll. My only role is to tell Father Petar. All of the secrets are for all of the world, none are just for the parish or the Church. My role is not to distribute the secrets to the world."

Father Petar said, "Three days before it happens, I will be able to tell everybody what will happen: where, at what time, hour and minute, and how long it will be lasting."

Author Janice Connell reported that, on December 24, 1982 [the correct date is December 25, 1982], Mary told Mirjana, "*Mirjana, I selected you and told you all that is necessary. I transferred to you many horrors that you must carry worthily. Think of me and think about how many tears I have shed because of these horrors. You must always be courageous.*"

In my interview of Mirjana on October 23, 2010, I told her regarding the report of author Janice Connell, "There are reports that you said that the secrets involve what Our Lady herself described as *'many horrors.'* She replied, 'I did not say that.' (See Appendix B). I was very surprised by her answer.

The late, authoritative theologian, Father Renée Laurentin, recorded Mirjana's message of October 25, 1985 regarding "the realization of the First Secret." He wrote,

> **Mirjana**: "When she appeared, the Blessed Virgin greeted me, *'Praised be Jesus.'* Then she spoke of unbelievers;
>
> *They are my children. I suffer because of them. They do not know what awaits them. You must pray more for them.*
>
> "We prayed with her for the weak, the unfortunate, the forsaken. After the prayer, she blessed us. Then she showed me, as in a film, the realization of the First Secret. The earth was desolate.
>
> *It is the upheaval of a region of the world.* "She was precise. I cried."
>
> "Why so soon? I asked."
>
> *In the world, there are so many sins. What can I do, if you do not help me. Remember, that I love you.*
>
> "How can God have such a hard heart?"
>
> *God does not have a hard heart. Look around you and see what men do, then you will no longer say that God has a hard heart.*
>
> *How many people come to church, to the house of God, with respect, a strong faith, and love of God? Very few! Here you have a time of grace and conversion. It is necessary to use it well.*
>
> **Mary to Mirjana**:
>
> *Pray very much for Father Pero [Petar], to whom I send a special blessing. I am a mother, that is why I come. You must not fear for I am there.*

Father Pero [Petar] Ljubicic had been chosen by Mirjana to unveil to the world the first three warnings, three days before the event. (*Messages and Teachings of Mary At Medjugorje, Chronological Corpus of the Messages*, Laurentin, René, and LeJeune, René, Milford, Ohio: The Riehle Foundation, 1988).

95

So, in my interview with Mirjana on October 23, 2010, I said, "There are many reports that you had an apparition on October 25, 1985, and an interview with a priest (some say Father Petar) the next day in which you said that you were shown a vision of the First Secret. You allegedly said that it was played before you as though it were a film and that Our Lady told you, '*It is the upheaval of a region of the world*.' Could you tell me about that?"

She emphatically replied, "I did not have any apparition on October 25, 1985; I did not see that and I did not say that." Then I was even more surprised than I was at her denial of the "*many horrors*" reported by author Janice Connell.

Mirjana emphasized that her last apparition occurred on December 25, 1982, when she received her tenth and last secret. She had no apparitions after that, she said, especially on October 25, 1985, as I had mentioned to her, except on her birthday, until 1987. Since then, she said, she had received apparitions on the second of every month. (See Appendix B).

Mirjana's denial that Our Lady told her on December 25, 1982, that she had "*transferred to* [her] *many horrors that you must carry worthily*," her denial that the First Secret contained a vision of "*the upheaval of a region of the world*," and her denial of her apparition and First Secret message of October 25, 1985 were not made with deception. They were made with conviction.

In an interview with Sabrina Čović-Radojičić, Mirjana said,

> I will always tell the truth and will die for the truth if it is linked with God and religion. When the apparitions started I was a young girl, but I would never have had the idea of denying Jesus or the apparitions out of fear. Imagine a young girl of 15 or 16 years of age at that time, facing the SUP, which is today's MU, 52 [secret service organizations] alone with those investigators in a suit and tie. Imagine how insignificant I could feel, alone against them. However, I would never have thought of lying. I listened to what they told me. I acted according to their orders. I was ready to die for my God. I was so proud of that!

However, the following denials of Mirjana are contradicted by the foregoing reports: her denial of the "*horrors*" that Our Lady had reminded her of on December 25, 1982; her denial of the vision and message of October 25, 1985; and her denial of the statement that the First Secret was *"the upheaval of a region of the world."*

On December 25, 1982, when Mirjana's visions were suspended, the Blessed Virgin Mary told her, according to the different translations, that she had shown her *"many horrors"* (as reported by Janice Connell), many *"terrible things"* (as reported by Father René Laurentin), and *"many abominations"* (as reported by Sabrina Čović-Radojičić). Here is the translation of the December 25, 1982 message reported by Father Laurentin,

> *Now you will have to turn to God in the faith like any other person. I will appear to you on the day of your birthday and when you will experience difficulties in life. Mirjana, I have chosen you, I have confided in you everything that is essential. I have also shown you many terrible things. You must now bear it all with courage. Think of me and think of the tears I must shed for that. You must remain courageous. You have quickly grasped the messages. You must also understand now that I have to go away. Be courageous.*

Moreover, Father Laurentin reported that on November 6, 1982, the month before, Mirjana had been frightened by the Eighth Secret [she corrected that and told me that it was the Seventh Secret] and prayed to Our Lady "to preserve humanity from this calamity," but she replied that *"it is not possible to avoid entirely the chastisement."* Father Laurentin reported,

> Frightened by the Eighth [Seventh] Secret, Mirjana prayed to the Blessed Virgin to preserve humanity from this calamity. Our Lady replied,
>
> > *I have prayed; the punishment has been softened. Repeated prayers and fasting reduce punishments from God, but it is not possible to avoid entirely the chastisement. Go on the streets of the city, count those who glorify God, and those who offend him. God can no longer endure that.*

It is also reported that Mirjana had an apparition and message on October 25, 1985, regarding the First Secret and that it was reported by Father Laurentin that Mirjana said that Our Lady "showed me, as in a film, the realization of the First Secret. The earth was desolate. *'It is the upheaval of a region of the world.'* She was precise. I cried."

Mirjana's denials of the apparitions, the visions, and the messages of December 25, 1982, regarding *"many horrors"* and of October 25, 1985, regarding the First Secret are contradicted by the reports. Perhaps her emphatic denials are the fruit of a psychological phenomenon known as Denialism whereby a person denies the reality of something because it is too horrific to believe it. Or perhaps Our Lady mercifully blocked her memory from carrying the burden of *"many horrors"* for so many years.

The apparition of October 25, 1995, was confirmed by author Michael H. Brown who wrote, "In 1985, the day after she was shown a visual preview of the First Secret [October 26,] Mirjana gave Father Ljubicic several hints about the nature of the warnings. She said the first was 'nothing good' and that it was more severe than some of the others. She was asked whether the warning would be spiritual or physical. 'It has to be seen,' she replied. 'This has to shake us up so the world will start thinking.'" (*The Final Hour*, Brown, Michael H, Queenship Publishing Company, Goleta, CA, July 1, 1997, p. 246).

Moreover, as reported by author Dr. Thomas Petrisko, Mirjana had *three* apparitions and messages concerning the First Secret: October 25, 1985; November 30, 1985; and February 15, 1986.

During the fall and winter of 1985-1986, theologian Father Robert Faricy lived in Medjugorje for several months. He also confirmed that Mirjana had an apparition and message on October 25, 1985, and an interview with Father Ljubicic on the same day. He wrote, "Our Lady had showed her, as in a film, the coming of the first of the Ten Secrets. It will be a severe warning to the world." (*Medjugorje Journal: Mary Speaks to the World*, Faricy, Robert and Rooney, Lucy, Franciscan Press, June 1, 1988).

The following month, Mirjana received a *second* apparition of the First Secret. Father Laurentin reported, "On November 30, 1985, Mirjana had another apparition during which she again saw, as in a film, the unfolding of the first message. 'It will be unhappy; it will be a sorrowful sign,' she confirmed." (*The Apparitions at Medjugorje Prolonged: A Merciful Delay for a World in Danger*, Laurentin, René, Riehle Foundation, 1987, p. 30).

Almost 3 months later, Mirjana experienced yet another special apparition and a *third* vision and message of the First Secret. Father Faricy wrote, "The chief news was that yesterday, Saturday, February 15, [1986,] Mirjana had a vision of Our Lady at her house here in Bijakovići and, during it, she saw again the First Secret, as though in a film." (*Medjugorje Journal: Mary Speaks to the World*, Faricy, Robert and Rooney, Lucy, Franciscan Press, June 1, 1988, p.136).

So, there are three authoritative reports that Mirjana had apparitions concerning the First Secret, each of which confirmed the other: October 25, 1985; November 30, 1985; and February 15, 1986. Mirjana's denials of the reports of these three appariitions can be explained only by her.

Mirjana's interview with Father Petar Ljubicic on October 26, 1985, is very clear and important. Father Petar is the priest whom Mirjana had previously chosen to be the recipient of the First Secret. Moreover, Mirjana gave the interview only one day after her apparition when her memory was very fresh. Mirjana told Father Petar in the following poor translation,

> The First Secret will not be a pleasant thing. It will be something people will hear about for a long time....The people of Medjugorje will know immediately that it is in connection with the secrets. It will be something that everyone, everywhere, will immediately hear of it.

> But this does not mean that people will rush to the place where the First Secret has just occurred. Certainly no one wants to see disasters, anguish, and bad luck. I do not think this kind of thing attracts people at all. Why should people go and see things like that? One thing is going to see a sign, another is going to see suffering or a disaster. Who would, for example, go to Italy to see a dam collapse? The First Secret will get people thinking about God.

> [During the apparition of October 25, 1985, Mirjana saw the First Secret as in a film.]

> This shook me more than anything else. This was, of course, due to seeing the First Secret. If people saw the First Secret, as was shown to me yesterday [October 25,]

everyone would certainly be shocked enough to look at themselves and everything around them in a completely new way. Now I know things that are not particularly pleasant. I believe that if everyone knew the same things, each of these people would be shocked and look at our world in a completely different light.

It will last for a while. It will be visible; it is necessary to shake the world a little. It will cause the world to stop and think. (Source: *Medjugorje Italia*).

In her October 26, 1995, interview with Father Petar, Mirjana said that Mary told her, "*It is necessary to pray a great deal until the First Secret is revealed. But in addition to that, it is necessary to make sacrifices as much as possible, to help others as much as it is within our abilities, to fast — especially now, before the First Secret. She said that we are obliged to prepare ourselves.*"

Mirjana told Father Petar that there would be spiritual conversions during the First Secret's manifestation. Then he asked her, "Do you think that there will still be those who will remain hardened—despite the explicit, tangible, visible signs, and warnings? She responded, "Yes, of course, just as there always were. Even today, so many see the obvious works of God, yet they simply reject him because they are so hardened, just as the Pharisees did." (See Appendix B).

The only details that Mirjana has revealed regarding any of the Ten Secrets is of the First Secret. However, she did reveal that after the first two secrets occur, they will be followed by a permanent sign that God will leave on the hill of the apparitions.

The Sign

After the first two secrets, God will leave a visible, supernatural, indestructible, and permanent sign on the hill where Mary first appeared in Medjugorje. She said, "*Be converted! It will be too late when the sign comes. Beforehand, several warnings will be given to the world. Hurry to be converted. I need your prayers and your penance."* (April 25, 1983).

Father Vlašić reported in his letter to St. John Paul II, "After the admonitions, the visible sign will appear on the site of the apparitions in Medjugorje for all the world to see. The sign will be given as a testimony to the apparitions and in order to call the people back to the faith. The witness of Mirjana will be a confirmation of the apparitions and a stimulus for the conversion of the world."

Mirjana told Padre Livio in his interview in 2001, "There will be a sign on the hill of the apparitions. It will be like a gift for all of us because we will see that the Madonna is here for us as our mother. It will be very beautiful and a very visible sign that can't be made with human hands; it will be something from the Lord that will remain. I know the date of the sign."

Regarding the sign, Father Petar asked Mirjana in his interview of October 26, 1985, whether one would be able to understand it as something tangible. She replied, "Yes, the sign will be indestructible and permanent. Naturally, it will be clear to everyone that it is not something constructed and erected. Nobody will be able to say that it was brought and placed in that particular spot by, let us say, someone from Medjugorje."

The sign will be given for the atheists. The faithful already have signs and must themselves become a sign for the atheists. The faithful must not wait for the sign before they convert. This time is a time of grace for us. We can never thank God enough for his grace. This time is for deepening our faith and our conversion. When the sign comes, it will be too late for many. As a mother, Mary cautions us because she loves us.

Regarding the sign, Mary further said,

> *The sign will come; you must not worry about it. The only thing I would want to tell you is to be converted. Make that known to all my children as quickly as possible. No pain, no suffering is too great for me in order to save you. I will pray to my Son not to punish the world, but I plead with you, be converted.*

You cannot imagine what the Eternal Father will send to earth. That is why you must be converted. Renounce everything. Do penance. Express my thanks to all my children who have prayed and fasted. I carry all this to my Divine Son in order to obtain an alleviation of his justice against the sins of mankind.

I thank the people who have prayed and fasted. Persevere and help me to convert the world. (June 24, 1983).

Mirjana told Father Vlašić in his interview on January 10, 1983, "First, some secrets will be revealed — just a few. Then the people will be convinced that Our Lady was here. Then they will understand the sign. When Jakov [another visionary] said that the mayor will be the first one to run to the hill, he meant that generally, people of the highest social class. They will understand the sign as a place or occasion to convert. They will run to the hill and pray, and they will be forgiven. When I asked Our Lady about unbelievers, she said, *'They should be prayed for, and they should pray.'* But when I asked again, recently, she said, *'Let them convert while there is time.'* She did not say they should be prayed for."

Medjugorje is not the first place where Our Lady promised a sign. The Blessed Virgin Mary also appeared at Fatima, Portugal, in 1917. She warned the world then to convert or to experience a worse war [World War II] than World War I, which was then ravaging Europe. Mary said that war is a punishment for sins. As she has promised at Medjugorje, Mary also promised at Fatima to leave a sign to confirm her warnings of chastisements. She promised that there would be a great public miracle for all to see "*so that all may believe.*" She prophesied the exact date and place of this miracle — October 13, 1917, at Fatima.

On that date, approximately 100,000 people witnessed the "Miracle of the Sun." The sun appeared to defy all cosmic laws. It "danced" and spun in the sky and suddenly fell to earth. After a rainfall, the sun broke through the clouds and appeared as an opaque, spinning disc in the sky, "like the most magnificent fire wheel that could be imagined, taking on all the colors of the rainbow and sending forth multicolored flashes of light," according to an eyewitness.

The sun then suddenly fell to the earth in a zigzag pattern causing the previously muddy ground and the wet clothes of the witnesses to become completely dry. Eyewitness José Maria de Almeida Garrett, Professor at the Faculty of Sciences of Coimbra, Portugal, said, "One heard a clamor, a cry of anguish breaking from all the people. The sun, whirling wildly, seemed all at once to loosen itself from the firmament and, blood red, advance threateningly upon the earth as if to crush us with its huge and fiery weight. The sensation during those moments was truly terrible."

Many thought that it was the end of the world, but the sun returned to its place in the sky.

The sign and the fulfillment of the secrets announced at Medjugorje will be a confirmation to the world of the reality of the apparitions of the Blessed Virgin Mary there and an incentive for the conversion of the world. It will help all people to come to believe and know the love of the one true God. Don't wait, now is the time to turn to God! We must open our hearts and begin to change our lives starting today, starting right now!

Mirjana has not commented on the Fourth, Fifth, Sixth or Eighth of the Ten Secrets, but she has commented on the chastisement secrets.

Chastisement Secrets

Concerning the chastisement secrets, Mirjana told Father Vlašić in her interview with him on January 10, 1983,

> I can tell you that the Eighth Secret is worse than the other seven. [Mirjana subsequently corrected this statement and told me that it was the Seventh Secret that was worse and that it was lessened.] I prayed for a long time that it might be less severe. Every day, when Our Lady came, I pestered her, asking that it be mitigated. Then she said that everyone should pray that it might be lessened. So, in Sarajevo, I got many people to join me in this prayer. Later, Our Lady told me that she'd been able to have the secret lessened. But then

she told me the Ninth Secret and it was even worse. The Tenth Secret is totally bad and cannot be lessened whatsoever. I cannot say anything about it, because even a word would disclose the secret before it's time to do so.

Mirjana told Padre Livio, "I asked Our Lady if it was possible that at least part of that secret [the Seventh] will change. She said that we had to pray. We prayed a lot and she said that she changed a part, but now we cannot change it anymore, because it is the will of the Lord that must be realized."

She told him, "It is not possible to be abolished altogether. Only one part of it was removed. Our Lady told me that it was mitigated, but now that it must be realized. I do not ask anything more about these things because this is the will of the Lord and it should be done."

Regarding the lessening or mitigation of the punishment, Mary told Mirjana on November 11, 1982, "*I have prayed. The punishment has been softened. Repeated prayers and fasting reduce punishments from God, but it is not possible to avoid entirely the chastisement. Go on the streets of the city, count those who glorify God and those who offend him. God can no longer endure that.*"

Although Mirjana said that the Tenth Secret "cannot be lessened *whatsoever*," Mary said that "it is not possible to avoid *entirely* the chastisement." This should give us hope that the chastisement need not happen *entirely* and that it may still be lessened.

The threatened biblical chastisement of the destruction of the city of Nineveh was entirely avoided because the people repented. (See Jonah chapter 3). The threatened biblical chastisement of the destruction of Sodom and Gomorrah could have been avoided if enough people had repented, but they did not and the twin cities were destroyed. (See Genesis chapter 19). So, we should repent and respond to Mary's requests in order to avoid or mitigate the threatened chastisements.

Let us take hope in the words of Cardinal Joseph Ratzinger, later Pope Benedict XVI, who interpreted the vision of the Third Secret of Fatima. He wrote on June 26, 2000, "The future is not, in fact, unchangeably set. The vision speaks of dangers and how we might be saved from them. There is no immutable destiny, that faith and prayer are forces which can influence history and that in the end prayer is more powerful than bullets and faith more powerful than armies....What remains...[is] the exhortation to prayer as the path of 'salvation of souls' and, likewise, the summons to penance and conversion."

So, as Jesus said, we should be not afraid.

Be Not Afraid

In an interview at Medjugorje on October 3, 2009, Mirjana said, "I would like to recommend that you not talk about chastisements, because Our Lady came in Medjugorje to help us and not to destroy us. She said, *'What I started in Fatima, I will finish in Medjugorje. My heart will triumph.'* If our Heavenly Mother's heart will triumph, what is there to fear?"

In the same interview, Mirjana said, regarding the end of the world, "Well, the one who dies tomorrow, for that person the end of the world will happen tomorrow. That person will encounter God tomorrow. So, it is not important to talk about it at all. It is important to talk about ourselves, to think of myself. What is my soul like? Is it ready to encounter God now, this very moment?"

She told Sabrina Čović-Radojičić in an interview, "Our Lady said, *'What I started in Fatima, I will finish in Medjugorje. My heart will triumph.'* If Our Lady's heart will triumph, then why should we wear ourselves out with anything? What should we be afraid of? We should be afraid of sin! That should be our fear; not the secrets. You should only be worried about whether you'll praise the Lord

"I think that with these words [of Our Lady] she said a lot. Now I let everyone reflect on what this means. Knowing that Mother's heart will triumph...isn't it a blessing for her children? My children know that they will be happy if I win, because this means that I do the good for them. If the heart of our Heavenly Mother is going to triumph, everything is going to be right for us. Mother will triumph; she will beat the evil."

In another interview with Sabrina, she said "We are all on the way of conversion, on the way of love. We all strive to know God and his love. We should always say to people, 'Don't be afraid! Don't be afraid of meeting your Mother! Don't be afraid of meeting her Son, our God. Why should you be afraid if he is your Father? Why are you not worthy of meeting him? If Our Lady is your Mother, why should you be unworthy of meeting this Mother with your heart? We are all called to this, because she is with us. She is among us.'"

She also told Sabrina, "I'd like to say once again to everybody, 'Don't be afraid! Have confidence in our Heavenly Mother. Put your life in her hands. If your life is in her hands, what should you be afraid of? Fear is a weakness. If I pray and if God is with me, who can do me any harm? This gives me the enthusiasm and motivation.'"

Mirjana told Padre Livio in his interview, "The Madonna always says not to talk about the secrets, but to pray. She says, '*Whoever relates to me like a mother, and to God like a father, has no fear.*' The Madonna teaches us not to worry about the future and not to waste time speaking about the secrets, but to be ready to meet the Lord at any moment."

She concluded, "I do not understand why you should be afraid. I just want to say to all my brothers and sisters that you need not fear. The only ones that should be afraid are those who do not give the Lord first place in their hearts. If you have Our Lord and Our Lady in the first place of your heart, of what should you be afraid? That's why I do not want people to think that you should be afraid. There can be no fear if God and Our Lady are in first place in your heart."

Jesus said, "Fear is useless, what is needed is trust." (Mark 5:36). Visionary Mirjana Soldo has no fear. She is a joyful woman with a devoted husband and two daughters. When asked why there would be secrets, Mirjana said, "I only know it is God's will and all that is to happen. But I do want to say that there is no reason to fear, because the Blessed Mother does not want faith to come from fear. That faith does not last. There is no reason to fear. She said that if we love God, we have peace of joy, — *no matter what transpires.*"

Because we are God's children, we should not fear anything. St. Paul reminds us that nothing can separate us from Christ's love.

(See Romans 8:38-39). Therefore, we should look to the future in a trusting spirit.

Our response to the requests of the Blessed Virgin Mary and our openness to the Holy Spirit's guidance and protection will be our help. All things work for good for those who love God (see Romans 8:28), so all prophesied secrets, with their warnings and chastisements, will ultimately lead us to an everlasting experience of love, peace, and joy.

I told Mirjana that I wrote my book not to scare people, but to help them to prepare for the secrets, warnings, and chastisements so that they don't happen or they are mitigated because the people convert and believe and pray and fast like Our Lady has asked us to do.

She responded, "That's very good that you wrote the book not to scare people. This is important because a mother never scares her children and never gives them a reason to be afraid. She gives them hope and love. Blessed Mary is not coming to Medjugorje so that we are afraid of the future, but so that we have love and peace in the future with her."

She told me, "The most important thing is to respond to Mary's requests for conversion, faith, prayer and fasting, and not to be fearful of any secrets."

I asked Mirjana to comment on Father Petar's statement, "Everything is closer and closer, God has to do something very quickly."

She said, "We can comment in many ways, but, maybe I'll be in front of God tomorrow. I won't have time to wait for secrets; I must change myself today. I always tell the pilgrims, 'Don't talk about secrets, don't think about secrets, think of yourself, think of today, where are you today with God? Because you don't know what you will have tomorrow.'"

Mirjana told Padre Livio, "Not only must we be ready in the future and face the future with great preparation, but we all have to be prepared at all times, because we do not know when God will call us. We must be ready at any moment and live every day in intimate union with God." We never know when we'll be called to a period of trial.

A Period of Trial

In his 1983 letter to St. John Paul II, Father Vlašić wrote,

Mirjana related an apparition she had on December 26, 1982 in which Satan appeared to her and asked Mirjana to renounce the Madonna and to follow him. That way she could be happy in love and in life. He said that following the Virgin, on the contrary, would only lead to suffering. Mirjana rejected him, and immediately the Virgin arrived and Satan disappeared. Then the Blessed Virgin gave her the following message in substance,

> *Excuse me for this, but you must realize that Satan exists. One day he appeared before the throne of God and asked permission to submit the Church to a period of trial. God gave him permission to try the Church for one century. This century is under the power of the devil; but when the secrets confided to you come to pass, his power will be destroyed. Even now he is beginning to lose his power and has become aggressive. He is destroying marriages, creating divisions among priests and is responsible for obsessions and murder. You must protect yourselves against these things through fasting and prayer, especially community prayer. Carry blessed objects with you. Put them in your house and restore the use of holy water.*

Mirjana told Father Vlašić in his 1983 interview with her,

The Virgin told me that God and the devil conversed, and the devil said that people believe in God only when life is good for them. When things turn bad, they cease to believe in God. Then people blame God, or act as if he does not exist.

God, therefore, allowed the devil one century in which to exercise an extended power over the world, and the devil chose the twentieth century. Today, as we see all around us, everyone is dissatisfied; they cannot abide each other. Examples are the number of divorces and abortions. All this, Our Lady said, is the work of the devil....

The devil is not in them, but they're under the influence of the devil, although he enters into some of them. To prevent this, at least to some extent, Our Lady said we need communal prayer, family prayer. She stressed the need for family prayer most of all. Also, every family should have at least one sacred object in the house, and houses should be blessed regularly....

[The devil is especially active today] through people of weak character, who are divided within themselves. Such people are everywhere, and they are the easiest for the devil to enter. But he also enters the lives of strong believers....

Mirjana continued in her interview with Father Vlašić, in 1983, "Nobody believes—hardly anybody. For example, Our Lady told me that the faith in Germany, Switzerland, and Austria is very weak. The people in those countries model themselves on their priests, and if the priests are not good examples, the people fall away and believe there is no God. You know very well that the situation of the world is horrible. There are wars in every part of the world. The situation is very tense. The world has become very evil. It cares about faith very little."

Father Svetozar wrote that Mirjana once said, "God cannot take it anymore!" She told Father Vlašić, "Nowadays, people curse God, Jesus Christ, his Mother, his Father, day in and day out, habitually. Besides, people have fallen into very evil ways, so that they live in evil routinely. It's no wonder that God is at the end of his patience."

Here Mirjana is applying human limitations to God, but she makes her point of how she sees the state of the world in relation to Mary's messages to her. Mary herself said, "*Go on the streets of the city, count those who glorify God and those who offend him. God can no longer endure that.*" (November 11, 1982).

In her 1983 interview with Father Vlašić, Mirjana explained that the century given over to Satan was generally the twentieth century: "part of which is in the twentieth century, until the First Secret is unfolded." The implication is that Satan's power will continue into the twenty-first century and will only be destroyed sometime after the First Secret "unfolds."

When Mary's warnings are revealed, people will ask, "What are we to do?" The answer is the same answer that St. Peter gave to the Jews when they asked the same question after they heard the mighty wind at Pentecost. St. Peter told them, "Repent and be baptized, every one of you, in the name of Jesus Christ for the forgiveness of your sins; and you will receive the gift of the Holy Spirit." (Acts 2:38).

Despite the explicit warnings and the tangible, visible sign that will be left to confirm them, Mirjana thinks that there will still be those who will not be ready, and will not respond, but will remain hardened. She said, "Those are the ones who have shut their souls to God."

How should we respond to Our Lady's requests and prepare for the secrets?

7. How to Prepare for the Secrets

The Blessed Virgin Mary comes to Medjugorje bringing us urgent messages from God. The summary of her messages is that peace can come only from God through conversion and faith, maintained by the sacraments (especially Confession and the Eucharist), prayer and fasting, reading Scripture, and the use of sacramentals.

All adults have the capacity to know that God exists. The sin of the world lies in that there is no interest or time for God. Mary comes to tell the world that God exists and that peace is necessary for the salvation of the world.

Peace

Mary said, "*I have come here as Queen of Peace to tell the world that peace is necessary for the salvation of the world. In God, one finds true joy from which true peace is derived.*" (June 16, 1983).

She also said, "*Jesus is the King of Peace, and only he can give you the peace that you seek.*" (December 25, 1995).

Mirjana told Father Vlašić that Mary introduced herself as the Queen of Peace because, "the situation of the world is horrible. There are wars in every part of the world. The situation is very tense. Peace is needed — a just and simple peace. First, peace in the soul. If a person has it in his soul, he is surrounded by it. Peace comes as result of faith in God and surrender to him as a consequence of prayer, penance, and fasting."

Peace is the natural desire of every human heart. However, peace is not obtainable by any human peace program or from money, drugs, power, or anything else without Jesus Christ who said, "Without me you can do nothing." (John 15:5).

Jesus said, "Peace I leave with you; my peace I give to you. Not as the world gives do I give it to you. Do not let your hearts be troubled or afraid." (John 15:27). Peace is a gift from God that cannot be earned by our effort, imposed by political effort, or gained by any human means whatsoever. As Mary said, only Jesus can give us the peace that we seek.

St. John Paul II said, "In the end, peace is not essentially about structures but about people. Certain structures and mechanisms of peace — juridical, political, economic — are of course necessary and do exist, but they have been derived from nothing other than the accumulated wisdom and experience of innumerable gestures of peace made by men and women throughout history who have kept hope and have not given in to discouragement. Gestures of peace spring from the lives of people who foster peace first of all in their own hearts. They are the work of the heart and of reason in those who are peacemakers (see Matthew 5:9)." (Message for the Celebration of the World Day of Peace, January 1, 2003).

Peace is not merely the absence of external conflict. It is a positive interior quality, which is a gift from Jesus (see John 14:27), beginning in our hearts and flowing like a river to our family, neighbors, friends, and society, gathering them all in its current. We seek and yearn for this peace because God has instilled this yearning in us so that we will rest in him.

St. Augustine said, "You have made us for yourself, O Lord, and our hearts are restless until they rest in you." Only then will we experience God's own peace which is beyond all understanding. (See Philippians 4:7).

Each of us must truthfully answer the eternal questions, "Who am I?, Why am I?, and What is my destiny?" The meaning of being human is that we are dependent creatures of God our Creator, who made us for himself out of his love for us and gave us great dignity.

The psalmist said, "What are humans that you are mindful of them, mere mortals that you care for them? Yet you have made them little less than a god, crowned them with glory and honor." (Psalm 8:5-6).

We have dignity because we are created with mortal bodies in God's image (see Genesis 1:26) with intellect, wills, and immortal souls. We are called to know him, to love him, and to serve him on earth so that we will have happiness and eternal life with him in Heaven. "He merited for us life by the free shedding of his own blood. In him, God reconciled us (see 2 Corinthians 5:18-19; Colossians 1:20-22) to himself and among ourselves; from bondage to the devil and sin he delivered us, so that each one of us can say with the Apostle: The Son of God 'loved me and gave himself up for me. (Galatians 2:20).'" (Vatican II, *Pastoral Constitution on the Church in the Modern World*, 22). St. Paul also said, "You have been purchased at a price." (1 Corinthians 6:20).

Jesus said that eternal life is to know the one true God, and the one whom he sent, Jesus himself. (See John 17:3). Those who believe in him have eternal life. (See 1 John 5:13). We "believe in him" through faith that he is true God and true man, our Lord and Savior. We humbly submit to all that he revealed that we should believe and do, and to the authoritative teaching of the one true Church that he founded.

"The way we may be sure that we know him is to keep his commandments. Whoever says, 'I know him,' but does not keep his commandments, is a liar, and the truth is not in him. But whoever keeps his word, the love of God is truly perfected in him. This is the way we may know that we are in union with him: whoever claims to abide in him ought to live just as he lived." (1 John 2:1-6). Through this union with him we become a mysterious new creation and partake of God's own life of grace and truth for all eternity. Jesus Christ fully reveals man to himself and we see our divine destiny to live with him in eternal life and happiness.

Even without this divine revelation, we can know that God exists by reason alone, without faith. God created us as rational animals with mortal, material bodies and immortal, immaterial souls with intellects to know the truth, and wills to do the good. We come to know this by our reasoning powers alone, unaided by God's revelation. "For what can be known about God is evident…, because God made it evident. Ever since the creation of the world, his invisible attributes of eternal power and divinity have been able to be understood and perceived in what he has made." (Romans 1:19-20).

As a result, those who deny God's existence, or act as if he does not exist, have no excuse and they do not accord him glory as God or give him thanks. Instead, they become vain in their reasoning; their senseless minds are darkened and they have no peace. (See Romans 1:20-21). "They exchanged the truth of God for a lie and revered and worshiped the creature rather than the Creator." (Romans 1:25). We see this in our own world today.

Not only can we know the truth of God's existence by our unaided reason, we can also know his will for us to do good and avoid evil and his law to love God and our neighbor. In the depths of his conscience, man detects a law which he does not impose upon himself, but which holds him to obedience. Always summoning him to love good and avoid evil, the voice of conscience, when necessary speaks to his heart: do this, shun that. For man has in his heart a natural law written by God; to obey it is the very dignity of man; according to it he will be judged. (See Romans 2:15-16). Conscience is the most secret core and sanctuary of a man. There, he is alone with God whose voice echoes in his depths. In a wonderful manner, conscience reveals that law which is fulfilled by love of God and neighbor. (See Matthew 22:37-40; Galatians 5:14). (Vatican II, *Pastoral Constitution on the Church in the Modern World*, 16).

Those who deny God, who do not listen to his voice and disobey his law, are handed over by him "to their undiscerning mind to do what is improper." (Romans 1:28). And what do the deniers of God do that is improper? They degrade their bodies through lust and unnatural homosexual relations. (Romans 1:24-27). "They are filled with every form of wickedness, evil, greed, and malice; full of envy, murder, rivalry, treachery, and spite. They are gossips and scandalmongers and they hate God. They are insolent, haughty, and boastful in their wickedness, and rebellious toward their parents. They are senseless, faithless, heartless, ruthless. Although they know the just decree of God that all who practice such things deserve death, they not only do them but give approval to those who practice them." (Romans 1:29-32).

They lose the peace of God and freely choose eternal death. "We know that the judgment of God on those who do such things is true." (Romans 2:2). "[He] will repay everyone according to his works: eternal life to those who seek glory, honor, and immortality through perseverance in good works, but wrath and fury to those who selfishly disobey the truth and obey wickedness." (Romans 2:6-8).

On the contrary, those who conform their wills to the will of God through conversion, faith, prayer, and fasting, and keep his Commandments, have a clear conscience and the gift of his peace.

Pope Benedict XVI recognized that peace is a gift from God alone and is built and preserved only when human beings can freely seek and serve him in their hearts, in their lives, and in their relationships with others. He said,

> The truth, goodness, happiness, and abundant life which each man and woman consciously or unconsciously seeks are given to us by God. In longing for these gifts, each person is seeking his Creator, for "God alone responds to the yearning present in the heart of every man and woman." (Post-Synodal Apostolic Exhortation *Verbum Domini*, 23). Humanity, throughout history, in its beliefs and rituals, demonstrates a constant search for God and "these forms of religious expression are so universal that one may well call man a religious being." (*CCC* 28). The religious dimension is an undeniable and irrepressible feature of man's being and acting, the measure of the fulfilment of his destiny and of the building up of the community to which he belongs. Consequently, when the individual himself or those around him neglect or deny this fundamental dimension, imbalances and conflicts arise at all levels, both personal and interpersonal. This primary and basic truth is the reason why, in this year's Message for World Day of Peace, I identified religious freedom as the fundamental path to peace. Peace is built and preserved only when human beings can freely seek and serve God in their hearts, in their lives, and in their relationships with others." (*New Year Address to Diplomatic Corps,* January 10, 2011).

When people neglect these eternal truths and the call to peace, conflicts arise. Father Svetozar Kraljević wrote in *The Apparitions of Our Lady at Medjugorje*, "The world was called to peace, but it went to war [the Yugoslavian Civil War.] Precisely ten years after Mary appeared, the first explosions of war were heard. We wonder what we shall miss again. And what shall take place in the future?"

The future is in the secrets. We should respond now to Mary's request for peace and not miss it again. We can possess anything in this world, but if we do not have peace, we have nothing. The only true peace is the one that Jesus gives. However, this peace is not obtainable, as Mary said, unless we repent (convert,) believe (have faith,) reconcile with God and one another (go to Confession,) pray (especially the Rosary,) and fast.

The angels greeted the shepherds of Bethlehem and said, "Glory to God in the highest, and on earth peace among men with whom he is pleased." (Luke 2:14). Pope Benedict XVI said, "The angel's greeting to the shepherds on the night of Christ's birth in Bethlehem reveals an unbreakable link between the relationship of men and women with God and their own mutual relationships. Peace on earth cannot be found without reconciliation with God, without harmony between Heaven and earth." (*Address to the Roman Curia*, December 22, 2006).

Conversion

Mirjana told Father Vlašić, "Our Lady said people should prepare themselves spiritually, be ready, and not panic; be reconciled in their souls. They should be ready for the worst, to die tomorrow. They should accept God now so that they will not be afraid. They should accept God, and everything else. No one accepts death easily, but they can be at peace in their souls if they are believers. If they are committed to God, he will accept them. This means total conversion and surrender to God. I say to all people: Convert! — the same as she said, '*Convert while there is time!*'

"Do not abandon God and your faith. Abandon everything else, but not that!" she continued. "I ask priests to help their people, because priests can cause them to reject their faith. After a man has been ordained, he must really be a priest, bring people to the

Church. The most important point is that the people convert and pray." Each of us must answer the question that God asked Fred Beretta before his Miracle on the Hudson, *"Will you reconcile and trust? You must choose."* [You may read his story in the Preface.]

Conversion is a total interior change of heart which proceeds from our repentance, reconciliation, and the submission of our wills to seek first the Kingdom of God. (See Matthew 3:2; 6:33). We turn from following our own wills to follow the will of God, from our values to his, and abandon, in trust, everything that takes us away from him.

The call of the prophets is to repent, meaning to convert, to turn to God, to change our ways, and to be reconciled with him and one another. Mary's first appearance at Medjugorje was on the Feast of St. John the Baptist. This is significant since he was the last of the prophets before Jesus. Between them, all righteousness was fulfilled. (See Matthew 3:15). They both gave the same call, "Repent, for the Kingdom of Heaven is at hand." (Matthew 3:2; 4:17).

Jesus has sent his Mother to Medjugorje for the same reason that he sent St. Paul to the pagans — "To open their eyes, so that they may turn from darkness to light, from the dominion of Satan to God, and receive, through faith in me, forgiveness of their sins and a share in the inheritance of the sanctified." (Acts 26:18).

The prophet Ezekiel spoke in God's name and said, "As I live, says the Lord God, I swear I take no pleasure in the death of the wicked man, but in the wicked man's conversion, that he may live." (Ezekiel 33:10-11).

The prophet Jeremiah called the Jews to conversion and said, "Cleanse your heart of evil." (Jeremiah 4:14). Jesus said, "For from the heart come evil thoughts, murder, adultery, unchastity, theft, false witness, blasphemy. These are what defile a person." (Matthew 15:19-20).

Conversion consists of a radical reformation of our hearts and lives by which we then acknowledge and confess our sins, turning from the values of the world to those of Jesus Christ and believing in and accepting the Gospel message and his person as the Son of God and our personal Lord and Savior. Through conversion, we turn from sin and selfishness, submit to Jesus as Lord of our minds and hearts, and change our ways of thinking and acting. True repentance requires a contrite heart (see Psalm 51:17) and sorrow for sin and a firm purpose to amend our lives and to avoid the near of occasions of sin in the future.

One of the greatest conversion stories of all time is that of Saul of Tarsus who became St. Paul. He testified how he first opposed the Gospel and persecuted Christians but was converted when Christ appeared to him on the road to Damascus. (See Acts 22:3-16). Paul's encounter with the person of Christ radically changed his life and opened his eyes to the truth of the Gospel. Pope Benedict XVI reflected on the significance of Paul's conversion for all Christian people,

> Paul's conversion matured in his encounter with the Risen Christ; it was this encounter that radically changed his life. What happened to him on the road to Damascus is what Jesus asks in today's Gospel: Saul is converted because, thanks to the divine light, "he has believed in the Gospel." In this consists his and our conversion: in believing in Jesus dead and risen and in opening to the illumination of his divine grace. In that moment, Saul understood that his salvation did not depend on good works fulfilled according to the law, but on the fact that Jesus died also for him, the persecutor, and has risen. This truth by which every Christian life is enlightened thanks to Baptism completely overturns our way of life. To be converted means, also for each one of us, to believe that Jesus "has given himself for me," dying on the Cross (see Galatians 2:20) and, risen, lives with me and in me. Entrusting myself to the power of his forgiveness, letting myself be taken by his hand, I can come out of the quicksands of pride and sin, of deceit and sadness, of selfishness and of every false security, to know and live the richness of his love. (January 25, 2009).

God's grace brings pardon and absolution for our sins, especially through the sacrament of Confession, by which we are reconciled to God and one another and become his friends and the friends of one another. This causes, through his grace, an interior transformation producing fruits of prayer, self-denial, and charity. (See Acts 26:20). This is the foundation of all Christianity. (See

Hebrews 6:1-2). Mary especially recommended the monthly reception of the sacrament of Confession. (See Appendix A.)

Mirjana told Father Vlašić, "Evil things will happen because the world has become very evil. It cares about faith very little."

Faith

Mary said, *"Faith is a vital element but one cannot compel a person to believe. Faith is the foundation from which everything flows."* (November 31, 1981).

Jesus said, "This is the work of God: have faith in the one he sent." (John 6:29). "Without faith, it is impossible to please him." (Hebrews 11:6).

Before his ascension to Heaven, Jesus appeared to his apostles and said, "Go into the whole world and proclaim the Gospel to every creature. Whoever believes and is baptized will be saved; whoever does not believe will be condemned." (Mark 16:15-18).

Faith is the submission of our intellect and will to God's revelation, in particular to the good news of the new covenant of eternal salvation through the forgiveness of our sins. (See Mark 1:15; Hebrews 9:26; Romans 3:24-26). "[Jesus Christ] is mediator of a new covenant: since a death has taken place for deliverance from transgressions under the first covenant, those who are called may receive the promised eternal inheritance." (Hebrews 9:15). We believe God's promises because he is all-good and will not deceive us.

Faith is not contrary to reason, but a belief in the person and message of Jesus Christ as a living witness accredited by God through his works (see Matthew 11:2-6; John 5:36; John 10:25, 37; John 14:11); his character (see John 8:46-59); and his doctrine (see John 7:16-17) and confirmed in his resurrection (see Romans 1:4). Faith is both preceded and assisted by God's grace.

After John the Baptist was put in prison, Jesus went into the Galilee region of Israel and proclaimed the good news of God. He said, "The time has come. The Kingdom of God is near. Repent and believe the good news!" (Mark 1:14-15). So, in addition to conversion (repentance), we must *believe* his good news.

We should believe the proclamation of Jesus, because he demonstrated that "the Kingdom of God was not a matter of talk, but of power." (1 Corinthians 4:20). "He went around all of Galilee, teaching in their synagogues, proclaiming the Gospel of the Kingdom, and curing every disease and illness among the people. His fame spread to all of Syria, and they brought to him all who were sick with various diseases and racked with pain, those who were possessed, lunatics, and paralytics, and he cured them." (Matthew 4:23-24).

The Kingdom of God. The good news (Gospel) that Jesus proclaimed was that the Kingdom of God was near. This Kingdom is not a geographical area on the earth, like Israel. Moreover, it is not an historical event which is fixed in time, like the kingdom of King Herod.

The Kingdom of God is the same as the Kingdom of Heaven. It is eternal life and its beginning may be enjoyed now. (See Matthew 25:34, 46; John 3:15). "For God so loved the world that he gave his only Son, so that everyone who believes in him might not perish but might have eternal life." (John 3:16).

The Kingdom of God is also the person of Christ himself and his Church. The members of his Kingdom are the children of God who enter it through conversion, faith, baptism, and the forgiveness of sins, and through the acceptance of the person of Jesus Christ and the teachings of his Church, which is his Kingdom on earth. The final realization of his Kingdom will occur in the glory of his second coming. (See Matthew 24:26-31). The Kingdom of God has come (see Luke 11:20; Matthew 4:17) and will come (see Luke 9:27), for which we are to pray (see Matthew 6:10).

The Kingdom of God is the Reign of God and his sovereignty and authority over all peoples and nations forever. (See Psalm 103:19; Zechariah 14:9,16; Revelation 15:4). His Kingdom is universal and everlasting (see Daniel 4:3); it is meant for all humankind, and all people are called to become members of it. It is full of glory, power, and splendor. (See Psalm 145:11-13). It is "righteousness, peace, and joy in the Holy Spirit." (Romans 14: 17).

At one and the same time, the Kingdom of God has arrived and is arriving towards a perfect realization. Its presence is not two events but two stages of the same event, one of which is here while the other is an object of hope and prayer. The Kingdom of God is inaugurated in Jesus Christ himself (see Matthew 12:25-28; Vatican II, *Dogmatic Constitution on the Church*, 5) and moves towards its perfect realization by means of his Church. (See Matthew 10:7; 16:19). Jesus revealed the Kingdom of God by his intervention into the world with his teachings, miracles, and exorcisms, which radically overthrew the Kingdom of Satan. (See Mark 3:27).

This Kingdom reveals itself through Jesus to all people who should submit to it in faith. The Kingdom comes to us individually as an offer of pardon to be freely accepted by reforming our lives and believing in and surrendering to the sovereignty of God in the person of Jesus Christ. Those who fail to reform must face his judgment. (See Matthew 11:20-24).

The blessings of the Kingdom to those who submit to it are the forgiveness of their sins (see Mark 2:5); God's provident care (see Matthew 6:33); and the gift of God's Holy Spirit (see Acts 2:38). In the future, God "will wipe every tear from their eyes, and there shall be no more death or mourning, wailing, or pain," (Revelation 21:4) "and they shall reign forever and ever." (Revelation 22:5).

Baptism. We enter the Kingdom of God through Baptism. When the mighty, noisy wind of Pentecost blew in Jerusalem in 33 A.D., the Jews there knew that they had experienced a supernatural sign. When the first warning comes, three days after its announcement from Medjugorje, the world will know that it experienced a fulfilled prophecy. Then, like the Jews in Jerusalem, almost 2000 years ago, the people will say, "What are we to do?" (Acts 2:37).

The answer to that question today is the same answer that St. Peter gave to the Jews, "Repent and be baptized, every one of you, in the name of Jesus Christ for the forgiveness of your sins; and you will receive the gift of the Holy Spirit." (Acts 2:38).

Conversion and faith are culminated in the sacrament of Baptism. Those who have converted but are unbaptized must be baptized.

Jesus told Nicodemus, "Amen, Amen, I say to you, no one can enter the Kingdom of God without being born of water and Spirit." (John 3:5). All of the faithful must be baptized and receive the sacraments of Confession, Eucharist, and Confirmation.

Baptism is the sign and the reality of being cleansed from sin. The unbaptized should be prepared for this and the other sacraments through the Catholic Church's Rite of Christian Initiation for Adults (RCIA.)

Conversion is not a single act; we are all in need of continual conversion and that's why Mary asks us to receive the sacrament of Confession monthly.

In the sacrament of Baptism, we die to sin and our old life and rise to a new life in Jesus Christ in the hopes of our rising from the dead to have eternal life in glory with him. St. Gregory of Nazianzus, a seventh century Church Father, tells us, "Let us be buried with Christ by Baptism to rise with him; let us go down with him to be raised with him; and let us rise with him to be glorified with him."

Pope Benedict XVI said, "I would like to encourage all of the faithful to rediscover the beauty of being baptized and belonging to the great family of God and to giving a joyous witness to their own faith so that they might bear the fruits of goodness and concord."

He noted how each baptized person "acquires the character of son from the name Christian, indisputable sign that the Holy Spirit brings man to be born 'again' from the womb of the Church." He continued, "Blessed Antonio Rosmini says that 'the baptized person undergoes a secret but most powerful operation by which he is raised up to the supernatural order, he is placed in communication with God.'" (January 9, 2011).

"Therefore, the Church announces the good tidings of salvation [being saved from eternal death and sin] to those who do not believe so that all men may know the true God and Jesus Christ whom he has sent, and may be converted from their ways, doing penance. (See John 17:3; Luke 24:27; Acts 2:38). To believers, also, the Church must ever preach faith and penance." (Vatican II, *The Constitution of the Sacred Liturgy*, 9).

Our response to hearing the good tidings of salvation is governed by the Second Vatican Council, which stated,

> "The obedience of faith" (Romans 16:26; 2 Corinthians 10:5-6) is to be given to God who reveals an obedience by which man commits his whole self freely to God, offering "the full submission of intellect and will to God who reveals," and freely assenting to the truth revealed by him. (Vatican II, *The Dogmatic Constitution on Divine Revelation*, 1:5).

Prayer and Fasting

Prayer and fasting maintain conversion and faith which are inextricably linked in the chain of peace. Prayer should calmly and peacefully proceed from an interior desire for union with God, without preoccupation to distractions.

Mary said, "*Pray with great meditation. Do not look at your watch all the time but allow yourself to be led by the grace of God. Do not concern yourself too much with the things of this world but entrust all that in prayer to our Heavenly Father. If one is preoccupied, he will not be able to pray well because internal security is lacking.*" (June 16, 1983).

According to Father Svetozar, a priest asked the visionaries to ask Mary whether we should pray to Jesus or to her. Mary responded, "*Pray to Jesus. I am his Mother, and I intercede with him, but say all your prayers to Jesus. I will help you pray, but the strength of your prayers is more important.*"

Mirjana told Father Vlašić, "When we pray, we pray to God. In return, we receive peace of soul, tranquility. We have opened our hearts to God, so that God can enter and when we have God in our heart and soul, we cannot cause evil to anybody. We will not curse — do anything evil. We will do good. We also have to pray for others. For example, I always pray for nonbelievers because they do not know what is missing in their lives. They have no idea of how much they may have to suffer later. I pray that God will convert them, that he will give them a sign, that he will open their souls so that they can accept the faith.

"Much can be done through prayer and fasting," Mirjana continued. "Our Lady has said that prayer can stop wars and prevent catastrophes. Prayer and fasting! Of course, prayer can help a struggling human who does not accept God and religion. Moreover, we are obliged to pray that such a person's heart will be opened. Again, I talk to many nonbelievers in Sarajevo and try to explain things to them so that they will gain at least a little understanding. Sometimes, it is not their fault; they received no religious training when they were young. Or later, when they abandoned their faith, no one tried to help them. I pray that God will open such hearts."

Mirjana told Father Vlašić how she prayed. "I pray the Rosary and I pray for an hour or two, depending on how much time I have. But usually never less than one hour. I pray that God will give me the strength of soul that I can again think and behave normally. I also pray for unbelievers, for their conversion. And for the secrets….When I pray, something comes to me, because I immerse myself in prayer. Then it's as if I'm speaking with someone. I express things in the way I think they should be said, all the while talking to God. Then I go back to saying the regular kind of prayers. Then I pray again in my own words. I say all this out loud.

"If we pray for a particular need," Mirjana continued, "we should emphasize exactly that: 'Dear God, I'm praying to be healed of my illness.' Pray like that. But pray from your heart, from the bottom of your soul, with feeling. It does not have to be a 'regular' prayer, but a conversation with God. 'God, you see my suffering. You know how I am. I'm not complaining, my cross is not too difficult to bear; but I would like to be on my feet again so that I can move around in the world.' Like that: conversation, then prayer."

Mirjana concluded, "I believe that sick people should speak and pray to God for one hour every day, intimately. I'm sure it would restore their souls and that God would grant them grace. Our Lady always recommended faith, prayer, and penance. She never mentioned anything special for anybody, whether they were sick or healthy. But, she said we should direct our prayers: *I am praying for such-and-such.* And we should pray with concentration, not race through the words of Our Father. The main thing is not to say the words of a prayer, but to feel them."

In an interview at Medjugorje on October 3, 2009, Mirjana said, "We can always pray better and we grow in that. I always recommend to everybody, do not waste your time judging yourself in your own prayer. Pray and God will help you. Sometimes you just feel like you prayed great, sometimes not, but Our Lady always offers her hand as mother and she will always raise you up. Do not forget, God is love and he loves you and he knows you and it is important that you desire to come closer to him and he will help you."

Mirjana continued, "Our Lady asks us to pray from the heart. I understand that to mean that every word that comes out of my mouth would pass through my heart first. So, when I say, 'Hail Mary,' then I truly greet Mary with my heart. When I say, 'full of grace,' then I feel within myself how much grace Our Lady gives me and to everyone. It is never a repetition for me because I always feel some new, different things when I pray the Hail Mary.

"For example," she continued, "when I reflect that Our Lady was assumed into Heaven, I think about her. I talk with her. I ask her about how she felt and all that she thought. I do not see her. I do not hear her, but just with my heart. Try that. If your thoughts still wander, put the Rosary aside and talk with Our Lady and tell her why, what your burden is and why you can't be still and pray. Whatever you have in your heart, give it to her."

Mirjana told me that she wanted "to ask everybody to pray for those who do not recognize the love of God yet. Because when we pray for them, we pray for us, for our future, because who of us can say, 'I am a good believer, I'm doing everything that God wants?' And when we pray for them, we pray for us."

Jesus is a model for prayer whom we should imitate. He often prayed all night long, even to the point of sweating blood. (See Luke 22:44). He condemned any prayer that is said for the sake of notice. (See Matthew 6:5). He remarked upon the brief petition for pardon uttered by the tax collector as the prayer that justifies a man. (See Luke 18:10). In our prayer, we should recognize the unredeemed sin within us, offer it to Jesus for his redemption, and continually yearn to be closer to God. The more we pray, the more we are conformed to the mind of Christ and live as a child of the Father.

Mary especially recommended the reading of Scripture, the Rosary, the use of sacramentals, and, as the best prayer, the celebration of the Eucharistic liturgy. (See Appendix A).

Pope Benedict XVI said, "As believers, we are convinced that prayer is a true force. It opens the world to God. We are convinced that God listens and that he can act in history. I think that if millions of people—believers—would pray, it could really be a force that could influence and contribute to the advancement of peace." (Aboard the Papal Plane, May 8, 2009).

Mary asked us, *"Pray to the Holy Spirit for my Son to be impressed within you. Pray that you can be apostles of the divine light in this time of darkness and hopelessness. This is a time of your trial. With a Rosary in hand and love in the heart set out with me. I am leading you towards Easter in my Son. Pray for those whom my Son has chosen that they can always live through him and in him, the High Priest. Thank you."* (March 2, 2012).

Mary has asked us to pray with her and to pray as much as possible, including the Rosary every day. She said, *"In addition, I want them to fast on Wednesdays and Fridays."* (August 14, 1984).

Mirjana told Father Vlašić, "Sick people do not have to fast. If they do not fast, it is not a sin for them. They can do another good deed instead. For those who are able to fast, it is not enough that they do a good deed instead. We did not discuss fasting except on bread and water. But probably she meant we should fast only on bread and water. Everyone who wants to receive something from God or have God's help, must fast."

In her interview at Medjugorje on October 3, 2009, Mirjana said, "When I'm fasting, I'm proving to myself that I am the boss of my own body and that I can do for God anything I want, that nothing can stop me. And with this fasting, I'm showing God that with this little, I am ready to do even more if that is what he desires. Through fasting, my prayer is stronger. I feel closer to him."

Jesus is also a model person for fasting. He fasted in the desert for 40 days and 40 nights after his Baptism. (See Luke 4:2). He said that certain demons could not be cast out except through prayer and fasting. (Matthew 17:21; Mark 9:29). Jesus condemned the appearance of self-denial. (See Matthew 6:16-18). External fasting without interior love of God and neighbor are really works for one's self. True fasting that delights the Lord involves more of charity than self-denial. (See Isaiah 58:6-7; Matthew 9:13).

Mary especially recommended, as *"the best fast,"* fasting on bread and water on Wednesdays and Fridays. We fast on these days because Wednesday is the day that Judas made the arrangement to betray Jesus and Friday is the day that they crucified him. (See Appendix A).

Mary asked for all of this prayer and fasting in order to maintain our peace and to mitigate worldly chastisements. She makes these requests as a mother concerned for our temporal and eternal welfare, aware of the evil rampant in the world, and for warning us of chastisements. She said, *"Through fasting and prayer one can stop wars, one can suspend the natural laws of nature."* (July 21, 1982).

The world is involved in a supernatural battle between the forces of good and evil. Only supernatural weapons can be effective in such a battle. St. Paul tells us to "put on the armor of God so that you may be able to stand firm against the tactics of the devil. Our battle is not against human forces but against the principalities and powers, the rulers of this world of darkness, the evil spirits in regions above." (Ephesians 6:11-12).

The supernatural weapons requested by Mary at Medjugorje are conversion and faith, maintained by prayer and fasting. Prayer and fasting will help to bring about peace. Mary said that peace is necessary for the salvation of the world and that she is the Queen of Peace.

Total Consecration to Jesus through Mary

On October 25, 1988, Mary also asked us at Medjugorje to consecrate ourselves to her Immaculate Heart. On November 8, 1983, Mary had revealed to Medjugorje visionary, Jelena Vasij, such a consecration.

When we consecrate ourselves to the Immaculate Heart of Mary we totally entrust and dedicate ourselves to Jesus through Mary as our Mediatrix. This is the consecration that St. John Paul II made to her as the Mediatrix of All Graces and he took as his motto *Totus Tuus* [Totally Yours.] He wrote,

> This role of Mary, [as the Mediatrix of All Graces,] totally grounded in that of Christ and radically subordinated to it, "in no way obscures or diminishes the unique mediation of Christ, but rather shows its power." This is the luminous principle expressed by the Second Vatican Council which I

have so powerfully experienced in my own life and have made the basis of my episcopal motto: *Totus Tuus* [Totally Yours.] The motto is, of course, inspired by the teaching of Saint Louis Marie Grignion de Montfort who explained in the following words Mary's role in the process of our configuration to Christ: "Our entire perfection consists in being conformed, united, and consecrated to Jesus Christ. Hence the most perfect of all devotions is undoubtedly that which conforms, unites, and consecrates us most perfectly to Jesus Christ. Now, since Mary is of all creatures the one most conformed to Jesus Christ, it follows that among all devotions that which most consecrates and conforms a soul to our Lord is devotion to Mary, his holy Mother, and that the more a soul is consecrated to her the more will it be consecrated to Jesus Christ." (*The Rosary of the Virgin Mary*, 1:15).

The Pope referred to St. Louis de Montfort who wrote the book, *True Devotion to Mary,* in which he teaches total consecration to Jesus through Mary as a means of renewing our baptismal promises. By this total consecration, we renounce Satan, his pomps and works, and permanently dedicate ourselves to Jesus through Mary, giving her our bodies and souls, our goods, and even the merits of our good works for her disposition according to her will. (See Appendix A*).

Knowing how to prepare for the Ten Secrets of Medjugorje should help us to persevere in this present state of the world and the state of the Church.

8. The State of the World

Cardinal Robert Sarah addressed a conference in Paris on May 25, 2019 regarding the state of the world. He said,

> I am convinced that this civilization is living through its mortal hour. As once during the decline and fall of Rome, so today the elites care for nothing but increasing the luxury of their daily lives, and the people have been anaesthetized by even more vulgar entertainments.
>
> As a bishop, it is my duty to warn the West: behold the flames of barbarism threaten you! And who are these barbarians? The barbarians are those who hate human nature. The barbarians are those who trample the sacred under foot. The barbarians are those who despise and manipulate life and strive for "human enhancement!"...
>
> The West is blinded by its lust for wealth! The lure of money that liberalism instills in hearts lulls the peoples to sleep! Meanwhile, the silent tragedy of abortion and euthanasia continues. Pornography and gender ideology mutilate and destroy children and adolescents. We have become so used to barbarity that it no longer even surprises us!...
>
> Underneath the surface of its fantastic scientific and technological accomplishments and the appearance of prosperity, Western civilization is in a profound state of decadence and ruin! Like Notre-Dame Cathedral [that had recently burned,] it is crumbling. It has lost its reason for being: to show forth and lead others to God.

In the third millennium we are experiencing cataclysmic events. The state of the world is worse than it was at the time of the Great Flood. There are great evils that the world has never experienced to this extent before, such as the dissolution of the family through no-fault divorce, same-sex sexual acts, same-sex false marriage, false transgenderism, contraception, abortion, embryonic experimentation, suicide, euthanasia, the sex trade, the drug trade, addictions, unjust wars, genocides, terrorism, ecological destruction, and business and political corruption.

Never has God been less believed, adored, or obeyed. Never has God been more ignored, disobeyed, and blasphemed. Many people live as if God does not exist. Many people are their own gods, believing and doing whatever they want. Many people are self-absorbed materialists; many seek only money, glory, and power. Few people seek to know, love, and serve God and to be eternally happy with him in Heaven. The world is becoming more worldly and less godly.

In 1984, St. John Paul II wrote in *Reconciliation and Penance,* "The restoration of a proper sense of sin is the first way of facing the grave spiritual crisis looming over man today. But the sense of sin can only be restored through a clear reminder of the unchangeable principles of reason and faith which the moral teaching of the Church has always upheld."

On January 8, 2009, Pope Benedict XVI addressed representatives of the 177 countries which have diplomatic relations with the Vatican. In his "State of the World" address, he said, "Today, more than in the past, our future is at stake, as well as the fate of our planet and its inhabitants, especially the younger generation which is inheriting a severely compromised economic system and social fabric."

In a later interview with journalist Peter Seewald, the Pope said, "There are, of course, signs that frighten us, that worry us. But there are also other signs with which we can connect and which give us hope. We have indeed spoken at length already about the scenario of terror and danger...."

The Pope then referred to the drug trade and sex trade and continued,

You see, man strives for eternal joy; he would like pleasure in the extreme, would like what is eternal. But when there is no God, it is not granted to him and it cannot be. Then he himself must now create something that is fictitious, a false eternity.

This is a sign of the times that should be an urgent challenge to us, especially as Christians. We have to show, and also live this accordingly, that the eternity man needs can come only from God. That God is the first thing necessary in order to be able to withstand the afflictions of this time. That we must mobilize, so to speak, all the powers of the soul and of the good so that a genuine coin can stand up against the false coin and in this way the cycle of evil can be broken and stopped.

The important thing…is that a need for healing exists, that man can understand again somehow what redemption means. Man recognizes that if God is not there, existence becomes sick and man cannot survive like that. That he needs an answer that he himself cannot give. (*Light of the World*, Peter Seewald, Ignatius Press, Ft. Collins, CO 80522, 2010).

In his traditional Christmas greeting to the Roman Curia on December 20, 2010, Pope Benedict XVI spoke of the parallels that exist between our state of the world and the decline of the Roman Empire.

The Pope noted, "There was no power in sight that could put a stop to this decline. All the more insistent, then, was the invocation of the power of God: the plea that he might come and protect his people from all these threats. The disintegration of the key principles of law and of the fundamental moral attitudes underpinning them burst open the dams which until that time had protected peaceful coexistence among peoples."

We see in our world today what the Pope described in the decline of Rome. He said, "The sun was setting over an entire world. Frequent natural disasters further increased this sense of insecurity."

Comparing our world to Rome, the Pope said, "For all its new hopes and possibilities, our world is at the same time troubled by the sense that moral consensus is collapsing, consensus without which juridical and political structures cannot function. Consequently, the forces mobilized for the defense of such structures seem doomed to failure."

"Alexis de Tocqueville, in his day," the Pope continued, "observed that democracy in America had become possible and had worked because there existed a fundamental moral consensus which, transcending individual denominations, united everyone. Only if there is such a consensus on the essentials can constitutions and law function. This fundamental consensus derived from the Christian heritage is at risk wherever its place, the place of moral reasoning, is taken by the purely instrumental rationality of which I spoke earlier.

"In reality, this makes reason blind to what is essential. To resist this eclipse of reason and to preserve its capacity for seeing the essential, for seeing God and man, for seeing what is good and what is true, is the common interest that must unite all people of good will. The very future of the world is at stake."

Without God, society and the world have no final goal and no reason to distinguish good from evil. In 2019, Pope Emeritus Benedict XVI wrote, "When God dies in a society, it becomes free, we were assured. In reality, the death of God in a society also means the end of freedom...because the compass disappears that points us in the right direction by teaching us to distinguish good from evil. Western society is a society in which God is absent in the public sphere and has nothing left to offer it. And that is why it is a society in which the measure of humanity is increasingly lost." (*Notes on the Abuse Scandal,* April 10, 2019).

Father Petar, designated recipient of Mirjana's First Secret, said, "Everything is closer and closer. Never in the whole world has the situation been so sad and so bad....Never in history have there been so many sinners and unbelievers. We are feeling that something has to happen very quickly. It cannot continue like this much longer. God has to do something very quickly!"

Father Petar gave a long answer to a question about his thoughts of when the secrets of Medjugorje would be revealed. At the Panel

Discussion at the Notre Dame Medjugorje Conference on May 27, 2007, he said,

> We are in the process of patiently waiting for when that's going to take place. From the very beginning, Our Lady was preparing Mirjana how she would reveal those secrets. I was present several times on such discussions that Our Lady had with Mirjana. I saw she was crying sometimes, and my question was, "Why are you crying?" She said, "I am crying because what she's announcing that would take place—it's no good, it's very serious."

> As I look into the situation in which the world is today, I have the feeling that this should take place very soon. The world cannot go on as it is, under the present condition. Something has to take place. Some intervention from Heaven has to take place. It appears as though everything is going towards perdition, but we know that for those that love, God works for good in all events, because God can even write in crooked lines the right way.

> What I would like to emphasize is what is most important—that we should not look for the time when it would take place, but put emphasis on: Are we ready to face it when it does take place? He who lives the Gospel in accordance to expectations of the Gospel and Christ has nothing to fear. When Jesus comes, such a person will be ready.

In 1976, when St. John Paul II was Cardinal Karol Wojtyla, he gave a retreat to the Roman Curia. He said that we may be "experiencing the highest level of tension between the Word and the anti-Word in the whole of human history….We may now be wondering if this is the last lap along that way of denial which started out from around the tree of the knowledge of good and evil. To us, who know the whole Bible from Genesis to Revelation, no stretch of that route can come as a surprise. We accept with trepidation, but also with hope, the inspired words of the Apostle Paul, 'Let no man deceive you in any way, because first it is necessary for the rebellion to come, and for the man of sin, the son of perdition to reveal himself.'" (2 Thessalonians 2-3).

The "way of denial" that began with the Fall of Adam and Eve by the taking of the forbidden fruit of the tree of the knowledge of good and evil may now have arrived at its "last lap."

The outrages offered by this most sinful generation to the all holy majesty of the one true God are greater than ever before in the history of mankind; Yes, far worse than even in the time of Noah and the flood. The world is in great need of divine cleansing.

However, not only the world requires divine cleansing, but the Church is also in need of purification in light of its present state.

9. The State of the Church

It seems that the Church is in a state of crisis arising from apostasy with the loss of faith and sense of sin. This led to widespread sexual immorality in the laity through contraception, fornication, and adultery, all of which led to abortion. Sexual immorality in the clergy led to widespread sexual abuse of minors, homosexual acts amongst the clergy, and enabling of the abusers and the active clerical homosexuals.

Those sins led to corruption in the administration of the Church and its finances and to heterodox statements of faith and morals within the hierarchy. They arose from a false sense of mercy at the expense of the salvation of souls and the pursuit of the Great Commission of Jesus to make disciples of all nations "teaching them to observe all that I have commanded you." (See Matthew chapter 28). And those sins have led to a decentralized Church leaving national bishops' bureaucracies free to pursue heterodoxy in faith and morals.

In 1969, Cardinal Joseph Ratzinger, later Pope Benedict XVI, gave a series of radio speeches later published in the book *Faith and the Future.* He spoke about the present state of the Church and its future. He said that he was convinced that the Church was going through an era similar to the Enlightenment and the French Revolution. He explained, "We are at a huge turning point in the evolution of mankind. This moment makes the move from medieval to modern times seem insignificant."

He compared the present state of the Church to that at the time of Pope Pius VI who was abducted by troops of the French Republic and died in prison in 1799. The Church was fighting against a force which intended to annihilate it definitively, confiscate its property, and dissolve religious orders. Today's Church could be faced with a similar situation if priests are merely reduced to social workers and the work of the Church becomes mostly political.

He said, "The process [of renewal] will be long and wearisome as was the road from the false progressivism on the eve of the French Revolution — when a bishop might be thought smart if he made fun of dogmas and even insinuated that the existence of God was by no means certain — to the renewal of the nineteenth century."

He prophesied that the future Church "will become small and will have to start pretty much all over again. It will no longer have use of the structures it built in its years of prosperity. The reduction in the number of faithful will lead to it losing an important part of its social privileges. It will be a more spiritual Church and will not claim a political mandate, flirting with the Right one minute and the Left the next. It will be poor and will become the Church of the destitute."

He continued, "The big talk of those who prophesy a Church without God and without faith is all empty chatter. We have no need of a Church that celebrates the cult of action in political prayers. It is utterly superfluous. Therefore, it will destroy itself. What will remain is the Church of Jesus Christ, the Church that believes in the God who has become man and promises us life beyond death."

He prophesied that "when all the suffering is past, a great power will emerge from a more spiritual and simple Church" and that this renewed Church will be a sign of hope for those who have not come to know the love of God. Then, and only then, Cardinal Ratzinger concluded, will they see "that small flock of faithful as something completely new: they will see it as a source of hope for themselves, the answer they had always secretly been searching for. "

Our Lady told Father Gobbi, *"The great trial has arrived for your Church. Those errors which have brought people to the loss of the true faith have continued to spread. Many pastors have been neither attentive nor vigilant and have allowed many rapacious wolves, clothed as lambs, to insinuate themselves into the flock in order to bring disorder and destruction."* (*To the Priests* 437).

On March 25, 2005, Cardinal Joseph Ratzinger, later Pope Benedict XVI, recited the following words at the 9th Station of the Way of the Cross on Good Friday at the Colosseum, while St. John Paul II was dying,

> Should we not also think of how much Christ suffers in his own Church? How often is the holy sacrament of his presence abused, how often must he enter empty and evil hearts! How often do we celebrate only ourselves, without even realizing that he is there! How often is his Word twisted and misused!
>
> What little faith is present behind so many theories, so many empty words! How much filth there is in the Church, and even among those who, in the priesthood, ought to belong entirely to him! How much pride, how much self-complacency! What little respect we pay to the sacrament of Penance, where he waits for us, ready to raise us up whenever we fall!
>
> All this is present in his Passion. His betrayal by his disciples, their unworthy reception of his body and blood, is certainly the greatest suffering endured by the Redeemer; it pierces his heart. We can only call to him from the depths of our hearts: *Kyrie eleison* (Lord, have mercy.)

The state of the Church is heterodox, meaning it is moving away from orthodoxy in some respects. Jesus excoriated the scribes and Pharisees as frauds and hypocrites and for weighing people down with laws that they themselves did not follow. He told the people to do everything that they were told to do, but not to follow their bad example.

Now the frauds and hypocrites in the Church are taking away some laws that they think are weighing the people down in an attempt to lighten a burden that Jesus said is already light and whose yoke is easy. Ironically, they call those who criticize them "modern-day scribes and Pharisees."

Because of Pope Francis' ambiguous language and actions, many cardinals, bishops, and priests are now teaching that those men and women who are divorced and civilly remarried without an annulment and who are sexually active without repentance and

Confession may discern in their consciences that they may receive the Eucharist. They even go so far as to say that they might have a duty to receive the Eucharist for the sake of preserving their illicit marriage and for the sake of their children.

Some bishops are now blessing the false marriages of same-sex people and welcoming them to receive the Eucharist. These sacrilegious communions will only further weaken the Church, according to the teaching of St. Paul. (See 1 Corinthians 11:30).

A conference, held in Rome on April 7, 2018, was called *Catholic Church: Where Are You Going? Only a Blind Man Can Deny That There Is Great Confusion in the Church.* Cardinals, bishops, priests, and lay faithful issued a Declaration in which they testified to the Church's unchanging teaching on marriage, the sacraments, and absolute moral commandments. A contingent from the audience shouted out, "People of God, stand up! We are the ones who have to act!"

Cardinal Raymond Burke called the Vatican's response to the "scandalized reactions" from across the globe "highly inadequate," because it failed to reassert the Church's teaching on the immortality of the soul and the existence of Hell. He said it also failed to state that Pope Francis repudiates the "erroneous and even heretical ideas" attributed to him.

The *Catholic Church: Where Are You Going?* conference issued a Final Declaration that stated, "We are convinced that persons who are divorced and civilly remarried, and who are unwilling to live in continence, are living in a situation that is objectively contrary to the law of God, and therefore cannot receive Eucharistic Communion."

At the conference, Cardinal Walter Brandmüller, former president of the Pontifical Committee for Historical Sciences, said that the faithful not only have the "right of free speech" in the Church, based on "the sense of faith and love," but also that they — according to their knowledge, responsibility, and prominent positions — "sometimes even have the duty to communicate [their opinion] to their spiritual shepherds when it is about the well-being of the Church." He therefore concludes, "It would be time for the Magisterium to pay appropriate attention to this witness of faith."

The People of God are encouraged by the Second Vatican Council (see *Lumen Gentium*, 33) to be a living witness and instrument of the mission of the Church, in virtue of the very gifts bestowed upon them and in accordance with the authentic tradition of the Church. They should testify and confess to the truths of the Church listed below by the Final Declaration of the Conference *Catholic Church, Where Are You Going?*, held in Rome on April 7, 2018,

1) A ratified and consummated marriage between two baptized persons can be dissolved only by death.

2) Therefore, Christians united by a valid marriage who join themselves to another person while their spouse is still alive commit the grave sin of adultery.

3) We are convinced that there exist absolute moral commandments which oblige always and without exception.

4) We are also convinced that no subjective judgment of conscience can make an intrinsically evil act good and licit.

5) We are convinced that judgment about the possibility of administering sacramental absolution is not based on the imputability of the sin committed, but on the penitent's intention to abandon a way of life that is contrary to the divine commandments.

6) We are convinced that persons who are divorced and civilly remarried, and who are unwilling to live in continence, are living in a situation that is objectively contrary to the law of God, and therefore cannot receive Eucharistic Communion.

It seems, as Pope Benedict XVI said while he was still the Pope, that the greatest persecution of the Church does not come from outside enemies but arises from sin in the Church.

Idols at the Amazon Synod

At the Amazon Synod in Rome in 2019, people placed statues in the Vatican Gardens. They were of the Amazonian Pachamama (Mother Earth.) Some bowed down to the ground and prostrated themselves before it. Cardinal Gerhard Müller, formerly the head of the Congregation for the Doctrine of the Faith, called the statues "idols."

The idols showed a naked woman in late term pregnancy. Idolaters turn to her for fertility, good ecology, and good fortune, instead of turning to the one true God and trusting in his goodness and providence. The Pachamama is an object of veneration, a goddess to which some Bolivians sacrifice llamas, especially their fetuses. It is an earth deity worshiped by some Peruvians and rooted in pagan Incan beliefs and practices.

Bishop José Luis Azcona, of Marajó in the Amazon region, confirmed that Pachamama is a pagan goddess and denounced the rituals at the Vatican. In his homily on October 16, 2019, in Brazil, he said, "In those rituals there is the devil, there is magic. The invocation of the statues in front of which even some religious have bowed in the Vatican (and I will not mention the religious order to which they belong) is the invocation of the mythical power of Mother Earth, to which they are asking blessings upon humanity or offering gestures of gratitude. These are scandalous demonic sacrileges, especially for the little ones who can't discern."

Moreover, some of the idols were brought into Santa Maria, a Catholic Church, and displayed there. God's first commandment is, "I am the Lord your God, you shall have no false gods before me." (Exodus 20:3). "You shall not carve idols for yourselves in the shape of anything in the sky above or on the earth below or in the waters beneath the earth; you shall not bow down before them or worship them." (Exodus 20:4-5).

Idolatry is the greatest offense against Jesus King of All Nations. Idolatry denies his Sovereign and Divine Kingship and the acknowledgment of his supreme authority over all creation. It denies the absolute and supreme authority granted to him by his Father. This authority must be recognized by all and re-acclaimed by his Church.

The *Catholic Encyclopedia* teaches that, "Considered in itself, idolatry is the greatest of mortal sins. For it is, by definition, an inroad on God's sovereignty over the world, an attempt on his divine majesty, a rebellious setting up of a creature on the throne that belongs to him alone."

When the prophet Ezekiel was brought in spirit by God into the Temple, he saw the idols of the house of Israel. Then he saw, "about twenty-five men, with their backs to the Temple of the Lord, and their faces toward the east, worshiping the sun toward the east."

Then God said to Ezekiel, "Have you seen this, O son of man? Is it too slight a thing for the house of Judah to commit the abominations which they commit here, that they should fill the land with violence, and provoke me further to anger? Lo, they put the branch to their nose. Therefore, I will deal in wrath; my eye will not spare, nor will I have pity; and though they cry in my ears with a loud voice, I will not hear them." (Ezekiel 8:16-18).

Likewise, at the church of Santa Maria during the Amazon Synod, some of the pews were turned around from the altar to face the Pachamama idol. About twenty-five people sat upon the pews, with their backs to the altar and the Blessed Sacrament and with their faces toward the idol. They sat "with their backs to the Lord's Temple" as did the "about twenty-five men" that Ezekiel saw. Will God now deal "in wrath" with us, as he told the prophet Ezekiel?

St. Athanasius, writing in his *History of the Arians*, even takes the introduction of idols into churches in the fourth-century Egyptian persecution to be the worst possible wickedness: "When was ever such iniquity heard of? when was such an evil deed ever perpetrated, even in times of persecution? They were heathens who persecuted formerly; but they did not bring their idols into the churches....This is a new piece of iniquity. It is not simply persecution, but more than persecution, it is a prelude and preparation for the coming of Antichrist."

We should turn to the one true God, face him in reparation, and implore him to end these sacrileges. Let us join Bishop Athanasius Schneider who encouraged all Catholics to offer prayers and reparation for "the abomination of the veneration of wooden idols perpetrated in Rome during the Amazon Synod."

In a November 2019 interview regarding the idols at the Amazon Synod, Archbishop Carlo Maria Vigano, former Apostolic Nuncio to the United States, said,

> The abomination of idolatrous rites has entered the sanctuary of God and has given rise to a new form of apostasy, whose seeds — which have been active for a long time — are growing with renewed vigor and effectiveness. The process of the internal mutation of the faith, which has been taking place in the Catholic Church for several decades, has seen with this Synod a dramatic acceleration towards the foundation of a new creed, summed up in a new kind of worship [*cultus*.] In the name of inculturation, pagan elements are infesting divine worship in order to transform it into an idolatrous cult....

> Idolatry seals apostasy. It is the fruit of the denial of the true faith. It is born of mistrust in God and degenerates into protest and rebellion....

> We cannot remain indifferent to the idolatrous acts that we have witnessed and left us dumbfounded. These assaults against the holiness of our Mother Church demand from us a just and generous reparation. It is urgent that we rediscover the meaning of prayer, reparation, and penance, of fasting, of the "little sacrifices, of the little flowers," and, above all, of silent and prolonged adoration before the Blessed Sacrament....

> The Amazonian paradigm is therefore not the end of the transformation process at which the "pastoral-revolution" promoted by the current papal magisterium aims. It serves as a catwalk to ferry what remains of the Catholic edifice towards an indistinct Universal Religion....

> Jesus prophesied, "When you see the desecrating sacrilege...there will be a great tribulation, such as has not been from the beginning of the world until now, no, and never will be." (Matthew 24:15, 21).

In May 2010, on his way back to Rome from his visit in Fatima, Pope Benedict XVI said about the Fatima message that "there is also the fact that attacks on the Pope and the Church come not only from without, but the sufferings of the Church come precisely from within the Church, from the sin existing within the Church."

He continued, "This too is something that we have always known, but today we are seeing it in a really terrifying way: that the greatest persecution of the Church comes not from her enemies without, but arises from sin within the Church, and that the Church thus has a deep need to relearn penance, to accept purification, to learn forgiveness on the one hand, but also the need for justice."

The Pope then insisted that the message of Fatima is still valid for our time when he said, "We would be mistaken to think that Fatima's prophetic mission is complete."

In May, 2020, author Peter Seewald released *Benedict XVI – A Life*. It is an authorized biography of Pope Emeritus Benedict XVI based upon interviews with him in 2019.

Benedict said, "A century ago, anyone would have thought it absurd to talk about homosexual marriage. Today those who oppose it are excommunicated from society."

He said, "It's the same thing with abortion and creating human life in the laboratory. It is only natural for people who oppose same-sex unions and abortion to fear the 'spiritual power of the Antichrist.'

"Modern society is in the middle of formulating an anti-Christian creed, and if one opposes it, one is being punished by society with excommunication....The fear of this spiritual power of the Antichrist is then only more than natural, and it really needs the help of prayers on the part of an entire diocese and of the Universal Church in order to resist it," Benedict said.

"The real threat to the Church....is in the global dictatorship of purportedly humanist ideologies," he emphasized.

"Events have shown by now that the crisis of faith has above all led to a crisis of Christian existence."

It seems that because of the terrible evils in the State and the Church, God is left with no recourse but to chastise humanity.

However, Our Lady has trained us to prepare for the Ten Secrets, and their warnings and chastisements, that will soon come to the world. She has told us to see the signs of the times and to follow her simple strategy of using the supernatural weapons requested by her at Medjugorje of conversion and faith, maintained by prayer and fasting. Prayer and fasting will help to bring about peace. Mary said that peace is necessary for the salvation of the world and that she is the Queen of Peace. May her promised New Era of Peace come quickly!

Let there be peace on earth and let it begin with you!

On September 2, 2019, Our Lady appeared to Mirjana and said, "*I am telling you that it is high time for you to kneel before my Son to acknowledge him as your God, the center of your life.*" Father Livio Fanzaga, Director of Radio Maria in Medjugorje, translated the original message. He said, "I believe that the time of secrets coincides with the 40th year of appearances." That year is 2021. We should also be mindful that in her July 25, 2019 message, Our Lady told another visionary, Marija, "*Little children, trials will come and you will not be strong, and sin will reign but, if you are mine, you will win, because your refuge will be the Heart of my Son Jesus. Therefore, little children, return to prayer until prayer becomes life for you in the day and the night. Thank you for having responded to my call.*"

Pope Benedict XVI, in his last words at the end of his final Wednesday Audience on February 27, 2013, said, "Let us call upon the maternal intercession of the Virgin Mary, Mother of God and Mother of the Church, that she may accompany each of us and the whole ecclesial community; to her let us commend ourselves with deep confidence. Dear friends! God guides his Church, he sustains it always, especially at times of difficulty. Let us never lose this vision of faith, which is the one true way of looking at the journey of the Church and of the world. In our hearts, in the heart of each of you, may there always abide the joyful certainty that the Lord is at our side: he does not abandon us, he remains close to us, and he surrounds us with his love. Thank you!"

In 2019, Rome journalist Robert Moynihan asked Archbishop Carlo Maria Vigano in an interview, "But what is your message really: that God is about to chastise the Church, as Nineveh was threatened with destruction, or do you believe there is still a chance to renew the Church, through prayer and a renewal of priestly and lay spirituality?"

The Cardinal replied, "The two possibilities you offer are not mutually exclusive. There may be both a chastisement, which will shake and diminish the Church, and also a reform and renewal of the Church, making her more resplendent in holiness. Both are possible."

Will *you* be ready when the "trials will come," as Mary prophesied? Could these "trials" refer to the Ten Secrets? Will the secrets soon be revealed as a prelude to the Triumph of the Immaculate Heart of Mary and the New Era of Peace?

10. The Triumph of the Immaculate Heart of Mary and The New Era of Peace

"What I Started at Fatima, I Will Finish in Medjugorje.
My Heart Will Triumph."

St. John Paul II told the Archbishop of Slovakia, Pavel Hnilca, "Medjugorje is the continuation of Fatima, it is the completion of Fatima." (*Why He is a Saint*, Oder, Slawomir, p. 169).

In my interview of Mirjana, she told me, "I want to say one thing that is very important. Blessed Mary said, '*What I started at Fatima, I will finish in Medjugorje. My heart will triumph.*' ... We should think about the messages and what she asked for us, so that we can help her Immaculate Heart to triumph."

What Mary started at Fatima was a movement towards the Triumph of Her Immaculate Heart through her requests for the daily Rosary, the devotion (consecration) to her Immaculate Heart, the First Saturday devotion and the Consecration of Russia to her Immaculate Heart.

She said, "*If my requests are heeded, Russia will be converted, and there will be peace. If not, she will spread her errors throughout the world, causing wars and persecutions of the Church. The good will be martyred, the Holy Father will have much to suffer, and various nations will be annihilated. In the end, my Immaculate Heart will triumph. The Holy Father will consecrate Russia to me, and she will be converted, and a period of peace will be granted to the world.*"

However, the response to her requests was insufficient and, as Mary prophesied, Russia "*spread her errors throughout the world,*" *causing wars and persecutions of the Church."* These errors of Russia resulted in the killings of over 100 million innocent people in Russia, China, North Korea, Cuba and the killing fields of Cambodia.

Because Our Lady of Fatima prophesied the annihilation of nations if her requests were not heeded, and they were not, she reaffirmed her Fatima prophecy at Akita, Japan, in 1973. She prophesied, *"If men do not repent and better themselves, the Father will inflict a terrible punishment on all humanity. It will be a punishment greater than the deluge [the Great Flood] such as one will never have seen before. Fire will fall from the sky and will wipe out a great part of humanity...."* Since then, on October 25, 1985, she apparently reaffirmed her Fatima and Akita prophecies at Medjugorje to the visionary Mirjana. She prophesied that the First Secret was *"the upheaval of a region of the world."* Yet the errors of Russia continue to be spread.

These errors began with Karl Marx. He was a pioneer Communist who co-authored, with Frederick Engels, the pamphlet *The Communist Manifesto* on February 21, 1848. Marx falsely taught that the history of society was governed by economics and class division between the workers and the capitalists. He taught that the working class was oppressed by capitalists and urged them to rebel. These errors helped to cause the violent Russian Revolution that began on October 25, 1917 and resulted in the deaths of millions of innocent people.

The errors of Russia include militant atheism, materialism, the elimination of private property, and state dictatorship.

In 1937, Pope Pius XI wrote, regarding the spread of the errors of Russia, that Communists "considered Russia the best-prepared field for experimenting with a plan elaborated decades ago, and who from there continue to spread it from one end of the world to the other... Our words are now receiving sorry confirmation from the spectacle of the bitter fruits of subversive ideas, which we foresaw and foretold, and which are... threatening every other country of the world." (*Divini Redemptoris*, n. 24, 6).

In 1984, Yuri Bezmenov, a former Russian KGB officer who defected to the United States, described the spread of these errors of Russia and Communist world aggression as a "total war against humanity and human civilization" that would be conducted by the process of ideological subversion.

Marxists spread the errors of Russia to the world through violence as well as non-violent infiltration of societies with ideologies that would transform their cultures. These ideologies now include identity politics and so-called "gender theory" that cause division in the social order between the so-called "oppressed", such as those who practice sexual deviancy and false transgenderism, and their so-called "oppressors."

Through today's Marxist ideology of "political correctness", their opponents are shamed, silenced and boycotted. These ideologies were adopted and are now promoted by some people in the most influential components of the American culture, including the establishments of Education, Law, Politics, Entertainment, Sports and Media.

Militant totalitarian Communism in Russia ended with the dissolution of the Soviet Union on December 26, 1991. However, the errors of Russia still persist throughout the world through the ideologies of neo-Marxism, cultural Secularism and Socialism in the Socialist countries of China, North Korea, Vietnam, Cuba and Venezuela.

The ideologies and the goals of today's Marxists have brought the errors of Russia to the United States through movements such as Black Lives Matter, founded by three self-proclaimed Marxists.

In the words of one Black Lives Matter leader, [we] "should burn down this system and replace it." The Black Lives Matter online manifesto opposes the "Western-prescribed nuclear family structure" and seeks to free "ourselves from the tight grip of heteronormative thinking." Dr. Carol M. Swain, a former Black professor at Vanderbilt University, said, "It's very clear to me that the Black Lives Matter organization is about something bigger than Black people, that it really is pushing a Socialist, Marxist agenda." This is how the errors of Russia still spread.

Today's Marxists have the revolutionary false hope of peace on earth through their human efforts alone. They want to live as John Lennon wrote in his song *Imagine.* They want to imagine, as he sang, that there's no heaven or hell and no religion; to live just for today with all the people living life in peace. However, these dreams are always nightmares that end in chaos and death, as in the Russian Revolution.

The beginning of the Russian Revolution on October 25, 1917, is a significant date for the Blessed Virgin Mary. Perhaps that is why she revealed her First Secret message to Mirjana on October 25, 1995 of "*the upheaval of a region of the world.*"

Perhaps Our Lady will reveal the First Secret on some future October 25 that will culminate in the Triumph of Her Immaculate Heart and the end of the errors of Russia that remain in the world today.

Author Dr. Thomas Petrisko wrote in his book on Fatima and Medjugorje, "Was God, by giving Mirjana the vision of the First Secret on this specific date [October 25], trying to irrefutably mark that he is the Lord of history, that he was in control of the beginning and the end of the hellish, atheistic nightmare that fell upon the world? Perhaps time will shed more light on this question."

Let us remember that Mary said at Fatima, "*In the end, my Immaculate Heart will triumph. The Holy Father will consecrate Russia to me, and she will be converted, and a period of peace will be granted to the world.*"

The Triumph of the Immaculate Heart of Mary

On July 13, 1917, Mary told the three child visionaries at Fatima, "*In the end, my Immaculate Heart will triumph....and a New Era of Peace will be granted to the world.*"

As long ago as February 2, 1634, Our Lady of Good Success at Quito, Ecuador, alluded to her triumph. She said, "*In order to dissipate this black cloud that prevents the Church from enjoying the clear day of liberty, there will be a formidable and frightful war....This night will be most horrible, for, humanly speaking, evil will seem to triumph. This, then, will mark the arrival of my hour, when I, in a marvelous way,*" *will dethrone the proud and cursed Satan, trampling him under my feet, and fettering him in the infernal abyss. Thus, the Church and Country will be finally free of his cruel tyranny."*

In 1988, Jesus King of All Nations told his Secretary, "…my Kingdom, my Reign, is near at hand. *"The kingdom of God."* (1 Corinthians 6:10)….My Most Holy Mother is preparing the great triumph. The Triumph of Her Immaculate Heart ushers in the Reign of my Love and Mercy." (*Journal* 7, 14). The Kingdom of God, for which Christians have prayed for over 2000 years, will come soon with the Reign of Jesus King of All Nations through the Triumph of the Immaculate Heart of Mary.

As Jesus is the head of the Mystical Body of Christ, the Church, so Mary is its heart and we are its humble feet, walking our pilgrimage in faith, directed by the head through the heart. This heart is like a prism diffusing all graces from the pure light of the Holy Trinity, in all its varied colors, to us. It is the gate of Heaven through which passes the love of God to renew the whole world.

The word "heart," as used in Scripture, often means the higher part of the soul, the interior perfections. With reference to Mary, it refers to her Immaculate Conception, fullness of grace, and blessedness. (See Luke 1:28, 42).

Mary's Immaculate Heart exists in her glorified body which still loves and suffers for all humanity. Mary's heart is immaculate because it is without sin as a consequence of her Immaculate Conception. It is the center of her ever-virgin being which perfectly loves God and us. As she is united with the Sacred Heart of Jesus, so, too, is she united with our hearts and our lives, joys, and sorrows.

Her Immaculate Heart also symbolizes her interior life (see Luke 2:19, 51) where she reflected on her joys and sorrows, her virtues and hidden perfections, her virginal love for God, and her maternal love for Jesus and all humanity.

Her heart is also the heart of a mother, a real living motherly heart which watches over us, hears our cries, and helps us by her tender care for us.

She knows at every moment everything that concerns us — our fears, anxieties, faults, temptations, and sins. As our Spiritual

Mother, her Immaculate Heart mediates our prayers to God and dispenses God's graces to us. She is the Mediatrix of All Graces.

As a mirror, her heart reflects the most pure light of the Trinity, where the Father finds his design intact and perfectly realized and from which he receives his greatest Glory from any creature.

The centrality of her being is symbolized by her physical heart, as the seat of her love, and her spiritual heart, as the seat of her interior perfections and her entire interior affective and moral life.

Mary revealed at Fatima that Jesus wants to establish in the world devotion to her Immaculate Heart. If we truly love Our Lady, we should heed her request and consecrate ourselves to her Immaculate Heart. Jacinta, one of the Fatima visionaries, said that God has entrusted peace to the Immaculate Heart of Mary. Mary, in turn, told Sister Lucia, another one of the visionaries, that she would be her refuge and the way that would lead her to God.

St. John Paul II believed that the apparitions to the visionaries at Medjugorje were a continuation and fulfillment of the apparitions at Fatima. On October 3, 2009, Mirjana said that Mary told her, *"What I started in Fatima, I will finish in Medjugorje. My heart will triumph."*

Cardinal Joseph Ratzinger, later Pope Benedict XVI, explained the meaning of the Triumph of the Immaculate Heart of Mary in *The Message of Fatima,* May 13, 2000,

> In biblical language, the "heart" indicates the center of human life, the point where reason, will, temperament, and sensitivity converge, where the person finds his unity and his interior orientation. The "Immaculate Heart" is a heart which, with God's grace, has come to perfect interior unity and therefore "sees God." (See Matthew 5:8). To be "devoted" to the Immaculate Heart of Mary means therefore to embrace this attitude of heart, which makes the *fiat*—"your will be done"—the defining center of one's whole life. It might be objected that we should not place a human being between ourselves and Christ. But then we remember that Paul did not hesitate to say to his communities: "imitate me" (1 Corinthians 4:16; Philippians 3:17; 1 Thessalonians 1:6; 2 Thessalonians 3:7, 9). In the Apostle [Paul,] they could see concretely what it meant to

follow Christ. But from whom might we better learn in every age than from the Mother of the Lord?...

At the conclusion of his commentary, Cardinal Ratzinger explained the meaning of the expression, "my Immaculate Heart will triumph." He said,

> What does this mean? The Heart open to God, purified by contemplation of God, is stronger than guns and weapons of every kind. The *fiat* of Mary [her Yes! to become the Mother of Jesus,] the word of her heart, has changed the history of the world, because it brought the Savior into the world — because, thanks to her Yes!, God could become man in our world and remains so for all time. The Evil One has power in this world, as we see and experience continually; he has power because our freedom continually lets itself be led away from God. But since God himself took a human heart and has thus steered human freedom towards what is good, the freedom to choose evil no longer has the last word. From that time forth, the word that prevails is this: "In the world you will have tribulation but take heart; I have overcome the world" (John 16:33). The message of Fatima invites us to trust in this promise.

Nine years later, Pope Benedict XVI offered a prayer on the Feast of Our Lady of Fatima,

> [Mary], you promised the three children of Fatima that "*in the end, my Immaculate Heart will triumph.*" May it be so! May love triumph over hatred, solidarity over division, and peace over every form of violence! May the love you bore your Son teach us to love God with all our heart, strength, and soul. May the Almighty show us his mercy, strengthen us with his power, and fill us with every good thing. (See Luke 1:46-56). (At Caritas Baby Hospital in Bethlehem, May 13, 2009).

One year after that, the next anniversary of the first apparition of Our Lady of Fatima, Pope Benedict XVI said in his homily at Fatima, "We would be mistaken to think that Fatima's prophetic message is complete." He went on to look forward to the 2017 centenary of Fatima, expressing his hope that "the seven years which separate us from the centenary of the apparitions" may "hasten the fulfillment of the prophecy of the Triumph of the Immaculate Heart, to the glory of the Blessed Trinity."

The Triumph of the Immaculate Heart of Mary began with St. John Paul II's collegial consecration of the world to her Immaculate Heart on March 25, 1984. This triumph is not just one event but rather an ongoing process.

Our Lady told Father Gobbi, of the Marian Movement of Priests, that the Triumph of Her Immaculate Heart *"will be a cause of amazement even to the angels of God, a joy to the saints in Heaven, a consolation and great comfort for all the just on earth, mercy and salvation for a great number of my straying children, and a severe and definitive condemnation of Satan and his many followers. In fact, at the very moment when Satan will be enthroned as Lord of the World and will think himself now the sure victor, I myself will snatch the prey from his hands. In a trice, he will find himself empty-handed, and, in the end, the victory will be exclusively my Son's and mine. This will be the Triumph of My Immaculate Heart in the world."* (*To the Priests* 29).

Our Lady then explained to Father Gobbi, *"This victory will take place with the fall of practical atheism throughout all the world, with the defeat of the Masonic and Satanic forces, with the destruction of the great power of evil, and with the full triumph of God in a world, then completely purified by the great merciful chastisement."* (*To the Priests* 579).

Our Lady also told Father Gobbi, *"The Triumph of My Immaculate Heart will be realized through a new birth of Jesus in the hearts and the souls of my poor wandering children. Only have confidence and do not let anxiety or discouragement take hold of you. The future that awaits you will be a new dawn of light for the whole world, now at last made clean."* (*To the Priests* 89).

On December 19, 2019, Archbishop Carlo Maria Vigano, former Apostolic Nuncio to the United States, released a statement titled "Mary Immaculate Virgin Mother—*Acies Ordinata, Ora pro nobis.*" He wrote,

> Over these last decades, the Mystical Body has been slowly drained of its lifeblood through unstoppable bleeding. The Sacred Deposit of Faith has gradually been squandered, dogmas denatured, worship secularized and gradually profaned, morality sabotaged, the priesthood vilified, the Eucharistic Sacrifice protestantized and transformed into a convivial Banquet....

Now the Church is lifeless, covered with metastases and devastated. The people of God are groping, illiterate and robbed of their faith, in the darkness of chaos and division. In these last decades, the enemies of God have progressively made scorched earth of two thousand years of Tradition....

The advent of the Antichrist is inevitable; it is part of the epilogue of the History of Salvation. But we know that it is the prerequisite for the universal triumph of Christ and his glorious Bride....

Now it is our turn! The Triumph of the Immaculate Heart of Mary — Coredemptrix and Mediatrix of All Graces — passes through her "little ones," who are certainly frail and sinners but are absolutely opposed to the members enlisted in the Enemy's army. "Little ones" consecrated without any limit whatsoever to the Immaculate, in order to be her heel, the most humiliated and despised part, the most hated by hell, but which together with her will crush the head of the infernal Monster....

The Church is shrouded in the darkness of modernism, but the victory belongs to Our Lord and his Bride. We desire to continue to profess the perennial faith of the Church in the face of the roaring evil that besieges her. We desire to keep vigil with her and with Jesus, in this new Gethsemane of the end times; to pray and do penance in reparation for the many offenses caused to them.

Jesus King of All Nations said, "Evil has already been defeated. Along with its fruit which is death, it has been nailed to the Cross. *"the cross of Christ."* (Galatians 6:12). It and its father [Satan] have been completely vanquished." *(Journal* 748-750).

The Triumph of the Immaculate Heart of Mary means the triumph of goodness over the evil state of the world. It is the triumph of grace over sin, of faith over atheism, of love over hate, of virtue over vice, and of life over death. It is the triumph of a loving motherly heart who wants to save her spiritual children on earth from evil and, by her intercession, to obtain the grace from her Son, Jesus, for him to do so, to reconcile them to himself, and to obtain a New Era of Peace.

The New Era of Peace

In the history of the world, God has brought purifying chastisements from which faithful remnant people were protected. For example, Noah and his family were a protected remnant after the Great Flood. Eras of peace followed such chastisements. They include the fall of the Tower of Babel and the confusion of languages; the Great Flood; the destruction of Sodom and Gomorrah; and the destruction of the Jewish Temple and the city of Jerusalem.

Although the prophecies of the Ten Secrets of Medjugorje may fill some people with fear and dread, there is still a horizon of hope and trust for what lies beyond it: the New Era of Peace that emerges from the Culture of Death. Jesus said, "fear is useless, what is needed is trust!" (Luke 8:50).

On December 31, 1986, Our Lady told Father Gobbi, "*Pray in order to give thanks to the Heavenly Father, who is guiding human events toward the fulfillment of his great plan of love and of glory....Peace will come, after the great suffering to which the Church and all humanity are already being called, through their interior and bloody purification. Peace will come, after the event of the terrible chastisement, which I have already announced to you beforehand, at the dawn of the century of yours....And peace will come to you from the Triumph of My Immaculate Heart, as that space of time, which has been granted by the Lord to humanity for repentance and for its conversion, is about to come to an end. Even now, the great events are coming about, and all will be accomplished at a faster pace, so that there may appear over the world, as quickly as possible, the new rainbow of peace which, at Fatima and for so many years, I have already been announcing to you in advance.*" (*To the Priests* 343).

Our Lady of Fatima started a movement to avert her prophesied chastisements of the spread of Communism and the annihilation of nations if people did not respond to her requests. She started a movement towards the Triumph of Her Immaculate Heart and a New Era of Peace through her call to prayer and the sacraments.

156

She requested the recitation of the daily Rosary and the practice of her first Saturday devotion in reparation for the offenses against her sorrowful and Immaculate Heart by attending Mass; receiving Communion; reciting the Rosary; meditating on the Mysteries, for at least 15 minutes, and confessing our sins within 8 days before or after the first Saturday. All of this will help to bring her promised *"finish in Medjugorje."* The "finish" will be the Triumph of Her Immaculate Heart and the New Era of Peace.

On July 13, 1917, Mary told the three visionary children at Fatima, *"An Era of Peace will be granted to the world."* On June 25, 1995, Mary said at Medjugorje, *"Pray for peace so that, as soon as possible, a time of peace, which my heart waits for impatiently, may reign."*

Cardinal Mario Luigi Ciappi, theologian for Popes Pius XII, John XXIII, Paul VI, John Paul I, and John Paul II, said, "Yes, a miracle was promised at Fatima, the greatest miracle in the history of the world, second only to the Resurrection. And that miracle will be an era of peace, which has never really been granted before to the world." (*The Apostolate's Family Catechism*, p. 35).

St. John Paul II said on January 1, 2000, "God loves all men and women on earth and gives them the hope of a New Era, an era of peace. His love, fully revealed in the Incarnate Son, is the foundation of universal peace." (*Message of Pope John Paul II for the Celebration of the World Day of Peace,* January 1, 2000).

On September 10, 2003, St. John Paul II said, "After purification through trial and suffering, the dawn of a New Era is about to break." (General Audience).

Mirjana said that when the First Secret entrusted to her is realized, the power of Satan will be broken. She explained that the century given over to Satan was generally the twentieth century: "part of which is in the twentieth century, until the First Secret is unfolded." The implication is that Satan's power will continue into the twenty-first century and will only be destroyed after the First Secret "unfolds."

The Triumph of the Immaculate Heart will bring the New Era of Peace. However, Our Lady of Fatima did not give us any details of this. Through other sources, we learn that the Era of Peace may encompass and include the following features: the Reign of Jesus

King of All Nations and its recognition on earth; the New Pentecost; the Kingdom of the Divine Will; and the Renewal of the Church, Mankind, and of All Creation. (See, generally, the *Journal* of the Jesus King of All Nations Devotion.)

This will be the restoration of all things in Christ.

The time of the arrival of the restoration of the Kingdom of Christ *"is relative to and dependent on the disposition of souls who wish to receive so great a good, as well as on the effort of those who must apply themselves in being its trumpet-bearers by offering up the sacrifice of heralding in the New Era of Peace."* (Jesus to Luisa Piccarreta, *The Gift of Living in the Divine Will in the Writings of Luisa Piccarreta*, n. 1.11.6, Rev. Joseph Iannuzzi).

When it arrives, there shall be one fold and one shepherd. Pope Pius XI prayed, "May God...shortly bring to fulfillment his prophecy for transforming this consoling vision of the future into a present reality....It is God's task to bring about this happy hour and to make it known to all....When it does arrive, it will turn out to be a solemn hour, one big with consequences not only for the restoration of the Kingdom of Christ, but for the pacification of...the world. We pray most fervently and ask others likewise to pray for this much-desired pacification of society." (*Ubi Arcani dei Consilioi*, (On the Peace of Christ in his Kingdom), December 23, 1922).

St. John Paul II said on November 6, 2002, "This is our great hope and our invocation, 'Your Kingdom come!' — a Kingdom of peace, justice, and serenity, which will re-establish the original harmony of creation." (General Audience).

Sister Lucia, a visionary of Fatima, said, "The period of peace does not refer to civil peace." This peace is not merely the absence of external conflict. It is a positive interior quality which is a gift from Jesus (see John 14:27). It is God's own peace which is beyond all understanding. (See Philippians 4:7).

Luz de Maria is an Argentinian mystic and mother. Bishop Juan Abelardo Mata, of Nicaragua, granted an *Imprimatur* on March 19, 2017 for her messages from Mary from 2009 to September 2017. These messages include the following prophecies, with some lack of clarity in the translation.

The Era of Peace is coming for mankind. [An] era in which everything will be reborn; man, purified and fused with God's Will, Creation, which will then feel in harmony with mankind. Total and complete happiness. Peace and harmony are coming. In order for mankind to overcome that great transition, it must first come to be purified and eradicate such a high degree of offenses with which my Son's Most Sacred Heart is hurt. Evil has entered the Church. The devil has infiltrated the Church causing some of my beloved to collapse in respect to faith and the dogmas. God is the same today, tomorrow, and always; the modernism that has transgressed tradition cannot change that. (Mary, January 30, 2011).

The new dawn will come for my children. Evil will not find a place among men and all will be peace. My children will see in all of Creation the seed of my love. My Mother will camp with her children; the lost gifts will be deserved by man again and I will see myself pleased in each human being. All of the Cosmos will vibrate with the beating of my heart to a single unique rhythm, and man will breathe my peace in total concordance. (Jesus, February 26, 2011).

The New Era of Peace may seem to be slow in coming, but it is not being delayed. God only wants to give enough time for people to repent and convert and return to him. Many will convert, even from among those who now deny the existence of God.

The New Era of Peace will be a gift from God and not earned by human effort. This peace is not obtainable without responding to Mary's pleas. It is the peace that St. John Paul II prayed for at the Basilica of Our Lady of Guadalupe,…"with the peace of God in our conscience, with our hearts free from evil and hatred we will be able to bring to all true joy and true peace, which comes to us from your Son, our Lord Jesus Christ, who with God the Father and the Holy Spirit lives and reigns forever and ever. Amen."

After the cleansing action of God's justice, Satan will be vanquished and humanity will live holy lives, almost without sin, almost a regaining of the paradise lost by the Original Sin of Adam and Eve. Unceasing love, happiness, and divine joy will signify this future clean world.

On May 13, 1995, the anniversary of her first apparition at Fatima, Our Lady prophesied to Father Gobbi that St. John Paul II would announce the New Era that would spring up after the purification of the earth.

She said, "*It is precisely through the sacrifice of this, the first of my beloved sons [St. John Paul II,] that divine justice will be espoused to a great mercy. After the time of the trial, which will be one of purification for all the earth, there will spring up upon the world the New Era foretold and announced by him [St. John Paul II]; and thus, in these final times, he invites you all to cross the bright thresholds of hope.*" (*To the Priests* 545).

Using almost the same exact language several years later, St. John Paul II wrote in *The Church in America*, "Now is the time of the New Evangelization to lead the People of God in America to cross the threshold of the third millennium with renewed hope." Later, he announced the New Era that Our Lady had prophesied would be announced by him. He wrote,

> At the dawn of the new Millennium, we wish to propose once more the message of hope which comes from the stable of Bethlehem: God loves all men and women on earth and gives them the hope of a New Era, an Era of Peace.
>
> His love, fully revealed in the Incarnate Son, is the foundation of universal peace. When welcomed in the depths of the human heart, this love reconciles people with God and with themselves, renews human relationships, and stirs that desire for brotherhood capable of banishing the temptation of violence and war. (*Message of Pope John Paul II for the Celebration of the World Day of Peace*, January 1, 2000).

At a general audience on February 14, 2001, he said that in the New Era brought by Christ, "God and man, man and woman, humanity and nature are in harmony, in dialogue, in communion."

The Pope continued, "The authentic New Era is nothing other than the re-establishment of the lost relationship between God and man. Christ must cancel the work of devastation, the horrible idolatry, violence, and every sin that the rebellious Adam has spread in the secular affairs of humanity and on the horizon of creation.

"He 'recapitulates' Adam in himself, in whom the whole of humanity recognizes itself; he transfigures him into Son of God; he brings him to full communion with the Father," the Pope explained.

Christ's New Era, the Pope announced, also embraces "nature itself...subjected as it is to lack of meaning, degradation, and devastation caused by sin," which will thus participate "in the joy of the deliverance brought about by Christ in the Holy Spirit."

St. John Paul II talked about this New Era again at an Address on September 10, 2003,

> God, in fact, is not indifferent before good and evil; he enters mysteriously the scene of human history with his judgment which, sooner or later, will unmask evil, defend the victims, and indicate the way of justice....
>
> However, the object of God's action is never ruin, pure and simple condemnation, the annihilation of the sinner. It is the prophet Ezekiel himself who refers to these divine words, "Do I indeed derive any pleasure from the death of the wicked?...Do I not rather rejoice when he turns from his evil way that he may live?...For I have no pleasure in the death of anyone who dies, says the Lord God. Return and live!" (Ezekiel 18:23, 32).
>
> In this light, one can understand the meaning of our canticle, brimming with hope and salvation. After the purification through trial and suffering, the dawn of a New Era is about to begin, which the prophet Jeremiah already announced when speaking of a "new covenant" between the Lord and Israel. (See Jeremiah 31:31-34).

In 2004, St. John Paul II again described the New Era of Peace. He said, "I once more express my conviction, born of faith, that God is even now preparing a great springtime for the Gospel." (*Address to U.S. Bishops of Boston and Hartford*, September 2, 2004).

Our Lady described the New Era to Father Gobbi on the Solemnity of the Assumption, August 15th, 1991, as the defeat of Satan and of his universal reign where "*Christ reigns in the splendor of his glorified body, and the Immaculate Heart of your Heavenly Mother triumphs in the light of her body, assumed into the glory of paradise.*" She said,

The New Era, which awaits you, corresponds to a particular encounter of love, of light, and of life between paradise, where I am in perfect blessedness with the angels and the saints, and earth, where you, my children, live in the midst of many dangers and innumerable tribulations. This is the Heavenly Jerusalem, which comes down from Heaven upon earth, to transform it completely and to thus shape the new heavens and the new earth.

The New Era, toward which you are journeying, is bringing all creation to the perfect glorification of the Most Holy Trinity. The Father receives his greatest glory from every creature which reflects his light, his love, and his divine splendor. The Son restores his Reign of grace and of holiness, setting free every creature from the slavery of evil and of sin. The Holy Spirit pours out in fullness his holy gifts, leads to the understanding of the whole truth, and renews the face of the earth.

The New Era, which I announce to you, coincides with the complete fulfillment of the divine will, so that, at last, there is coming about that which Jesus taught you to ask for, from the Heavenly Father: "your Will be done, on earth as it is in Heaven." (Matthew 6:10). This is the time when the divine will of the Father, of the Son, and of the Holy Spirit is being accomplished by the creatures. From the perfect fulfillment of the divine will, the whole world is becoming renewed, because God finds there, as it were, his new Garden of Eden, where he can dwell in loving companionship with his creatures.

The New Era, which is just now beginning, brings to you a full communion of life with those who have preceded you and who, here in paradise, enjoy perfect happiness. You see the splendor of the heavenly hierarchy; you communicate with the saints of paradise; you relieve the purifying sufferings of the souls who are still in Purgatory. You experience, in a strong and visible way, the consoling truth of the communion of saints.

The New Era, which I am preparing for you, coincides with the defeat of Satan and of his universal reign. All his power is destroyed. He is bound, with all the wicked spirits, and shut up in Hell from which he will not be able to get out to do harm in the world. Herein, Christ reigns in the splendor of his glorified body, and the Immaculate Heart of your Heavenly Mother triumphs in the light of her body, assumed into the glory of paradise.

This feast of mine, [the Assumption,] which bids you to look to your Heavenly Mother, assumed into Heaven, thus becomes for you a reason for deep joy and great confidence.

In the midst of the innumerable sufferings of the times through which you are living, you look upon me as a sign of sure hope and of consolation, because I am the luminous door which opens up the New Era that has been prepared for you by the Most Holy Trinity. (*To the Priests* 453).

Padre Livio told Mirjana in his interview with her that Mary, Queen of Peace, was coming to build us a new world of peace, the end of which is to bring us to the light of a closer relationship with God. Mirjana responded to him, "Yes, Yes. I'm sure that eventually we will see this light. We shall see the triumph of the Hearts of Our Lady and Jesus."

We confidently await this New Era of Peace in hope.

11. Hope for the World

Through the prophet Jeremiah, God announced, "I know well the plans I have in mind for you, says the Lord, for your welfare, not for woe! Plans to give you a future full of hope." (Jeremiah 29:11). According to St. Paul, "Hope will not leave us disappointed, because the love of God has been poured out in our hearts through the Holy Spirit who has been given to us." (Romans 5:5).

"Hope is the confident expectation of divine blessing." (CCC 2290). I asked Mirjana if she had this same confidence that we will receive God's blessing. She said, "Yes, Yes, because God is my Father and he loves us and he sends his Mother for so many years here to Medjugorje to help us to find Jesus, to find a good way, where we will meet Jesus and have real peace. Look at me. I am always joking, smiling, living my life with God and Blessed Mary with hope, because my faith is hope. I hope in God's love. I hope that he will judge me with love, I don't think about secrets."

Cardinal Joseph Ratzinger, later Pope Benedict XVI, wrote, "The vision of the third part of the 'secret' [of Fatima,] so distressing at first, concludes with an image of hope: no suffering is in vain, and it is a suffering Church, a Church of martyrs, which becomes a signpost for man in his search for God."

St. John Paul II recognized signs of hope for the world. He said, "With full confidence let us place under the vigilant intercession of Holy Mary...the prospect of the Third Millennium. The Third Millennium remains for us a horizon of very stimulating reflections, because it makes us look forward in hope. The Blessed Mary is the guide in the new exodus towards the future."

In his Apostolic Letter, *On the Coming of the Third Millennium,* he said, "Only God knows what the future holds. But we are certain that he is the Lord of history and directs it to his own end with our cooperation in hope. It will be the fulfillment of a divine plan of love for all humanity and for each one of us. That is why, as we look into the future, we are full of hope and are not overcome with fear. The journey...is a great journey of hope."

The Pope also said, "As the Third Millennium of the redemption draws near, God is preparing a great springtime for Christianity, and we can already see its first signs. Christian hope sustains us in committing ourselves fully to the New Evangelization and to the worldwide mission and leads us to pray as Jesus taught us: 'Thy will be done, on earth as it is in Heaven.' (Matthew 6:10)." (*Mission of the Redeemer*, 86).

In his Apostolic Letter, *On the Coming of the Third Millennium,* the Holy Father closed his remarks and said, "Christians are called to prepare...by renewing their hope in the definitive coming of the Kingdom of God, preparing for it daily in their hearts in the Christian community to which they belong, in their particular social context, and in the world history itself."

Appendices

A. How to Respond to Mary's Requests

This appendix shows how to respond to Mary's requests made at Medjugorje. Each "how to" section presents her requests, the teaching(s) for the requests and some practical applications.

How to Make a Good Confession

Mary's Requests

"Make your peace with God and among yourselves. For that, it is necessary to believe, to pray, to fast, and to go to Confession." (June 26, 1981).

"Pray, pray! It is necessary to believe firmly, to go to Confession regularly, and, likewise, to receive Holy Communion. It is the only salvation." (February 10, 1982).

"Whoever has done very much evil during his life can go straight to Heaven if he confesses, is sorry for what he has done, and receives Communion at the end of his life." (July 24, 1982).

"Monthly Confession will be a remedy for the Church in the West. One must convey this message to the West." (August 6, 1982).

"Do not confess through sheer habit, in order to remain the same after it. No, it is not good. Confession ought to give life to your faith. It ought to stimulate you and bring you back to Jesus. If Confession means nothing to you, really, you will convert with difficulty." (November 7, 1983).

Teaching

The Church's teachings on the sacrament of Confession (Penance) are contained in the *Catechism of the Catholic Church,* (CCC), sections 1420-1484. Confession is a sacrament. A sacrament is a sign instituted by Christ to give grace. The sign is also the reality. The sign of Confession is the priest's words of absolution which also really, not symbolically, absolve the sinner.

Jesus instituted the sacrament of Confession when he appeared to the apostles after his Resurrection and said, "Receive the holy Spirit. Whose sins you forgive are forgiven them, and whose sins you retain are retained." (John 20:23).

The sacrament of Confession is a gift of the mercy of God for the forgiveness of our sins. It reconciles us with God and his Church. In the sacrament, the priest acts in the person of Christ. He forgives the sins that we confess and for which we are truly sorry and have a firm purpose of not committing again.

It is called the sacrament of Confession because the confession of sins is an essential element of it. It is also called the sacrament of conversion because it makes sacramentally present Jesus' call to conversion. It is also called the sacrament of Penance because it consecrates the sinner's personal steps of conversion, penance, and satisfaction. It is also called the sacrament of Penance because it imparts to the sinner reconciliation with God and neighbor. Sin is, above all else, an offense against God, a rupture of our communion with him. At the same time, it damages communion with our neighbor and the Church.

During his public life, Jesus not only forgave sins, but he also received sinners at his table, a gesture that expresses God's forgiveness and our reconciliation with him. We should receive the sacrament of Confession regularly and, at a bare minimum, at least once a year for mortal sins.

Practical Application

Come to Jesus in the sacrament of Confession. He waits there for you in the person of the priest to grant you his pardon and mercy. Jesus never wearies from repentant sinners or ceases from hoping for their return. The greater their distress, the greater his welcome. Doesn't a father love a sick child with special affection? Are not his care and solicitude greater? So is the tenderness and compassion of the heart of Jesus more abundant for sinners than for the just.

The mercy of the heart of Jesus is inexhaustible. The callous and indifferent should know that his heart is a fire which will enkindle them because he loves them. The measure of his love and mercy for fallen souls is without limit. He wants to forgive you. He is ever there, waiting with boundless love for you to come to him. Do not be discouraged. Fearlessly throw yourselves into his arms! He is your father.

Only a baptized Catholic can receive the sacrament of Confession. For a non-Catholic Christian, it can be received only if there is a danger of imminent death. Three things are required for a valid sacramental confession:

1. You must examine your conscience to be aware of your sins and you must confess them. What did you do wrong? How did you offend God or harm your neighbor? Go through the Ten Commandments in your mind to see how you might have violated them.

2. You must be sorry for your sins and be repentant with a firm purpose to amend your life, to sin no more, and to avoid the near occasions of sin, that is, the situations, persons, and/or things that may lead you to sin.

3. You must complete the penance assigned to you by the priest as soon as possible. This is usually particular prayers, but, sometimes, it requires restoration of any harm committed such as returning or paying back for stolen or damaged property.

You should go to Confession at the regularly scheduled times or make a special appointment for a private confession with the priest. An appointment for a private confession is advisable for those who may take more time because they have committed a sin which requires possible counseling or they have not confessed in a long time.

When you arrive for Confession, you should examine your conscience and wait your turn at the confessional. When you enter the confessional, choose either a face-to-face confession or an anonymous confession behind the screen. Begin by blessing yourself with the Sign of the Cross and then saying, "Bless me Father, for I have sinned. It has been (the number) weeks (months or years) since my last Confession."

Then recite all of your sins and the approximate number of times that they were committed. You must confess all of the sins of which you are aware. Do not let fear or embarrassment of them hold you back from reciting them. The priest has probably heard them all before. Also, your confession is absolutely confidential. Under the Seal of Confession, the priest may never reveal your sins to anyone.

You may also ask the priest for advice regarding your sins. When you are finished, tell him that you are sorry for these sins and have a firm purpose to amend your life. Then the priest will briefly discuss the effects of your sins and will offer advice and encouragement on how to lead a better Christian life. He will give you a penance to perform and may ask you to say an Act of Contrition (a sample one is given below.) If you don't know it, or it isn't readily available, simply say something like, "I'm truly sorry for my sins and I resolve to sin no more."

Finally, he will absolve you of your sins through a prayer. At the end of his absolution, he will say, "I absolve you of your sins in the name of the Father, and of the Son, and of the Holy Spirit." Make the Sign of the Cross as he does this. He will then dismiss you by saying some variation of "go in peace." You reply, "Thanks be to God" and leave the confessional. As soon as possible, complete your penance and thank God that your sins have been forgiven!

Act of Contrition. "O my God, I am heartily sorry for having offended you. I detest all my sins because of your just punishment, but most of all because they offended you, my God, who are all good and deserving of all my love. I firmly resolve, with the help of your grace, to sin no more and to avoid the near occasions of sin. Amen."

How to Celebrate the Eucharist

Mary's Requests

"Mass is the greatest prayer of God. You will never be able to understand its greatness. That is why you must be perfect and humble at Mass, and you should prepare yourselves for it." (1983).

"You do not celebrate the Eucharist as you should. If you would know what grace and what gifts you receive, you would prepare yourselves for it each day for an hour at least." (1985).

"There are many of you who have sensed the beauty of the Holy Mass. Jesus gives you his graces in the Mass." (April 3, 1986).

"Let the Holy Mass be your life." (April 25, 1988).

Teaching

The Catholic Church's teachings on the Eucharist may be found in the *Catechism of the Catholic Church,* (CCC), sections 1322-1405. The Eucharist is a sacrament instituted by Christ at his Last Supper. The Eucharistic celebration or Mass is a sacrificial meal at which we pray, listen to the Word of God, and receive the body and blood of Jesus Christ, true God and true man, in communion with him and one another. The Mass *re*-presents to us the Last Supper of Jesus and his sacrifice on the Cross.

All Catholics are required, under pain of mortal sin, to attend Mass on Sundays and Holy Days of Obligation. Prepared by the sacrament of Confession, we must receive Communion at least once a year, preferably during the Easter Season. It is called "Mass" because it ends with our being sent forth (*missio* in Latin), so that we may fulfill God's will in our daily lives.

The Eucharistic celebration is both a *sacrifice* and a *meal*. it re-presents to us the sacrifice, in an unbloody manner, of Jesus Christ on the Cross on Good Friday. It also re-presents to us his Last Supper on Holy Thursday, the day before, where he gave his apostles his body and blood, under the appearances of bread and wine, in anticipation of his offering on the Cross the next day. He told them to do that in memory of him.

Sacrifice. In the times of the Old Testament, before Christ, God was really present in the sanctuary of the Temple of the Jews in the Holy of Holies. This contained the Ark of the Covenant, which contained the manna from the desert, the rod of Aaron, and portions of the Ten Commandment stones.

After the sacrifice of a lamb, its blood was sprinkled on the top of the Ark, which was called the mercy seat, in prayer for God's mercy for his people. The high priest was the only one who could enter the Holy of Holies and only on one day per year.

When Jesus was slumped, dying on the Cross, he shed his real blood as the true Lamb of God, meekly, silently, and innocently so that we would have the merciful forgiveness of our sins. The ultimate and perfect sacrifice was the giving of himself to the Eternal Father for the forgiveness of our sins. He said, "It is finished, Father into your hands I commend my spirit." (John 19:30).

Now when we celebrate the Eucharist, Jesus re-presents to us his sacrifice on the Cross in a real but unbloody manner. We do not see his glorified body, but through a supreme act of faith we believe that he is really and truly present, body and blood, soul and divinity, under the appearance of the bread and wine consecrated by the priest. It is called "Eucharist" because it is an action of thanksgiving to God.

Recipients of the Eucharist are not cannibals. Cannibals eat a dead person's body in a way that diminishes that person's body. Through the miracle of the Eucharist, we partake of the eternally life-giving glorified body of the very much alive Jesus Christ. Jesus said, "I am the *living* bread that came down from Heaven. Whoever eats this bread will live forever; and the bread that I will give is my flesh for the life of the world." (John 6:51).

The celebration of the Eucharist is a mystery of faith. Miraculous things take place during the celebration that have eternal effects: ultimate worship of God is made and grace is poured out on both those present and those for whom the Mass is offered.

The Mass is not a new sacrifice of Christ because Jesus is now glorified at the right hand of the Father in Heaven. Death no longer has power over him. The Christ present at Mass is the glorified Christ, as he now is in Heaven.

Because it makes present Christ's one sacrifice on the Cross, the Mass is both the source and summit of Catholic life. At Mass, the Church does not become present at the foot of the Cross in sorrow but, rather, in joyful celebration, offering and partaking of Christ's Sacrifice.

The celebration of the Mass is the most important thing that the Church does each day. The Mass is a mystery of faith because it is an unbloody re-presentation of the presentation of the bloody sacrificial death of Jesus Christ on the Cross at Calvary two thousand years ago, which he anticipated and *pre*-presented to us at his Last Supper. The Eucharistic celebration is not a repetition of Calvary; it is, rather, a making of the unique sacrifice of Calvary really present now, on the altar, in an unbloody manner. By a sacrifice, something is offered. If it is living, it is called a victim. In the Mass, Christ is both the victim and the priest, the same as on Calvary. He offers himself by the actions of the priest who acts in the person of Christ and offers himself to the Father in reparation for our sins.

Meal. At his Last Supper, Jesus celebrated the Passover Meal. The Passover Meal memorialized the original special meal that the Jews in Egypt ate, according to God's command, before their Exodus from Egypt under the cruel Egyptian Pharaoh. The lamb was sacrificed and its blood sprinkled on their doorposts and lintels so that the Angel of Death would "pass over" them but would kill the first-born of the Egyptians. This was God's punishment upon the Egyptians in order to free his people from their slavery. That night, the Jews ate the sacrificed lamb. That lamb died, as a ransom, in place of the firstborn of the Jewish households who were saved from death. Thereafter, they celebrated the Passover Meal in memory of the Exodus and God's liberation of them from the Egyptian Pharaoh.

During his Last Supper Passover Meal, Jesus anticipated his sacrifice on Calvary. He pre-presented it when he instituted the Eucharistic sacrifice: giving them what appeared to be bread and wine and saying, *"This is my body,...This is my blood."* He then told his apostles, the first bishops, *"Do this in memory of me."* (See Luke 22:19-20). So, when the ordained priest says the words of consecration over the bread and wine, by the almighty power of God, the bread is transubstantiated (changed in substance) into the body of Christ and the wine is changed into his blood.

Jesus instituted the Eucharist in order to perpetuate his sacrifice on the Cross throughout the ages, until he comes again, as a memorial of his death and resurrection. It is a sacrament of love, a sign of unity, a bond of charity, and a Passover (Paschal) Meal in which Christ is consumed, the mind is filled with grace, and a pledge of our future glory in Heaven is given to us. (CCC 1323).

Practical Application

You should gather together to celebrate the Eucharist in clothing and with gestures that convey the respect, solemnity, and joy of this moment when Jesus Christ presides, represented by the priest, and offers you his body and blood as our priest and victim.

The celebration of the Eucharist consists of the Liturgy of the Word and the Liturgy of the Eucharist. The Liturgy of the Word consists of readings from the Old Testament, the Psalms, and the New Testament. In preparation for this celebration, you should read and meditate on the readings of the Liturgy of the Word that will be presented at Sunday Mass. You should carefully and attentively listen to these readings and the homily proclaimed by the priest or deacon in order to accept the Scriptures as the Word of God and to be better able put them into practice.

You can also read and meditate on these readings and the readings of the daily Liturgy. The Scriptures for each day may be found at the website of the United States Conference of Catholic Bishops: *www.usccb.org/nab/today.shtml*. They may be also found in the magazine *Magnificat*. You may subscribe at *www.magnificat.com*.

At the Offertory, you should offer yourself with Jesus to the Father as a sacrificial gift along with the gifts of bread and wine that are presented. These will be changed through transubstantiation into his body and blood at the consecration by the priest. You sacrificially offer yourself in the hopes that you will be fully incorporated into the unity of his mystical body when you receive at Communion his real body and blood. You also offer gifts by donating to the collection.

No one may receive the body and blood of Christ unless he is a baptized Catholic, believes in the Real Presence, and lives the teachings of the Church. You must fast for one hour from food and liquids, except water, before receiving Holy Communion. You should not present yourself for reception of Communion unless you are in the state of grace.

If you are aware of serious, mortal sin, it must be confessed before a reception of Communion, because you are not in a state of grace. You should refrain from reception of Communion until you have done so. Otherwise, you may be guilty of an unworthy, sacrilegious Communion.

St. Paul wrote, "Whoever, therefore, eats the bread or drinks the cup of the Lord in an unworthy manner will be guilty of profaning the body and blood of the Lord. Let a man examine himself, and so eat of the bread and drink of the cup. For anyone who eats and drinks without discerning the body eats and drinks judgment upon himself." (1 Corinthians 11:27-29).

As you approach the minister of Communion, you should show a sign of reverence, such as a bow from the waist, say "Amen" after the Eucharistic minister says, "the body of Christ," and receive with the option of on your tongue or in your hand.

Then you may have the option to receive the blood of Christ, if it is available. Again, as you approach the minister of the blood, you should show a sign of reverence, such as a bow from the waist. After the Eucharistic minister says, "the blood of Christ," say "Amen," take the chalice, sip it, and return it to the minister. Then you should return to your seat and make an Act of Thanksgiving to God.

How to Read the Bible

Mary's Requests

"Dear children, today I call you to read the Bible every day in your homes and let it be in a visible place so as always to encourage you to read it and pray." (October 18, 1984).

"Every family must pray family prayers and read the Bible." (February 14, 1985).

Teaching and Practical Application

The Bible is not just one book but a library of books. It consists of forty-five books in the Old Testament (before Christ) and twenty-seven in the New Testament (after Christ.) The books contain history, wisdom, prophecy, and prayers. "The Word of God is living and active, sharper than any two-edged sword, piercing to the division of soul and spirit...discerning the thoughts and intentions of the heart." (Hebrews 4:12).

The Bible is a sacramental, a sign of God's presence that is an occasion for grace. By reading it, you share in the very life of God. (See 1 Peter 1:4). He is with you when you read it prayerfully.

The Bible is the Word of God that you should read not as some human work of the past, but as his living Word which is ever timely and speaks to you personally. You should read the Bible prayerfully, with the lifting of your mind and heart in a personal conversation with God who is the real Author.

God's Word in the Bible comes to you through human authors who wrote only what God intended for them to write, as guided by the Holy Spirit. It is God's revelation of the truth that is necessary for your salvation. It should be received by your mind in accordance with the teachings of the Church rather than through your own private interpretation. It is not a science text that teaches how the world originated.

You must understand what the author of each book is saying and how he is saying it. Is the literary form history, a real event, myth, parable, poem, prayer, vision, or prophecy? What is the literal meaning? Is the literal meaning the real meaning? What is the figurative meaning? What is the spiritual sense (the allegorical, moral, or heavenly sense?) What truth is the author trying to convey? Are you interpreting this in its context and according to its literary form and the teachings of the Church? How can you apply this truth to your own life?

A good reading program is to first read the New Testament Gospel of Mark and the Book of Acts. Then read the following fourteen Old Testament narrative and historical books; they will lead you chronologically through history from Creation to Christ: Genesis, Exodus, Numbers, Deuteronomy, Joshua, Judges, 1 Samuel, 2 Samuel, 1 Kings, 2 Kings, 1 Chronicles, 2 Chronicles, 1 Maccabees, and 2 Maccabees. This will give you an overall understanding of the life of Christ and of our salvation history.

Then go back and reread more slowly. Meditate by using your imagination, placing yourself in the scene and experiencing the actions, motives, and emotions of the participants. Ponder, listen, ask God questions, make a resolution to improve your life.

You can also read and meditate on the readings of the daily liturgy. They may be found on-line here: http://www.usccb.org/nab/today.shtml. They may be also found in the magazine *Magnificat*. You may subscribe at *www.magnificat.com*.

How to Pray

Mary's Requests

"Pray, pray, pray! When I tell you this, you do not understand it. Every grace is yours and you can receive them through prayer." (August 12, 1982).

"Prayer is a dialogue with God....Prayer is not a trifle. Prayer really is a dialogue with God." (October 20, 1984).

"Dear children! You are a chosen people and God has given you great graces. You are not conscious of every message which I am giving you. Now I just want to say – Pray, pray, pray! I don't know what else to tell

you because I love you and I want you to comprehend my love and God's love through prayer." (November 15, 1984).

"Dear children! Today again I call all of you to prayer. Only with prayer, dear children, will your heart change, become better, and be more sensitive to the Word of God. Little children, do not permit Satan to pull you apart and to do with you what he wants. I call you to be responsible and determined and to consecrate each day to God in prayer." (January 25, 1998).

Teaching and Practical Application

What is prayer? Prayer is the raising of our minds and hearts to God or the requesting of good things from him from a humble and contrite heart, the hidden center of our being. (CCC 2559). One of his disciples asked Jesus, "Lord teach us to pray." (Luke 11:1). Jesus didn't give him a long explanation. He just prayed aloud and said, "When you pray, this is what to say." Then he taught them the Lord's Prayer.

In the Lord's Prayer, we petition God for the holiness of his name, the coming of his Kingdom, the fulfillment of his will, the nourishment of our lives, the forgiveness of our sins, and our deliverance from temptation and evil.

Prayer expressions are vocal, meditative, or contemplative. (CCC 2699). Vocal prayer is prayer of words said aloud or silently in our minds, such as the Lord's Prayer or the Hail Mary prayer.

Meditative prayer is a quest of the mind to understand the why and how of the Christian life. Meditation engages thought, imagination, emotion, and desire. Christian prayer tries above all to meditate on the mysteries of Christ. (CCC 2708). For example, you can pray the Rosary by imagining the mystery, placing yourself as a participant in it, reflecting on its meaning or message, and have a silent interior dialogue with God.

Contemplative prayer is a quest from the heart for God alone. It is a gift that you can predispose yourself to receive in silence by quieting your mind and interior thoughts until you reach silent communion with God in humble faith beyond the senses. It is a gaze of faith fixed on Jesus, attentive to the Word of God in silent love. (*CCC* 2724).

Why should you pray? You should pray because God asks this of you. He tirelessly calls you to this mysterious encounter with himself. Prayer unfolds throughout the whole history of salvation as a reciprocal call between God and man. (*CCC* 2591).

You should pray so that you aren't put to the test. Jesus said, "Pray that you may not be put to the test. The spirit is willing but the flesh is weak." (Mark 14:38).

Where should you pray? Jesus often retired to deserted places and prayed. (See Luke 5:16). He also said, "When you pray, go to your private room, shut yourself in and pray to your Father who is in that secret place, and your Father who sees all that is done in secret will reward you." (Matthew 6:5-6).

However, Jesus didn't mean to limit your places of prayer to deserted places or your private rooms. You can pray from the depths of your heart anywhere. Jesus didn't mean "your private room" only literally, but also metaphorically, as the room of your heart, the center of your being. Above all, you should pray in a church, which is the proper place for liturgical prayer for the parish community and the privileged place for Eucharistic adoration. (*CCC* 2691).

To whom should you pray? You should pray to the Lord Jesus. Even though prayer is primarily addressed to the Father, you should invoke the name of Jesus by the power of the Holy Spirit. You pray in communion with the Blessed Virgin Mary because of her singular cooperation with the Holy Spirit. In this way, you magnify with her the great things the Lord has done for her and entrust your petitions and praises to her. (*CCC* 2680-2682).

For whom should you pray? You should pray for everyone in need and especially for those who persecute you. (See Matthew 5:44). Jesus set the example for us and prayed, "Father forgive them, they know not what they do." (Luke 23:34).

When should you pray? You should pray constantly (see 1 Thessalonians 5:16-17) and at all times in the Spirit. (Ephesians 6:18). If you get tired, you should remember that Jesus often prayed all night. (See Luke 6:12).

"We have not been commanded to work, to keep watch and to fast constantly, but it has been laid down that we are to pray without ceasing." (1 Thessalonians 5:17). You should pray especially at turning points in your life. Jesus set the example and prayed when he chose the twelve apostles to assist him in his mission and when he entered into his Passion.

How should you pray? You should pray as a person speaks to a friend. Moses spoke to the Lord face-to-face as a man speaks to his friend. (See Exodus 33:11). You should pray with the right heart in humility, like the tax collector, and not self-righteously, like the Pharisee. (See Luke 18:9-14). You should pray with the Holy Spirit who prays within you (see Romans 8:26); with your mind and spirit (see 1 Corinthians 14); with a right heart (see Acts 8:21-22); imploringly (see Luke chapter 11); and without losing heart (see Luke 18:1).

Jesus taught his parable on praying with persistence to obtain loaves of bread from a friend for an unexpected guest. (See Luke chapter 11). He taught you not to lose heart but to pray always, like the widow to the corrupt judge. (See Luke 18:1).

What intentions should you pray for? You should pray in praise of God, in adoration of him, in contrition for offending him, in thanksgiving for him, and in petition to him, especially for the coming of his Kingdom. You should pray for mercy (see Luke chapter 8); for healing (see James 13:16); and for unity (see John chapter 17). You should pray in intercession for the needs of others. These general forms of prayer are explained in sections 2626-2643 of the *Catechism of the Catholic Church.*

Whom should you pray through? You should pray through the intercession of the saints. Because they practiced heroic virtue and lived in fidelity to God's grace; they are proposed to you as models and intercessors. (CCC 828). "Being more closely united to Christ, those who dwell in Heaven fix the whole Church more firmly in holiness. They do not cease to intercede with the Father for us, as they proffer the merits which they acquired on earth through the one mediator between God and men, Christ Jesus. So, by their fraternal concern is our weakness greatly helped." (CCC 956).

You learn from the saints as models of holiness, particularly from the all-holy Virgin Mary, whom the liturgy of the Church celebrates in the rhythms of the Feast Days of the saints. (CCC 2030). Mary intercedes for you as she did at Cana when she asked her Son to meet the needs of a wedding feast. (See John chapter 2).

How to Pray in Adoration of the Most Blessed Sacrament

Saint Michael the Archangel appeared to the Secretary of the Jesus King of All Nations Devotion. He identified himself as "the Guardian of the Most Blessed Sacrament" and said that Christ, the God-man King, "…must be loved, adored, reverenced, and worshiped properly in this, the most excellent sacrament." (*Journal* 177).

St. Michael told Jesus' Secretary, "Let souls turn to me for renewed devotion to Our Lord in this Blessed Sacrament! He must be properly adored, loved, thanked, praised, and worshiped in this the Most Glorious Sacrament." (*Journal* 86).

This sacrament was instituted by Jesus at the Last Supper by the Eucharistic sacrifice of his body and blood. He did this in order to leave a memorial of his death and resurrection and to perpetuate his sacrifice until he comes again. (CCC 1323).

In the Eucharistic species, Jesus is really present in his glorified body and blood under the appearance of bread and wine. That is why we adore him in the Blessed Sacrament, not only during the celebration of Mass, but also at those other times when we adore him present in the tabernacle or exposed outside of it. (CCC 1378).

Jesus told his apostles that he would not leave them orphans. (See John 14:18). So, it is highly fitting that he should have wanted to remain present to his Church in the unique way of the Blessed Sacrament. As St. John Paul II wrote, "The Church and the world have a great need for Eucharistic worship. Jesus awaits us in this sacrament of love. Let us not refuse the time to go to meet him in adoration, in contemplation full of faith, and open to making amends for the serious offenses and crimes of the world. Let our adoration never cease." (*Dominicae cenae,* 3).

Jesus King of All Nations lamented to his Secretary the lack of devotion to him in the Blessed Sacrament. He appeals to us to come before the tabernacle and keep him company. He said,

My heart burns with love! Now more than at any other time in history, my heart meets with deafness, coldness, and hatred. Love is completely ignored. Even my faithful have little time for me. I await souls day and night in the tabernacle to no avail. *"they forgot the Lord their God;"* (Kings 12:9). How few of even my priests, my ministers, keep me company in my loneliness. (*Journal* 345).

Please dear souls, bought with my precious blood, come to me and give me your devotion, your love, and your time. I need your help in the divine work of saving souls. I appeal to you. Come to me in the Blessed Sacrament and pray for the salvation of souls. *"Come to me, all you that yearn for me, and be filled with my fruits;"* (Sirach 24:18). Come and give me the love of your human hearts which I long for. Come and quench the thirst of your God. (*Journal* 346).

During adoration of the most Blessed Sacrament, we can pray to Jesus through praise, adoration, contrition, thanksgiving, and petitions. We can remember those elements of prayer by using the acronym PACTS. We can also meditate on the love of his Sacred Heart for us, like St. John the Evangelist who rested his head on the heart of Jesus at the Last Supper.

St. John also witnessed Jesus' heart pierced by a lance during his crucifixion, from which gushed forth his blood and water on the Cross. We can meditate on this event as a symbol of the outflowing of the love, mercy, and graces from Jesus' Sacred Heart to us, especially through the sacraments of Baptism and Eucharist. We can recall the prayer that Jesus revealed to Saint Faustina in the Divine Mercy Devotion, "O blood and water, which gushed forth from the heart of Jesus as a fountain of mercy for us, we trust in you."

During adoration, we can also meditate on Mary's presence with John at the crucifixion and Jesus' entrustment of John to her as his Mother and his entrustment of her to him as her son, and to all of us as well, as her spiritual sons and daughters. As such sons and daughters, we should consecrate ourselves to Jesus through her Immaculate Heart.

Jesus told his Secretary, "...my throne on this earth remains in the hearts of all men. *"...in your hearts...by His grace."* (Colossians 3:16).

I most particularly reign in the most holy Eucharist, *"Take and eat; this is my body."* (Matthew 26:26) and in loving hearts that…*"Welcome Him, then, with all joy…"*(Philippians 2:29)…believe in me, that speak with me, and I tell you, my daughter, that I do speak in the hearts of all men." *(Journal* 197).

During adoration, we can place all of our petitions, our problems, needs, hopes, and petitions in the hands of Mary Mediatrix of All Graces and pray through her intercession and mediation for Jesus to respond to our requests through her. We can also repair for others who do not adore Jesus in the Blessed Sacrament by adoring him, and by talking, listening, and conversing with him intimately as with a friend. We can open our minds and hearts to him and tell him of our hopes, joys, sufferings, and sorrows and patiently await his response.

We can also maintain interior silence in reparation against the overwhelming noise of our culture and be attentive and listen to Jesus speak to us through our thoughts and emotions. We should be mindful of the Scriptures, "Be still, and know that I am God" (Psalm 46:10) and "For God alone my soul waits in silence, for my hope is in him." (Psalm 62:5).

We can remain quietly in the real presence of Jesus without saying anything. We can simply expose our souls to the penetrating radiance of his Eucharistic face, believing and trusting that he will act in us and do in us what none of us could do for ourselves. We should yield to his divine action and give him permission to act in us and upon us. We can resolve to abandon ourselves to his love, and then be at peace. We can honor his love by allowing him to love us. There is no more effective way to grow in holiness and to acquire the virtues that will make us his instruments. This is a great secret of holiness that we should practice.

If we do this, Jesus will make our hearts like unto his own and sanctify us by configuring us more to himself, uniting his Eucharistic heart to ours through the pierced heart of sorrow of his Mother and our Mother. This is the divine friendship that Jesus had with John, the beloved disciple, and this is the divine friendship that Jesus wants to share with us.

How to Pray the Rosary

Mary's Requests

"Recite the Rosary every day." (August 14, 1984).

"Dear children, today I am requesting you to start reciting the Rosary with deep faith, so that I will be able to help you. You, dear children, wish to receive graces but you do not pray and I cannot help you if you do not want to make a move. Dear children, I urge you to recite the Rosary so that the Rosary may become a task that you undertake with joy; in this way you will understand why I have been with you like this for so long: I want to teach you how to pray." (June 12, 1986).

"Dear children, again today I am urging you to pray and to abandon yourselves completely to God. You know that I love you and it is out of love that I come here to show you the path to peace and to the salvation of your souls. I want you to obey me and not to allow Satan to tempt you. Dear children, Satan is strong and that is why I ask you to pray, and to offer me prayers for those who are under his influence, that they may be saved. Be witnesses through your lives and offer up your lives for the salvation of the world. I am with you and I thank you. And then in Heaven you will receive the rewards that I have promised you from the Father. Therefore, children, do not worry about anything. If you pray, Satan will not be able to put any obstacles in your way, because you are God's children and he keeps an eye on you. Pray! Hold the Rosary constantly in your hands, as a sign for Satan that you belong to me. Thank you for having responded to my call!" (February 25, 1988).

Teaching

Mary asked St. Dominic to preach her Rosary to make his ministry more fruitful. In 1208, in Prouille, France, Dominic suddenly experienced an apparition of the Blessed Mother. She said, *"Wonder not that you have obtained so little fruit by your labors. You have spent them on barren soil, not yet watered with the dew of divine grace. When God willed to renew the face of the earth, he began by sending down on it the fertilizing rain of the Angelic Salutation [the Hail Mary.] Therefore, preach my Psalter [Rosary] composed of 150 Angelic Salutations and fifteen Our Fathers and you will obtain an abundant harvest."*

The Blessed Mother was referring to the ancient origin of the Rosary, which got its start with monks who recited the 150 Psalms (Psalter) and gave the laymen who wanted to participate (but couldn't memorize the Psalms) pouches of 150 pebbles, so they could recite an Our Father on each of them. The laity next developed a rope with 150 knots, then strings with fifty wood pieces, and soon the technique spread to other parts of Europe, where the faithful began to recite a Hail Mary with each piece of wood. Finally, it took its present form with 50 small beads for the Hail Marys and five large beads for the Our Fathers. This results in five decades for each of the Joyful, Luminous, Sorrowful, and Glorious Mysteries of the life of Christ.

St. John Paul II wrote in his Apostolic Letter, *On the Most Holy Rosary*, "To recite the Rosary is nothing other than to contemplate with Mary the face of Christ. At the start of a millennium which began with the terrifying attacks of 11 September 2001, a millennium which witnesses every day in numerous parts of the world fresh scenes of bloodshed and violence, to rediscover the Rosary means to immerse oneself in contemplation of the mystery of Christ who 'is our peace,' since he made 'the two of us one, and broke down the dividing wall of hostility.' (Ephesians 2:14)."

Practical Application

The word "Rosary" comes from Latin (*Rosarium*) and means a garland of roses, the rose being one of the flowers used to symbolize the Virgin Mary. It consists of various prayers prayed on beads, while meditating on "mysteries," which are events in the lives of Jesus and Mary. They are called "mysteries" because you can meditate on them but never fully comprehend them. There are four sets of mysteries, each of which contains five events. They are called the Joyful, Sorrowful, Luminous, and Glorious Mysteries.

You should meditate on the mysteries as you pray ten Hail Marys which constitutes a decade. Each mystery has five decades. You meditate on the events by using your imagination and placing yourself in the scenes as a witness to the event and think of the actions and emotions of those involved.

St. John Paul II said, "The Rosary is a prayer oriented, by its very nature, to peace. Not only because it leads us to pray it, supported by the intercession of Mary, but also because it makes us assimilate, together with the mystery of Jesus, his plan for peace. At the same time, with the serene rhythm of the repetition of the Hail Mary, the Rosary floods our spirit with peace and opens it to saving grace."

Rosary packages may be ordered from our website:
www.JKMI.com

St. John Paul II said that this is how we should pray the Rosary,

Announce each mystery to open up a scenario on which to focus our attention. The words direct the imagination and the mind towards a particular episode or moment in the life of Christ and/or Mary.

Listen to the word of God and follow the announcement of the mystery with the proclamation of a related biblical passage. As we listen, we are certain that this is the Word of God, spoken for today and spoken "for me."

Silence. After the announcement of the mystery and the proclamation of the Word, it is fitting to pause and focus one's attention for a suitable period of time on the mystery concerned, before moving into the vocal prayers.

Conclude each mystery with a prayer for the fruits specific to that particular mystery. The Rosary is then ended with a prayer for the intentions of the Pope.

You should try to make prayer a daily habit, especially the daily Rosary. You can begin this habit by praying at least one decade of the Rosary at a regular time and place. Then let this grow into the habit of the daily Rosary and, for those who are able, attendance at daily Mass, which Mary calls *"the best prayer."*

The Rosary Method

Make the Sign of the Cross and pray the "Apostles' Creed" while holding the Cross. (See all of the Rosary prayers in the following section, *The Rosary Prayers.*)

Pray the "Our Father" on the first large bead.

Pray three "Hail Marys" on the next three smaller beads.

Pray the "Glory Be."

Announce the First Mystery; then pray the "Our Father" on the large bead of the first decade.

Pray ten "Hail Marys," while meditating on the Mystery on the ten small beads.

Pray the "Glory Be" and the "Fatima Prayer," after each decade.

Before each decade, announce the next mystery followed by an "Our Father," on the large bead.

For each set of ten beads, pray ten "Hail Marys" on the small beads, while meditating on the Mystery.

After the Rosary, pray the Concluding Prayers.

As suggested by St. John Paul II, the Joyful Mysteries are prayed on Monday and Saturday, the Luminous on Thursday, the Sorrowful on Tuesday and Friday, and the Glorious on Wednesday and Sunday (except during Sundays of the Christmas season when the Joyful Mysteries are prayed and the Sundays of Lent when the Sorrowful Mysteries are prayed.)

The Rosary Prayers

*These prayers are each usually divided between the Leader (**L**) and the Responders (**R**). If you are alone, recite both parts.*

Sign of the Cross

L: In the name of the Father, and of the Son, and of the Holy Spirit.

R: Amen.

Apostles' Creed

L: I believe in God, the Father Almighty, Creator of Heaven and earth; and in Jesus Christ, his only Son, our Lord; who was conceived by the Holy Spirit, born of the Virgin Mary, suffered under Pontius Pilate, was crucified, died, and was buried. He descended into Hell. On the third day, he arose again. He ascended into Heaven and is seated at the right hand of the Father. He will come again to judge the living and the dead.

R: I believe in the Holy Spirit, the Holy Catholic Church, the communion of saints, the forgiveness of sins, the resurrection of the body, and life everlasting. Amen.

Our Father

L: Our Father who art in Heaven, hallowed be thy name. Thy Kingdom come. Thy will be done, on earth as it is in Heaven.

R: Give us this day our daily bread and forgive us our trespasses as we forgive those who trespass against us, and lead us not into temptation, but deliver us from evil. Amen.

Hail Mary

L: Hail Mary, full of grace, the Lord is with thee. Blessed art thou amongst women and blessed is the fruit of thy womb, Jesus.

R: Holy Mary, Mother of God, pray for us sinners now and at the hour of our death. Amen.

Glory Be

L: Glory be to the Father, and to the Son, and to the Holy Spirit.

R: As it was in the beginning, is now, and ever shall be, world without end. Amen.

Fatima Prayer

O my Jesus, forgive us our sins, save us from the fires of Hell. Lead all souls to Heaven, especially those in most need of thy mercy.

Concluding Prayers

Hail, Holy Queen

Hail, holy Queen, Mother of Mercy! Our life, our sweetness, and our hope! To thee do we cry, poor banished children of Eve; to thee do we send up our sighs, mourning, and weeping in this valley of tears. Turn then, most gracious Advocate, thine eyes of mercy toward us, and after this, our exile, show unto us the blessed fruit of thy womb, Jesus. O clement, O loving, O sweet Virgin Mary.

L: Pray for us, O Holy Mother of God.

R: That we may be made worthy of the promises of Christ.

L: Let us pray an Our Father, Hail Mary, and Glory Be for the intentions of the Pope.

The Rosary Mysteries

Joyful Mysteries of the Rosary

First Joyful Mystery: The Annunciation

"The angel Gabriel said to Mary, 'Hail, full of grace, the Lord is with you. Blessed are you among women....You shall conceive and bear a son, and you shall call his name Jesus....' Mary answered, 'Behold the handmaid of the Lord, be it done to me according to your word.'" (Luke 1:28, 31, 38).

Second Joyful Mystery: The Visitation

"Elizabeth was filled with the Holy Spirit and cried out in a loud voice, 'Blessed are you among women and blessed is the fruit of your womb....The moment your greeting sounded in my ears, the babe in my womb leapt for joy.'" (Luke 1:42-44).

Third Joyful Mystery: The Nativity

"And it came to pass while they were there, that the days for Mary to be delivered were fulfilled. And she brought forth her firstborn son and wrapped him in swaddling clothing and laid him in a manger, because there was no room for them in the inn." (Luke 2:6-7).

Fourth Joyful Mystery: The Presentation

"When the days of her purification were fulfilled, they took him up to Jerusalem to present him to the Lord...Simeon blessed them and said to his Mother, 'Behold, this child is destined for the fall and for the rise of many in Israel, and for a sign that shall be contradicted; and thy own soul a sword shall pierce.'" (Luke 2:22, 34-35).

Fifth Joyful Mystery: The Finding of the Child Jesus in the Temple

"After three days, they found him in the Temple, sitting in the midst of the teachers, listening to them, and asking them questions....And he returned with his parents to Nazareth and was obedient to them." (Luke 2:46, 51).

Luminous Mysteries of the Rosary

First Luminous Mystery: The Baptism of Jesus

"Jesus came from Galilee to Jordan in order to be baptized by John. But John stopped him, saying, 'I have need to be baptized by you.' Jesus answered, 'Let it be so now, for by us must all righteousness be fulfilled.' Jesus arose from the water and, behold, the heavens were opened and he saw the Spirit of God coming down like a dove and alighting upon him, a voice from Heaven said, 'This is my beloved Son in whom I am well pleased.'" (Matthew 3:13-17).

Second Luminous Mystery: The Wedding at Cana

"At the wedding in Cana, they had need of wine, and Mary, the Mother of Jesus, said to him, 'They have no more wine.' Jesus said to her, 'Woman, what is that to you and me?' Mary said to the servants, 'Do whatever he tells you.' Jesus said to the servants, 'Fill the six stone water pots with water.' When this was done, Jesus told them to take some to the master of the feast. When this man had tasted it he told the bridegroom, 'Why have you kept the best wine until now?' This was Jesus' first miracle showing his glory and his disciples believed in him." (John 2:1-12).

Third Luminous Mystery: The Proclamation of the Kingdom

At this time, Jesus began to preach and to say, "This is the time of fulfillment. The Kingdom of God is at hand. Repent and believe in the gospel." (Mark 1:14-15)

"So, I tell you, her many sins have been forgiven; hence, she has shown great love. But the one to whom little is forgiven, loves little." (Luke 7:47).

Fourth Luminous Mystery: The Transfiguration

"Jesus took Peter, James, and John, his brother, and brought them up into a high mountain and was transfigured before them. His face shone like the sun and his clothing was white as light. And behold, there appeared Moses and Elijah talking with him. A bright cloud overshadowed them and a voice said, 'This is my beloved Son in whom I am well pleased. Listen to him.' As they came down the mountain, Jesus commanded them, saying, 'Tell the vision to no man until the Son of Man has risen from the dead.'" (Luke 9:28-35).

Fifth Luminous Mystery: The Institution of the Eucharist

"When the evening came, Jesus sat down with the Twelve....And as they were eating, Jesus took bread and blessed it, and breaking it into pieces, he gave it to them, saying, 'Take and eat; this is my Body which will be given for you.' After supper, he took the cup and, after giving thanks, he gave it to them, saying, 'Drink you all of it, for this is the new covenant in my blood, which will be shed for you and for many for the forgiveness of sins'" (Matthew 26:20-28).

Sorrowful Mysteries of the Rosary

First Sorrowful Mystery: The Agony in the Garden

"Kneeling down, he began to pray, 'Father if it be your will, take this cup from me, yet not my will but yours be done.'...In his anguish, he prayed even more intensely, and his sweat became like drops of blood falling to the ground." (Luke 22:42-44).

Second Sorrowful Mystery: The Scourging at the Pillar

"Pilate released Barabbas to them. Jesus, however, he first had scourged, then he handed him over to be crucified." (Matthew 27:26).

Third Sorrowful Mystery: The Crowning with Thorns

"Weaving a crown of thorns, they fixed it on his head, and placed a reed in his right hand. To make fun of him they knelt before him saying, 'Hail, King of the Jews.' They spat on him and took the reed and kept striking him on the head." (Matthew 27:29-30).

Fourth Sorrowful Mystery: The Carrying of the Cross

"When the soldiers had finished mocking him,…they led him away to crucify him. On the way, they laid hold of a certain Simon of Cyrene, coming from the country, and upon him they laid the Cross to bear it after Jesus." (Matthew 27:31; Luke 23:26).

Fifth Sorrowful Mystery: The Crucifixion

"When they came to the place called the Skull, they crucified him.…Jesus said, 'Father, forgive them, for they do not know what they are doing.'…There was darkness over the whole land until the ninth hour…and Jesus cried out with a loud voice, 'Father, into your hands I commend my spirit.'" (Luke 23:33-34, 44, 46).

Glorious Mysteries of the Rosary

First Glorious Mystery: The Resurrection

"And looking up, they saw that the stone had been rolled back, for it was very large. On entering the tomb, they saw a young man sitting at the right side who said to them, 'Do not be afraid. You are looking for Jesus of Nazareth who was crucified. He is risen, he is not here. Behold the place where they laid him.'" (Mark 16:4-6).

Second Glorious Mystery: The Ascension

"Then, after speaking to them, the Lord Jesus was taken up into Heaven and took his seat at God's right hand." (Mark 16:19).

Third Glorious Mystery: The Descent of the Holy Spirit

"And there appeared to them parted tongues, as of fire, which settled upon each of them. And they were filled with the Holy Spirit and began to speak in foreign tongues, even as the Holy Spirit prompted them to speak." (Acts 2:3-4).

Fourth Glorious Mystery: The Assumption

"Arise, my beloved, my beautiful one, and come!...You are all beautiful, my beloved, and there is no blemish in you." (See Songs 2:10; 4:7).

Fifth Glorious Mystery: The Coronation

"A great sign appeared in the sky, a woman clothed with the sun, with the moon under her feet, and on her head a crown of twelve stars." (Revelation 12:1).

How to Fast

Mary's Requests

"The best fast is on bread and water. Through fasting and prayer one can stop wars, one can suspend the natural laws of nature. Works of charity cannot replace fasting....Everyone, except the sick, has to fast." (July 21, 1982).

"I should like the people in this period to pray with me. And to pray as much as possible! In addition, I want them to fast on Wednesdays and Fridays, and recite the Rosary every day." (August 14, 1984).

Teaching

Fasting means to make a sacrifice to God, to offer not only our prayers, but to also make our whole being participate in the sacrifice. We should fast with love, for a special intention, and to purify ourselves and the world.

"Jesus was led up by the Spirit into the wilderness to be tempted by the devil and he fasted forty days and forty nights." (Matthew 4:1-2). The season of Lent is a commemoration of Our Lord's fast which he undertook before entering into his public ministry. It was a time of preparation for the tremendous mission that lay before him. To do this, he denied himself food during those forty days and forty nights.

Christian fasting is distinct from fasting in other religions because its objective is to imitate Jesus and to come closer to God, not to ourselves. When we fast, we do not shut ourselves up inside, nor do we let it out and boast of our fasting. Rather, we unite ourselves with Jesus, who fasted in the desert. Our fast does not scorn the flesh since the Son of God took that flesh upon himself, becoming our brother. Depriving oneself and denying oneself are positive acts which aim at the encounter with Christ.

The Church defines abstinence as meatless meals and a fast as one meatless meal per day, with two lighter meals, and no eating in between meals. Fasting only relates to solid food, not to drink, so any amount of water or other beverages may be consumed.

Abstinence from all meat is to be observed by all people, 14 years and older, on Ash Wednesday and on all Fridays of Lent. Fasting is to be observed on Ash Wednesday and Good Friday by all who are between 18 and 59 years old.

For those whose health or ability to work would be negatively affected by fasting and/or abstinence, the regulations above don't apply. If a Friday in Lent coincides with a solemnity, the abstinence is not required. The Bishop of a diocese can modify these rules for those in his diocese. For example, it is not uncommon to give dispensations from the normal Lenten regulations if St. Patrick's Day (March 17) falls on a Friday during Lent.

Since the Fridays outside Lent are specified as penitential days by universal church law, but abstinence is not specified by the Bishops of the United States, it is left to the individual to choose the form this penance takes. Pastoral teachings have urged voluntary fasting on other days during Lent and voluntary abstinence on the other Fridays of the year.

Practical Application

The teachings above are the minimal regulations. Because of *"the great evils of our time"*, Mary asks more of us. She asks for the *"best fast,"* which is bread and water on Wednesdays and Fridays. Those unable or unwilling to fast on bread and water, as Mary requested, can fast from meat or from enjoyments such as smoking, drinking, television, computer time, excessive work, and play. They could also perform acts of mercy for others and/or give alms to the poor.

As St. John Paul II wrote, "Jesus himself has shown us by his own example that prayer and fasting are the first and most effective weapons against the forces of evil." (*The Gospel of Life*, 100).

So, let us pray and fast to avert the threatened chastisements.

How to Make the Total Consecration

Mary's Requests

"I would like to draw you closer to the Heart of Jesus. Therefore, dear children, I am asking you today to pray to my dear Jesus, in order that all your hearts may become his. I also ask you to consecrate yourselves to my Immaculate Heart. I desire you to consecrate yourselves personally, as families and as parishes, so that everything may belong to God through me. Therefore, dear children, pray that you may understand the true meaning of these messages that I give you. I do not want anything for myself, but all for the salvation of your souls. Satan is strong and therefore you, my little children, by constant prayer must draw close to my motherly Heart. Thank you for having responded to my call." (October 25, 1988).

Teaching

On June 13, 1917, Our Lady of Fatima told the three visionary children, *"My Immaculate Heart will be your refuge and the way that will lead you to God."*

One month later, she showed Hell to the three children and said, *"You have seen Hell where the souls of poor sinners go. To save them, God wishes to establish in the world devotion to my Immaculate Heart. If what I say to you is done, many souls will be saved and there will be peace."*

On May 13, 2000, at Fatima, Cardinal Ratzinger, later Pope Benedict XVI, explained the meaning of Our Lady's "Immaculate Heart." He said,

> In biblical language, the "heart" indicates the center of human life, the point where reason, will, temperament, and sensitivity converge, where the person finds his unity and his interior orientation. The "Immaculate Heart" is a heart which, with God's grace, has come to perfect interior unity and therefore "sees God." (See Matthew 5:8). To be "devoted" to the Immaculate Heart of Mary means therefore to embrace this attitude of heart, which makes the *fiat*—"your will be done"—the defining center of one's whole life. It might be objected that we should not place a

199

human being between ourselves and Christ. But then we remember that Paul did not hesitate to say to his communities: "imitate me." (1 Corinthians 4:16; Philippians 3:17; 1 Thessalonians 1:6; 2 Thessalonians 3:7, 9). In the Apostle [Paul,] they could see concretely what it meant to follow Christ. But from whom might we better learn in every age than from the Mother of the Lord?

On December 8, 1975, Mary told Father Gobbi, "*My Immaculate Heart: it is your safest refuge and the means of salvation which, at this time, God gives to the Church and to humanity....I have called you to trust, to complete abandonment, and to consecrate yourselves totally to my Immaculate Heart.*" (*To the Priests* 88)

Eleven years later, she told him,

In these times, you all need to hasten to take shelter in the refuge of my Immaculate Heart, because grave threats of evil are hanging over you.

These are first of all evils of a spiritual order, which can harm the supernatural life of your souls....There are evils of a physical order, such as infirmity, disasters, accidents, droughts, earthquakes, and incurable diseases which are spreading about....There are evils of a social order, such as divisions and hatred, famine and poverty, exploitation and slavery, violence, terrorism, and war.

To be protected from all these evils, I invite you to place yourselves under shelter in the safe refuge of my Immaculate Heart....My Immaculate Heart will become your strongest defense, the shield of protection which will safeguard you from every attack of my Adversary....For this reason, I say again to each one of you today that which I said at Fatima to my daughter, Sister Lucy, 'My Immaculate Heart will be your refuge and the sure way which will lead you to God.' (*To the Priests* 326).

The best way of satisfying Our Lady of Fatima's request to practice "devotion to her Immaculate Heart" is to respond to her request at Medjugorje "to consecrate yourselves to my Immaculate Heart."

The complete object of the consecration to the Immaculate Heart of Mary is the centrality of her being, symbolized by her physical heart, as the seat of her love, her interior perfections, and her entire interior affective and moral life.

St. John Paul II said, at Fatima, that "consecrating ourselves to Mary means accepting her help to offer ourselves and the whole of mankind to him who is holy, infinitely holy; it means accepting her help—by having recourse to her motherly Heart, which, beneath the Cross, was opened to love for every human being, for the whole world—in order to offer the world, the individual human being, mankind as a whole, and all the nations to him who is infinitely holy." (*The Sun Danced at Fatima,* Joseph A. Pelletier, Image Books 1983, 204-205).

The Total Consecration was the personal spirituality of St. John Paul II. His motto was *Totus Tuus* (Totally Yours.) He wore the Brown Scapular sacramental as a sign of his consecration. We should imitate his example.

St. Louis de Montfort wrote, "Now, Mary being the most conformed of all creatures to Jesus Christ, it follows that, of all devotions, that which most consecrates and conforms the soul to Our Lord is devotion to his Holy Mother, and that the more a soul is consecrated to Mary, the more it is consecrated to Jesus. Hence it comes to pass that the most perfect consecration to Jesus Christ is nothing else but a perfect and entire consecration of ourselves to the Blessed Virgin." (*True Devotion to Mary,* 120).

There is nothing new about this consecration, which St. Louis popularized. It has been practiced in the Church for over 900 years. St. Louis explains that the most perfect practice of true devotion to Mary is the total consecration to her, (*True Devotion to Mary,* 118, 120, 121), by which we set aside ourselves to be used by her to accomplish her will, which is in union with her Son's. She in turn mediates our sacrifice to Jesus.

A chalice in and of itself is earthly material, but when a priest pours wine into it and consecrates it, the chalice becomes sacred and the wine is transubstantiated into the blood of Christ.

So, too, are we mere earthen vessels (see Corinthians 4:7) but, when we are totally consecrated to the Immaculate Heart of Mary, she mediates the new wine of grace to us and transforms us into something sacred, the image of her Son, so that no longer do we live, but Christ lives in us as one. (See John 2:3-10; Galatians 2:20).

Total Consecration and the Parable of the Widowed Mother

Once there was a rich father who died, willing all of his property to his only son. The son's obedience had merited this inheritance. He was a just steward of his inheritance and used it to support his widowed mother and other children, whom she subsequently adopted.

Soon, thereafter, the natural son died, willing all of his inheritance, together with what he had gained by his own merits, to his widowed mother. His will named her as his executrix and trustee, as he trusted her to use his bequest for the benefit of herself and his adopted brothers and sisters.

On her part, the widowed mother simply carried out her son's will and dispensed his gratuitous bequest to her adopted children for their care and support.

On their part, the adopted children presented their needs to their mother and were most grateful to their brother and mother for their generosity in caring for them as their own. They dedicated their lives to their mother and, in love, fulfilled her every request. In imitation of their brother, they gave from themselves to their mother for her distribution to all who were in need. Never was there a more charitable family.

In like manner, God the Father gave all graces to his obedient, only Son, Jesus (see John 3:35), who merited them for our salvation. Jesus, in turn, willed all of these graces and his own merits from the Cross to his Mother and named her as his Mediatrix to dispense them according to his will, to us, his adopted brothers and sisters (see Romans 8:16-17), for our sanctification and salvation. Mary follows her Son's will and dispenses all graces to us with tender, maternal love.

On our part, we should present our needs to our Heavenly Mother and express profound gratitude for her cooperation in her Son's redemption and for caring for us as her own. We express this gratitude best by imitating the Father and the Son in total self-giving and by fulfilling her request through our total consecration to her Immaculate Heart.

St. Louis de Montfort's Act of Total Consecration

O Immaculate Mother, I (Name), a faithless sinner, renew and ratify today, in thy hands, the vows of my Baptism; I renounce forever Satan, his pomps and works; and I give myself entirely to Jesus Christ, the Incarnate Wisdom, to carry my cross after him all the days of my life, and to be more faithful to him than I have ever been before.

In the presence of all the heavenly court, I choose thee this day for my Mother and Mistress. I deliver and consecrate to thee, as thy slave, my body and soul, my goods, both interior and exterior, and even the value of all my good actions, past, present, and future; leaving to thee the entire and full right of disposing of me, and all that belongs to me, without exception, according to thy good pleasure, for the greater glory of God, in time and in eternity. Amen.

How to Use Sacramentals

Mary's Requests

"I invite you to place more blessed objects in your homes and that each one wear some blessed object on himself. Let all the objects be blessed. For then Satan will not tempt you so much, because you will be armed against him." (July 18, 1985).

Teaching and Practical Application

A blessed object is a sacramental, that is, any object over which an ordained clergyman (priest or deacon) has pronounced a blessing. The act of blessing sanctifies the object for use in prayer and devotion. The concept of blessing is prevalent in the Old Testament where it is conceived as a communication of life from God.

A sacramental is a sacred sign that signifies spiritual effects that are obtained by the intercession of the Church. Sacramentals take various forms from blessings to blessed objects. The blessed objects of devotion most used by Catholics are: holy water, candles, ashes, palms, crucifixes, medals, rosaries, scapulars, and images of our Lord, the Blessed Virgin Mary, and the saints. Sacramentals do not confer the grace of the Holy Spirit in the same way that the sacraments do, but, by the Church's intercessory prayer, they do prepare us to receive God's grace and dispose us to cooperate with it.

Just like with all sacramentals, there is no superstitious, magical benefit derived from simply wearing a medal. The efficacy of sacramentals depends upon the devotion, faith, and love of the person who uses them. As Christ was the invisible God made visible, so sacramentals, like sacraments, are visible signs of his invisible grace.

Sacramentals are sacred signs instituted by the Church. They prepare men to receive the fruit of the sacraments and sanctify different circumstances of life. (CCC 1677). Among sacramentals, blessings (of persons, meals, objects, and places) come first. Every blessing praises God and prays for his gifts. (CCC 1671).

The medals of Jesus King of All Nations and Our Lady of America are special sacramentals for protection.

Jesus said, "*It is my Most Holy Will and desire that there be a medal struck according to the likeness [of me] you have seen. I promise to offer the precious grace of final perseverance to every soul who will faithfully embrace this devotion....I promise to offer the grace of protection....This will especially be true of danger coming from natural disasters.*" (*Journal* 75).

The front side of the Jesus King of All Nations medal shows his image as the God-man King. On the rim of the border are the words "O Jesus King of All Nations, May Your Reign Be Recognized On Earth."

The reverse side of the medal shows St. Michael the Archangel, with the Eucharistic God-man King in the form of the Sacred Host and the Most Precious Blood,. He appears with a sword in his right hand and beneath his feet are the words, "Protect Us!" Jesus requested that around the border should appear the words, "At that time there shall arise Michael, the Great Prince, Guardian of your People." (Daniel 12:1).

Jesus promised those who wear the medal "the grace of protection in times of harm and danger. This will especially be true of danger coming from natural disasters."

The front side of the medal of Our Lady of America shows her image, surrounded by the words, "By thy holy and Immaculate Conception, O Mary, deliver us from evil."

The reverse side of the medal shows the Coat of Arms of the Christian family, with the Triangle of the Trinity and the Eye of Divine Providence on the shield of the Precious Blood through which sanctifying grace was made possible to fallen mankind.

The sanctification of the family, through imitation of the Holy Family, is represented by the Cross and the two lilies, on each of which is depicted a burning heart. The flaming sword is a symbol of divine love that is necessary for union with God, while the Rosary indicates our means of drawing close to the Holy Family through meditation on its mysteries.

The scroll at the top of the medal bears the inscription, "*Gloria Patri et Filio et Spiritu Sancto* (Glory be to the Father and to the Son and to the Holy Spirit.)" Below that is "*Jesu, Maria, Joseph* (Jesus, Mary, Joseph.)"

Sister Mildred, the visionary of the medal, wrote, "Those who wear the medal with great faith and fervent devotion to Our Lady will receive the grace of intense purity of heart and the particular love of the Holy Virgin and her Divine Son. Sinners will receive the grace of repentance and the spiritual strength to love as true children of Mary. As in life, so in death, this blessed medal will be as a shield to protect them against the evil spirits, and St. Michael himself will be at their side to allay their fears at the final hour." (*Diary* 17).

The sacramentals of the Rosary, the Brown Scapular, and the medals of Jesus King of All Nations and Our Lady of America may be ordered from our website:

www.JKMI.com

B. Interviews

The Medjugorje visionary, Mirjana Soldo, was interviewed several times. Excerpts of three of those interviews are included here: by Father Tomislav Vlašić in 1983; by Father Petar Ljubicic in 1985; and by the author, Dan Lynch, in 2010.

Interview with Visionary Mirjana Soldo by Father Tomislav Vlašić

This excerpt is from an interview on January 10, 1983 taken from the book, The Apparitions of Our Lady at Medjugorje, *by Father Svetozar Kraljević.* (Medjugorje, Bosnia-Herzegovina: Information Center "Mir" Medjugorje, 2005). *It has been edited by the author, who deleted irrelevant material.* [In the following, "**T**" is Father Tomislav Vlašić and "**M**" is Mirjana.]

T: Mirjana, we have not seen each other for some time, and I would like you to tell me about the apparitions of the Blessed Virgin Mary, and especially the events that are connected with you.

M: I have seen the Blessed Virgin Mary for eighteen months now, and I feel I know her very well. I feel she loves me with her motherly love, and so I have been able to ask her about anything I would like to know. I've asked her to explain some things about Heaven, Purgatory, and Hell that were not clear to me. For example, I asked her how God can be so unmerciful as to throw people into Hell, to suffer forever. I thought: If a person commits a crime and goes to jail, he stays there for a while and then is forgiven — but to Hell, forever? She told me that souls who go to Hell have ceased thinking favorably of God — have cursed him, more and more. So, they've already become a part of Hell, and choose not to be delivered from it.

Then she told me that there are levels in Purgatory: levels close to Hell and higher and higher toward Heaven. Most people, she said, think many souls are released from Purgatory into Heaven on All Saints' Day, but most souls are taken into Heaven on Christmas Day.

T: Did you ask why God allows Hell?

M: No, I did not. But afterward I had a discussion with my aunt, who told me how merciful God is. So, I said I would ask Our Lady how God could…

T: According to what you've said, then, it's as simple as this: people who oppose God on earth just continue their existence after death and oppose God in Hell?

M: Really, I thought if a person goes to Hell…Don't people pray for their salvation? Could God be so unmerciful as not to hear their prayers? Then Our Lady explained it to me. People in Hell do not pray at all; instead, they blame God for everything. In effect, they become one with that Hell and they get used to it. They rage against God, and they suffer, but they always refuse to pray to God.

T: To ask him for salvation?

M: In Hell, they hate him even more.

T: As for Purgatory, you say that souls who pray frequently are sometimes allowed to communicate, at least by messages, with people on earth, and that they receive the benefits of prayers said on earth?

M: Yes. Prayers that are said on earth for souls who have not prayed for their salvation are applied to souls in Purgatory who pray for their salvation.

T: Did Our Lady tell you whether many people go to Hell today?

M: I asked her about that recently, and she said that, today, most people go to Purgatory, the next greatest number go to Hell, and only a few go directly to Heaven.

T: Only a few go to Heaven?

M: Yes. Only a few — the least number — go to Heaven.

T: Did you ask about the conditions for a person to enter Heaven?

M: No, I didn't; but we can probably say what they are. God is not looking for great believers but simply for those who respect their faith and live peacefully, without malice, meanness, falsehood.

T: This is your interpretation, your understanding?

M: Yes. After I talked to Our Lady, I came to that conclusion. No one has to perform miracles or do great penance; merely live a simple, peaceful life....

T: Well, besides Heaven, Hell, and Purgatory, is there anything else new recently?

M: Our Lady told me that I should tell the people that many in our time judge their faith by their priests. If a priest is not holy, they conclude that there is no God. She said, "*You do not go to church to judge the priest, to examine his personal life. You go to church to pray and hear the Word of God from the priest.*" This must be explained to the people, because many turn away from the faith because of priests.

In our time, the Virgin told me, God and the devil conversed, and the devil said that people believe in God only when life is good for them. When things turn bad, they cease to believe in God. Then people blame God, or act as if he does not exist.

God, therefore, allowed the devil one century in which to exercise an extended power over the world, and the devil chose the twentieth century. Today, as we see all around us, everyone is dissatisfied; they cannot abide each other. Examples are the number of divorces and abortions. All this, Our Lady said, is the work of the devil.

T: You have said that the devil has entered into some marriages. Is his rule limited to those marriages?

M: No. That is just the beginning.

T: This behavior of people—they're under the influence of the devil. But the devil does not have to be in them?

M: No, no. The devil is not in them, but they're under the influence of the devil, although he enters into some of them.

To prevent this, at least to some extent, Our Lady said we need communal prayer, family prayer. She stressed the need for family prayer most of all. Also, every family should have at least one sacred object in the house, and houses should be blessed regularly....

T: Tell me where the devil is especially active today. Did she tell you anything about this? Through whom or what does he manifest himself most?

M: Most of all through people of weak character, who are divided within themselves. Such people are everywhere, and they are the easiest for the devil to enter. But he also enters the lives of strong believers—sisters, for example. He would rather "convert" real believers than nonbelievers. How can I explain this? You saw what happened to me. He tries to bring as many believers as possible to himself.

T: What do you mean, "what happened to me?" Is that what you talked about before?

M: Yes.

T: You have never discussed what happened into my tape recorder. Please try to describe it now, so I can record it.

M: It was approximately six months ago, though I don't know exactly and cannot say for sure. As usual, I had locked myself into my room, alone, and waited for Our Lady. I knelt down and had not yet made the sign of the cross, when suddenly a bright light flashed and a devil appeared. It was as if something had told me it was a devil. I looked at him and was very surprised, for I was expecting Our Lady to appear. He was horrible—he was like black all over and had a...he was terrifying, dreadful, and I did not know what he wanted. I realized I was growing weak, and then I fainted. When I revived, he was still standing there, laughing. It seemed that he gave me a strange kind of strength, so that I could almost accept him. He told me that I would be very beautiful, and very happy, and so on. However, I would have no need of Our Lady, he said, and no need for faith. "She has brought you nothing but suffering and difficulties," he said; but he would give me everything beautiful — whatever I want. Then something in me — I don't know what, if it was something conscious or something in my soul — told me: No! No! No! Then I began to shake and feel just awful. Then he disappeared, and Our Lady appeared, and when she appeared my strength returned — as if she had restored it to me. I felt normal again. Then Our Lady told me, *"That was a trial, but it will not happen to you again."*

T: Did Our Lady say anything else?

M: Nothing else. She told me it would not happen again and that she would talk to me about it later.

T: You said that the twentieth century has been given over to the devil?

M: Yes.

T: You mean the century until the year 2000, or generally speaking?

M: Generally, part of which is in the twentieth century, until the First Secret is unfolded. The devil will rule till then. She told me several secrets and explained them to me; and I have written them down in code letters, with dates, so I won't forget them. If, say, tomorrow a secret is to be revealed, I have a right, two or three days before, to pick whatever priest I want and tell him about it. For example: "The day after tomorrow, such-and-such will happen." The priest, then, is free to do as he thinks best with that information. He can write it out before it happens, then read it to others after it happens. He can also tell it to the people: "Tomorrow, such-and-such will happen." It's up to him to decide what to do with the information."

T: Were these secrets ever revealed before, to anybody in previous generations?

M: I can't answer that.

T: Since you've been told not to talk about them, I won't ask you to. That's all right—as it should be. But I'll ask you if you know when the secrets will be revealed.

M: I know. I know every date of every secret.

T: But you can't say anything about this?

M: I can't.

T: Can we suppose, then, that one of you might say that three secrets would be revealed before the great sign appears; then the rest of the secrets will be revealed, one by one? Is there anything to that?

M: Nothing like that, but something like this. First, some secrets will be revealed—just a few. Then the people will be convinced that Our Lady was here. Then they will understand the sign. When Jakov said that the mayor will be the first one to run to the hill, he meant that generally, people of the highest social class. They will understand the sign as a place or occasion to convert. They will run to the hill and pray, and they will be forgiven. When I asked Our Lady about unbelievers, she said, *"They should be prayed for, and they should pray."* But when I asked again, recently, she said, *"Let them convert while there is time."* She did not say they should be prayed for.

T: You can say nothing specifically until the moment Our Lady says you can?

M: Yes.

T: Can we say that some secrets belong only to you, personally?

M: No. None of the secrets are personally for me.

T: Not you, then, but Ivan [another Medjugorje visionary] has received personal secrets.

M: My secrets are for all mankind generally, for the world, Medjugorje, some other areas, and about the sign.

T: The sign will pertain to this parish?

M: Yes, to Medjugorje. But there is something else.

T: Something else?

M: Nothing for me personally.

T: You have been given the last of the secrets?

M: Yes, the Tenth.

T: Can you tell me what it relates to?

M: I cannot; but I can tell you that the Eighth Secret is worse than the other seven. [Mirjana subsequently corrected this statement and said that it was the *Seventh* Secret that was worse and that was lessened.] I prayed for a long time that it might be less severe. Every day, when Our Lady came, I pestered her, asking that it be mitigated. Then she said that everyone should pray that it might be lessened. So, in Sarajevo, I got many people to join me in this prayer. Later, Our Lady told me that she'd been able to have the secret lessened. But then she told me the Ninth Secret and it was even worse. The Tenth Secret is totally bad and cannot be lessened whatsoever. I cannot say anything about it, because even a word would disclose the secret before it's time to do so.

T: I won't press you. Anyway, though, the Tenth Secret has to do with what will definitely happen?

M: Yes.

T: Unconditionally?

M: Yes, it will happen.

T: What does Our Lady say? Can we prepare ourselves for what will happen?

M: Yes, prepare! Our Lady said people should prepare themselves spiritually, be ready, and not panic; be reconciled in their souls. They should be ready for the worst, to die tomorrow. They should accept God now so that they will not be afraid. They should accept God, and everything else. No one accepts death easily, but they can be at peace in their souls if they are believers. If they are committed to God, he will accept them.

T: This means total conversion and surrender to God?

M: Yes.

T: After these Ten Secrets, after these eighteen months of apparitions, what do you tell the people they should do? What do you say to priests, to the Pope and bishops, without revealing the secrets? What does Our Lady want us to do?…

M: I say to all people: Convert! — the same as she said. *"Convert while there is time!"* Do not abandon God and your faith. Abandon everything else, but not that!

I ask priests to help their people, because priests can cause them to reject their faith. After a man has been ordained, he must really be a priest, bring people to the Church.

The most important point is that the people convert and pray.

T: What is the greatest danger to mankind? What does it come from?

M: From godlessness. Nobody believes — hardly anybody. For example, Our Lady told me that the faith in Germany, Switzerland, and Austria is very weak. The people in those countries model themselves on their priests, and if the priests are not good examples, the people fall away and believe there is no God. I heard of a priest to whom a rich man had left money to build a home for old people, but instead, the priest built a hotel. Now all the people in that city have turned their backs on the faith, because how could a priest not fulfill the last wish of a dying man and, instead, build a hotel and make money for himself? Nevertheless, people must understand that they shouldn't scrutinize a priest's private life but listen to what he says through God — God's Word.

T: Why did Our Lady introduce herself as the Queen of Peace?

M: You know very well that the situation of the world is horrible. There are wars in every part of the world. The situation is very tense. Peace is needed — a just and simple peace. First, peace in the soul; then...

T: So, the message of Our Lady is a message of peace?

M: Yes, Primarily peace of the soul. If a person has it in his soul, he is surrounded by it.

T: Peace comes as result of faith in God and surrender to him.

M: Yes; as a consequence of prayer, penance, and fasting.

T: Our Lady tells us that peace can be achieved that way; but evil things will happen, nevertheless. Why?

M: They have to happen. The world has become very evil. It cares about faith very little. A while ago, I told you what she said when I decided to wear a cross around my neck. How many city people will say with approval, "What a sensible girl," and how many will say instead, "How stupid she is?"

T: I do not remember your saying that to me.

M: Our Lady was telling me at length how faith has declined. For example, now I live in the provincial capital, Sarajevo, and if I put a simple cross pendant around my neck and walked on the streets, how many people would say, or think to themselves, "What a sensible girl!" and what proportion would say or think, "What a stupid or old-fashioned girl?" Nowadays, people curse God, Jesus Christ, his Mother, his Father, day in and day out, habitually. Besides, people have fallen into very evil ways, so that they live in evil routinely. It's no wonder that God is at the end of his patience.

T: Why do you think the Blessed Mother always exhorts the world, over and over again, to prayer and penance?

M: When we pray, we pray to God. (That's what you said in your sermon last night.) In return, we receive peace of soul, tranquility. We have opened our hearts to God, so that God can enter and when we have God in our heart and soul, we cannot cause evil to anybody. We will not curse—do anything evil. We will do good.

T: But Our Lady also says that we should pray for others.

M: We have to pray for anyone we see who is—. For example, I always pray for nonbelievers, because they do not know what is missing in their lives. They have no idea of how much they may have to suffer later. I pray that God will convert them, that he will give then a sign, that he will open their souls so that they can accept the faith.

T: I understand that, with prayer, we open ourselves to God, but Our Lady always seems to stress the need of prayer for others—prayer and fasting. Do you think that prayer and fasting bring a proper balance into the world? Do you feel that prayer and fasting can even partially atone for all the sins of the world?

M: Yes, I do; it's possible. Much can be done through prayer and fasting. Our Lady has said that prayer can stop wars and prevent catastrophes. Prayer and fasting! Of course, prayer can help a struggling human who does not accept God and religion. Moreover, we are obliged to pray that such a person's heart will be opened. Again, I talk to many nonbelievers in Sarajevo and try to explain things to them so that they will gain a least a little understanding. Sometimes, it is not their fault; they received no religious training when they were young. Or later, when they abandoned their faith, no one tried to help them. I pray that God will open such hearts.

T: How do people react when you tell them such things? Do they accept you and what you say?

M: Well, it is usually in the classroom when I talk to people. They do not know that Our Lady has appeared to me. But they soon discover that I'm a believer, because when I hear somebody curse God, I ask them not to do it, at least not in front of me. Then they ask me if I believe, and I tell them I do. That way, we start a conversation, and I try to explain things: about God, who he is, and what he wants us to do. They seem to understand what I'm saying. Many, in fact, ask me to write out a prayer for them so they can say it at night. Really, they accept what I tell them. Only last night, I converted a grownup, a man. When you do something like that, convert somebody, you've introduced them to the faith, and you feel you've done something very important. A great feeling of peace comes into my soul, a special joy. Somehow, your whole soul starts to glitter.

T: Have you received any special messages for priests and bishops?

M: No; but a long time ago, she said that they should accept us, help us as much as they can, and pray more and do penance.

T: Priests and bishops, too?

M: Yes....

T: Did you ever ask about other apparitions in the world — Our Lady's apparitions in our time at other places?

M: She mentioned a man in Germany who caused panic among the people — on buses, trains, and the like — telling them, "*Convert! While there is yet time!*" There are many false prophets in our time, she said, throughout the world, who lie, claiming to see Our Lady or Jesus. This is a great sin, and we should pray for such people. In fact, she and I prayed for fourteen days, exclusively, for false prophets. They do not understand how grave a sin it is to lie about having visions....

T: What is your habit of praying now, and do you have favorite prayers?...

M: I pray the Rosary and I pray for an hour or two, depending on how much time I have. But usually never less than one hour. I pray that God will give me the strength of soul that I can again think and behave normally. I also pray for unbelievers, for their conversion. And for the secrets....

M: When I pray, something comes to me, because I immerse myself in prayer. Then it's as if I'm speaking with someone. I express things in the way I think they should be said, all the while talking to God. Then I go back to saying the regular kind of prayers. Then I pray again in my own words. I say all this out loud....

T: Do you know of any healing that's connected with you?

M: Yes, in Sarajevo. A man wrote to me and thanked me.

T: What happened?

M: I had all that in Sarajevo. I wrote it all down in my notebook. He was in a wheelchair, unable to walk, and he wrote me a very beautiful letter, full of strong emotions, telling me about his suffering. I asked Our Lady to help him, and she told me that he is a firm believer but that he should pray more. He prays, but not for himself. And he should pray for himself, that he might be healed. Anyway, he finally prayed, and I prayed, and after three months he wrote to me again and said he could walk a little. He can get on his feet and walk a little with one crutch. He wrote to thank me.

T: So, Our Lady said that if we pray for a particular need…

M: We should emphasize exactly that: Dear God, I'm praying to be healed of my illness. Pray like that. But pray away from your heart, from the bottom of your soul, with feeling. It does not have to be a "regular" prayer, but a conversation with God. "God, you see my suffering. You know how I am. I'm not complaining, my cross is not too difficult to bear; but I would like to be on my feet again so that I can move around in the world." Like that: conversation, then prayer.

T: How long should we pray?

M: I believe that sick people should speak and pray to God for one hour every day, intimately. I'm sure it would restore their souls and that God would grant them grace.

T: Did Our Lady ever recommend special devotions?

M: She always recommended faith, prayer, and penance. She never mentioned anything special for anybody, whether they were sick or healthy. But as I told you, she said we should direct our prayers, "I am praying for such-and-such." And we should pray with concentration, not race through the words of Our Father. The main thing is not to say the words of a prayer, but to feel them.

T: And fasting?

218

M: She said that sick people do not have to fast. If they do not fast, it is not a sin for them. They can do another good deed instead. For those who are able to fast, it is not enough that they do a good deed instead.

T: Does she say fasting must be on bread and water only, or are other kinds of fasting acceptable?

M: We did not discuss fasting except on bread and water. But probably she meant we should fast only on bread and water.

T: Everybody?

M: Yes—everybody who wants to receive something from God or have God's help.

T: Are there any other points you want to mention?

M: Not that I can remember.

Interview with Visionary Mirjana Soldo by
Father Petar Ljubicic

Mirjana gave the following interview to Father Petar Ljubicic on October 26, 1985, the day after she had her apparition and message regarding the First Secret. The source of the interview is the book Tower of Light. *(Brown, Michael, Tower of Light. Palm Coast, Florida: Spirit Daily Publishing, 2007, pp. 298-303). [In the following, "P" is Father Petar and "M" is Mirjana.]*

P: How would you assess the current situation around the world? How would you personally do all these things?

M: There never was an age such as this one, never before was God honored and respected less than now, never before have so few prayed to him; everything seems to be more important than God. This is the reason why [the Blessed Mother] cries so much. The number of unbelievers is becoming greater and greater. As they endeavor for a better life, to such people, God himself is superfluous and dispensable. This is why I feel deeply sorry for them and for the world. They have no idea what awaits them. If they can only take a tiny peek at these secrets, they would convert in time. Certainly, God always forgives all those who genuinely convert.

P: Did she perhaps alert us to other things you must do, in addition to praying and preparing for that time? Perhaps something concrete?

M: Yes, she told me it is necessary to pray a great deal until the First Secret is revealed. But, in addition to that, it is necessary to make sacrifices as much as possible, to help others as much as it is within our abilities, to fast—especially now, before the First Secret. She stated that we are all obliged to prepare ourselves.

P: Tell me how do you view the situation around you? How do you view the young people around you? I am referring to your peers, the ones you live and interact with?

M [then in her teens and studying in Sarajevo:] Father, I wish you only knew how I feel on some days! There are times when I feel that I could go mad. If Mary wasn't here, if she didn't fill me with strength, by now I would have surely gone mad....When I see how people believe, especially in Sarajevo, how they use God and his Name in their swearing, how thoughtless they are, how they curse God....These wretched ones have no idea what awaits them in the near future. It is then, as I observe them, that I take pity on them. I feel so sorry for them and pray and cry and pray, pray so much for them. I pray to Mary to enlighten their minds because, as Jesus said, they truly do not know what they do....And yet the first two secrets are not all that severe and harsh. What I mean is, yes, they are severe, but not as much as the remaining ones.

P: Are [the secrets] perhaps of a notable, distinct character, or more of a spiritual nature?

M: Distinct. Distinct.

P: Distinct?

M: Yes, distinct. It will be visible. It is necessary in order to shake up the world a little. It will make the world pause and think.

P: Something like a catastrophe?

M: No, it will not be anything as huge as that. That will come later. It will be something that will give the world something to think about seriously, allow it to see that she was indeed here, and to see and realize that there is God, that he exists.

P: After that, will there be anyone who will say, "This is some sort of a natural phenomenon" or along those lines?

M: Perhaps some staunch unbelievers might say something like that after the First and Second Secrets.

P: I am just curious whether anyone will be able to say, "I feel something, that something will happen soon," or something along those lines.

M: Well, you can see there are some rather peculiar things going on in the world. People are unhappy, dissatisfied, avarice reigns everywhere, hardly anyone admits that they ever have enough of anything. Yet, none of this gives any clues about the secret. This secret stands on its own. This secret will abundantly speak for itself and requires no prior clues or signals. [She is probably referring to the First Secret.]

P: Once again, concerning the First Secret, who will experience, see, and be convinced and then be able to say, "Truly, that which has occurred or is occurring is the manifestation of the secret?" Who will be able to see all that?

M: All those who will be here or in the place(s) where the secret will unfold.

P: Let me assume that this involves a specific place. All those who will wish to see and experience this sign or whatever the secret is, will they have to come to that particular place to see and experience this?

M: Well, Father, surely no one wishes to watch disasters, distress, and misfortune. I don't think that this kind of thing attracts people at all. Why would people go to see something of that sort? It is one thing to go and see a sign, quite another to go and see suffering or a disaster. Who would, for example, go to Italy to see a damn collapse? Who has that kind of a desire? I don't think that anyone does — and that is how it will be with this secret. Whatever is in the secret, it will, of course, be something that everyone, everywhere, will immediately hear about.

P: Tell me, if the secret involves a location rather than a condition or situation, wouldn't it be desirable to have as many people as possible see — to have as many eyewitnesses as possible — even though it may not be a joyful thing or something pleasant to look at?

M: Father, it will be obvious....It will be something that people will hear about very far.

P: Out of the Ten Secrets that each of you will receive — and you and Ivanka [Ivanković] already did [now also a third named Jakov Colo] — do you know which of them will be exactly the same? I mean, which secrets will be exactly the same for you, for Ivanka and others?

M: No, I don't know.

P: Someone said that only three of the secrets that each of you received are identical, that all the others are different.

M: The one about the sign is identical, I am positive about that because there will not be six different signs.

P: Not on the same spot.

M: The sign is the same sign. Personally, I never spoke about the secrets with any [of the others.] After all, in the same way that the secrets were entrusted to me, that is how they were entrusted to the others as well.

P: Thus far I have never spoken with you about the permanency of the sign. Each of you maintains persistently that it will be indestructible, permanent, and very large. Accordingly, one will be able to understand it as something tangible.

M: Yes, the sign will be indestructible and permanent. Naturally, it will be clear to everyone that it is not something constructed and erected. Nobody will be able to say that it was brought and placed in that particular spot by, let us say, someone from Medjugorje.

P: The sign's manifestation — will it be during the day or night? By asking that, am I encroaching on the secret?

M: Oh, that is a secret. I cannot answer because that touches upon....The secret already has a specific date and time.

P: Does the secret have a specified minute and second?

M: I know the exact day and the hour.

P: Do you anticipate that there may be some people, some souls, who will perhaps "feel" something, without anyone else's knowledge or anticipation, that something is about to happen and will, therefore, come in large numbers?

M: I do not know. But I did have the opportunity to ask Our Lady something to that effect. I do know that, during the secret's manifestation, there will be spiritual conversions.

P: There will be conversions.

M: Yes, there will be conversions.

P: Do you think that [of those who will convert] a majority of them will be those who were suspicious, who doubted, who didn't believe?…

M: There will be all kinds: those who were just suspicious, those who didn't believe it all, and others.

P: Do you think that there will still be those who will remain hardened—despite the explicit, tangible, visible signs and warnings?

M: Yes.

P: There will be?

M: Yes, there will be.

P: Yes, of course, just as there always were. Even today, so many see the obvious works of God, yet they simply reject him because they are so hardened, just as the Pharisees did.

M: Those are the ones who have shut their souls to God.

P: Let me touch upon Our Lady's lesson in her latest message. It seems that Our Lady is drawing attention to our greatest enemy, Satan. It seems that he is increasing his attacks, that he is attempting to create confusion and entangle the entire situation.

M: He is responsible for the unbelievers. Satan. This is why she said to bless the home with holy water on Saturdays. He is the one who makes people into unbelievers. Who else?

P: Do you think that Godlessness is growing or decreasing today?

M: Father, it is increasing. A miracle is necessary for Godlessness to decrease.

Interview with Visionary Mirjana Soldo by Dan Lynch

I knocked at the door of the home of Mirjana Soldo, one of the Medjugorje visionaries, just in time for my 8:45 a.m. appointment with her on October 23, 2010. There was no answer. After a few knocks, a nervous and embarrassed Mirjana walked up behind me and said that she wasn't ready and needed a few minutes. Then she turned and started to walk quickly away. I called after her, "There's no need to hurry, I'm not going anywhere."

I saw a table on her front patio and arranged it for our interview. I cleared one half of the table and placed two chairs at the end so that we would face each other kitty-corner. She arrived shortly thereafter and I greeted her. [In the following, "**D**" is Dan and "**M**" is Mirjana.]

D. Good morning Mirjana. My name is Dan Lynch. I'm from America. Thank you for receiving me at your home.

M. I don't know why you wanted to see me. [With a quizzical look.]

D. Oh, I'm sorry, I thought that it was explained to you. I'm an author. I wrote this book. [Showing her the first edition of my book.] It's called *The Ten Secrets of the Blessed Virgin Mary.* You're the only visionary that I used as a source for the book. I've read everything that you said about the secrets. However, there are some conflicting reports about what you have said about the secrets and I would like you to verify what I wrote in the book. I want to tell the whole truth.

D. Can we pray? [I raised my arms and prayed, "Come Holy Spirit, come by means of the powerful intercession of the Immaculate Heart of Mary, your well beloved spouse." We then prayed a Hail Mary together and I asked Our Lady, Queen of Peace, to pray for us.]

D. I'm from the State of Vermont. I'm married and have nine children and twenty grandchildren. I'm a retired judge and I've been in the Marian apostolate for over twenty years. I brought my wife and five of my children here to Medjugorje in 1988.

In 1994, in the middle of the war, I returned with 20 pilgrims to pray and fast for the end of the war. Father Svet [Svetozar Kraljević] and I led the pilgrims on a walking peace procession from Medjugorje to Mostar, carrying the 6-foot high Images of Our Lady of Guadalupe and Jesus King of All Nations.

I wrote this book primarily for the unbelievers, not to scare them, but to give them an incentive to convert and to believe. After the First Secret happens, just the way it will be described three days in advance by Father Petar, the unbelievers and many others will want to know what they should do. My book tells them what Our Lady requests and how to respond to her requests.

I think that it will be like Pentecost, when the Jews who were gathered in Jerusalem heard the mighty wind of the Holy Spirit and asked Peter, "What should we do?" Peter answered them, "Repent, and be baptized every one of you in the name of Jesus Christ for the forgiveness of your sins; and you shall receive the gift of the Holy Spirit!" (Acts 2:37-38). So, that's my background. Now can you tell me a little bit about your background and family?

M. I was born in Sarajevo and attended the University of Sarajevo for three years.

D. Did you get your degree?

M. No, it was impossible for me to continue my education because I could not receive permission from the Communist government. They knew me as a "visionary" and I was an enemy of the state which said, "God does not exist in Yugoslavia."

Both of my parents were born in Medjugorje and I used to come here to visit my grandparents when I lived in Sarajevo. The apparitions of Our Lady began here in 1981 while I was visiting. Later, I married my husband, Marco, and moved here in 1989. I have two daughters, Maria, who is now 19 and Veronica, who is now 16.

D. I won't ask you any questions about the details of the secrets or for you to violate any confidence with Our Lady. You know why?

M. Because a secret is a secret.

D. Yes, and do you know what Our Lady would do if I violated your confidence? She would slap me on the hand. [Slapping my right hand with my left as Mirjana laughs.]

M. I never ask Blessed Mary questions. I just listen to what she tells me. She told me, "Choose a priest to whom you will tell the *First* Secret." She emphasized the singular. She did not tell me to tell him all the secrets. I chose Father Petar. I'll tell him the First Secret ten days before it occurs. We will fast and pray together for seven days and then he will announce the secret three days before it occurs. I don't know if each of the secrets will be announced.

D. There are many reports that you had an apparition on October 25, 1985 and an interview with a priest (some say Father Petar) the next day in which you said that you were shown a vision of the First Secret. You allegedly said that it was played before you as though it were a film and that Our Lady told you, "*It is the upheaval of a region of the world.*" Could you tell me about that?

M. I did not have any apparition on October 25, 1985, I did not see that and I did not say that. [**D** is wide-eyed and surprised.]

[Author's note: Please read page 101 and learn that these denials of Mirjana are contradicted by three authoritative reports of three separate apparitions.]

My last apparition of Our Lady was on Christmas Day, 1982, when she gave me the Tenth and Last Secret. I had no apparitions after that except on my birthday [March 18] until 1987. Since then, I have received apparitions on the second of the month. Blessed Mary said that these apparitions are for "*those who do not know the love of God yet.*" And we are not to judge who has or does not have the love of God. Right? You should know that since you are a judge. [Said with a smile.]

D. There are also reports that you said that the secrets involve what Our Lady herself described as "*many horrors.*"

M. I did not say that.

On Christmas Day, 1982, I received the last of my Ten Secrets. Then Blessed Mary gave me all of the Ten Secrets. I received these Ten Secrets at the same time on one thing. It was like...[Mirjana pauses and looks up, searching for words] what the Queens wrote on 150 years ago.

D. You mean a scroll?

M. Yes! Blessed Mary presented it [the scroll] to me and it contained all Ten Secrets and I could immediately read it.

D. I hope you have it in a safe place.

M. Yes, it's in my house.

D. Okay, could you please go in and get it for me? [Said facetiously as Mirjana laughs.]

M. It was in my house in Sarajevo during the war and was brought from there to here in Medjugorje for safekeeping. Others have seen it and can see something, but they see it differently. I showed it to one of my cousins who saw it as a letter asking for help. I also showed it to a friend who saw it as a prayer. Since then, I have not shown it to anyone else because different people see it in different ways, and only I see it as containing the Ten Secrets.

D. There are reports that you will give the scroll to Father Petar before the First Secret, and he will be able to read it.

M. No, regarding my release of the First Secret, Blessed Mary told me, "*You will* tell *the priest ten days in advance.*" [Mirjana emphasized the word "tell" in contrast to the word "give."] Blessed Mary never told me to *give* him the scroll. My only role is to tell Father Petar. My role is not to distribute the secrets to the world.

D. Do each of you six visionaries have the same secrets?

M. We visionaries do not talk to each other about the secrets, so we don't know if we have the same secrets or not.

D. Is the sign one of the secrets or not?

M. It may or may not be a secret. I can't tell you.

D. There are conflicting reports about who the secrets are for. Some reports say that some of the secrets are for the Church and some for your parish. Who are the secrets for? Are some for the parish? Some for the Church or the world or what?

M. All of the secrets are for all of the world, none are just for the parish or the Church.

D. There are conflicting reports about which secret was lessened. Was it the Seventh Secret or the Eighth Secret that was lessened through prayer?

M. It was the Seventh Secret, not the Eighth Secret. After the Seventh Secret was lessened, Blessed Mary told me, "*Never ask this again.*" So, I have not asked for any other secrets to be lessened.

Why can't the secrets be beautiful? Blessed Mary gives us hope.

Now I really must go, I need to prepare lunch for the pilgrims staying here.

D. Oh, I'm sorry, I can come back. Duty first!

M. No, I'm sorry, I'm leaving tomorrow for Italy and have to get ready.

D. Oh, well, [stammering and caught off guard,] would you please give us a summary statement about the secrets?

M. I don't want to talk very much about the secrets, because secrets are secrets. I want to say one thing that is very important. Blessed Mary said, "*What I started at Fatima, I will finish in Medjugorje. My heart will triumph.*"

If the heart of our mother will triumph, we don't need to be scared of anything. It's only important to put our life in her hands and not to think about secrets. We should think about the messages and what she asked for us, so that we can help her Immaculate Heart to triumph.

D. So the most important thing is to respond to her requests for conversion, faith, prayer, and fasting and not to be fearful of any secrets?

M. Yes, look at us visionaries. Look at me. I am always joking, smiling, living my life with God and Blessed Mary with hope, because my faith is hope. I hope in God's love. I hope that he will judge me with love, I don't think about secrets.

D. And the *Catechism of the Catholic Church* defines hope as "the confident expectation of divine blessing." (CCC 2090). Do you have that confidence? That we will receive God's blessing?

M. Yes, Yes, because God is my Father and he loves us and he sends his Mother for so many years here to Medjugorje to help us to find Jesus, to find a good way, where we will meet Jesus and have real peace.

D. Is there anything else that you'd like to add?

M. Yes. I want to ask everybody to pray for those who do not recognize the love of God yet. Because when we pray for them, we pray for us, for our future, because who of us can say, "I am a good believer, I'm doing everything that God wants?" And when we pray for them, we pray for us.

D. And that's why I wrote this book, *The Ten Secrets of the Blessed Virgin Mary,* not to scare people but to help them to prepare for them so that they don't happen or they don't happen severely, because they convert and believe and pray and fast like Our Lady has asked us to do.

M. That's very good that you wrote the book not to scare people. This is important because a mother never scares her children and never gives them a reason to be afraid. She gives them hope and love. Blessed Mary is not coming to Medjugorje so that we are afraid of the future, but so that we have love and peace in the future with her.

D. So you hope that my book gives people hope?

M. I will pray.

D. Father Petar says, "Everything is closer and closer; God has to do something very quickly." Would you comment on that?

M. We can comment in many ways, but, maybe I'll be in front of God tomorrow. I won't have time to wait for secrets, I must change myself today. I always tell the pilgrims, "Don't talk about secrets, don't think about secrets, think of yourself, think of today, where are you today with God? Because you don't know what you will have tomorrow."

D. Thanks very much for seeing me Mirjana, can we get our picture taken?

M. Yes, of course.

[The picture is shown in the front of this book.]

C. The Prayers for Protection of the Jesus King of All Nations Devotion and Other Protection Prayers

The Jesus King of All Nations Devotion is a helpful aid for us to convert and to prepare for and protect against chastisements. The Devotion was granted the *Nihil Obstat* which is a declaration that it contains nothing contrary to faith or morals.

Jesus revealed his only medal in the world and promised us protection if we wore it. Jesus also promised us graces of forgiveness, conversion, healing, and peace, through the practice of the Devotion. The Devotion is practiced by the wearing of the medal; veneration of his image; adoration of the Blessed Sacrament; reception of the sacraments of Penance and the Eucharist; and recitation of the prayers that he revealed. These prayers are provided below.

The Novena in Honor of Jesus as True King

This simple Novena is a most generous gift from Our Lord. Jesus gave these extraordinary promises: "*I promise you that every time you say these Novena prayers I will convert ten sinners, bring ten souls into the One True Faith, release ten souls from Purgatory, many of whom are the souls of priests, and be less severe in my judgment of your nation.*"

The Novena consists of praying once a day over a period of nine days a set of one Our Father, one Hail Mary, and one Glory Be, recited before the following Novena Prayer:

O Lord our God, you alone are the Most Holy King and Ruler of all nations. We pray to you, Lord, in the great expectation of receiving from you, O Divine King, mercy, peace, justice, and all good things.

Protect, O Lord our King, our families and the land of our birth. Guard us, we pray, Most Faithful One! Protect us from our enemies and from your just judgment.

Forgive us, O Sovereign King, our sins against you. Jesus, you are King of Mercy. We have deserved your just judgment. Have mercy on us, Lord, and forgive us. We trust in your Great Mercy.

O most awe-inspiring King, we bow before you and pray; may your Reign, your Kingdom, be recognized on earth! Amen.

The Novena of Holy Communions

This Novena consists of offering nine consecutive Holy Communions in honor of Jesus King of All Nations. Jesus said, "*I desire that the faithful souls who embrace this devotion to me make a Novena of Holy Communions. They therefore shall offer me nine consecutive Holy Communions, and go to Confession during this Novena, if possible, in honor of me as 'Jesus King of All Nations.'*"

Jesus indicated that by "consecutive," he meant nine Communions, one after another, that the soul would receive. They need not be on nine calendar days in a row, just each Communion received, one after the other.

The powerful and unprecedented effects of this Novena were shown to Jesus' Secretary in a vision. She saw Jesus gazing up to Heaven. Nine times he gave a command and an angel came to earth. Jesus explained, "*My daughter, for those souls who will offer me [this] Devotion, I will bid an angel of each of the Nine Choirs, one with each Holy Communion, to guard this soul for the rest of its life on this earth.*"

Jesus wants us to pray this Novena for others and explains its necessity at this time, "*This Novena may be prayed with its promises for another soul, and that soul will also receive additional angelic protection. I urge my faithful ones to offer me this Novena again and again so that I*

*may continue to send down my holy angels for the protection and
assistance of other souls who cannot do this for themselves. In these end-
times, the power of the enemy has greatly increased. I see how greatly my
children are in need of my protection."*

In his great generosity, Jesus granted that, in addition to the
angelic protection, one may have a separate, unrelated intention for
this Novena. He promised, *"What they ask for in this Novena [of Holy
Communions,] if it be according to my Most Holy Will, I will surely grant
it. Let these souls ask from me without reservation."*

The Chaplet of Unity

Jesus spoke these words and promises concerning the Chaplet of
Unity,

*I, Jesus, Son of the Most High God, Who AM Sovereign Lord,
promise to hold out to the souls who pray my Chaplet of Unity the
Scepter of my kingship and grant them Mercy, Pardon, and
Protection in times of severe weather and plagues. I extend this
promise not only for yourselves, but also for individuals for whom
you pray. No, my beloved, sin and evils committed by mankind
are too great, no longer will I spare my judgment to correct the
conscience of mankind as a whole, but this Devotion and Chaplet
prayed with repentance, confidence, and love, will heal, save, and
unite souls to my Mercy who otherwise would be lost. Any harm
or danger, spiritual or physical, whether it be to soul, mind, or
body, will I protect these souls against, and clothe them over with
my own mantle of Kingly Mercy. To this I add the promise of the
assistance of my Most Holy Mother's mediation on their behalf.
Even if you die, you shall not be lost, for you shall know salvation
and union with me in the Kingdom of my Father, where we reign
with the Holy Spirit, eternally the Divine Trinity, One God.*

The Chaplet is recited on ordinary Rosary beads. Groups may
divide the recitation between the Leader (**L**) and the Responders
(**R**). If you are alone, recite both parts.

Recite on the large bead before each of five decades,

L: God our Heavenly Father, through your Son, Jesus, our
Victim-High Priest, True Prophet, and Sovereign King,

R: pour forth the power of your Holy Spirit upon us and open our hearts. In your Great Mercy, through the Motherly Mediation of the Blessed Virgin Mary, our Queen, forgive our sinfulness, heal our brokenness, and renew our hearts in the faith, and peace, and love, and joy of your Kingdom, that we may be one in you.

Recite on the ten small beads of each of the five decades,

L: In your Great Mercy,

R: forgive our sinfulness, heal our brokenness, and renew our hearts that we may be one in you.

Conclude in unison,

Hear, O Israel! The Lord our God is One God!

O Jesus King of All Nations may your Reign be recognized on earth!

Mary, our Mother and Mediatrix of All Grace, pray and intercede for us your children!

Saint Michael, great prince and guardian of your people, come with the holy angels and saints and protect us!

Prayer to Saint Michael the Archangel

Saint Michael the Archangel defend us in battle.

Be our protection against the wickedness and snares of the devil.

May God rebuke him, we humbly pray; and do Thou, O Prince of the Heavenly Host—by the divine Power of God—cast into Hell, Satan, and all the evil spirits who roam about the world seeking the ruin of souls. Amen.

Prayer to Our Guardian Angel

Angel of God, my guardian dear,

to whom God's love commits me here,

Ever this day, be at my side, to light and guard,

to rule and guide. Amen.

The Litany for the Healing of Our Land
By Dan Lynch

In light of the chastisements of pandemics, natural disasters, and violence, we should remember that Jesus has told us, "Let not your heart be troubled." (John 14:1). "In this world you will have trouble. But take heart! I have overcome the world." (John 16:33).

Jesus came to destroy the works of the devil (see 1 John 3:8), so we should not be fixated on the media reports of what are really chastisements. They should inspire our hearts to open in prayer and fasting for the victims and their families and not lead us to craven fear for our own safety. Jesus told us, "Fear is useless; what is needed is trust."(Luke 8:50).

We should not fear the works of the devil or the chastisements that God may allow but pray for their aversion or mitigation or the grace to endure them. We should embrace the Devotion to Jesus King of All Nations and focus our hope on the promise of Our Lady of Fatima for the Triumph of the Immaculate Heart of Mary and a New Era of Peace. "There is hope for your future, says the Lord." (Jeremiah 31:17).

God told King Solomon, "If then my people, upon whom my name has been pronounced, humble themselves and pray, and seek my face and turn from their evil ways, I will hear them from Heaven and pardon their sins and heal their land." (2 Chronicles 7:14).

It is a time to pray for the healing of our land from all evil.

So, let us humble ourselves, turn from our evil ways, and pray to Jesus King of All Nations that he will hear us from Heaven, pardon our sins, and heal our land. Let us pray the following *Litany for the Healing of Our Land* which concludes with *The Prayer in Honor of Jesus as True King*.

O Jesus King of All Nations, we humble ourselves, turn from our evil ways and pray that you will hear us from Heaven, pardon our sins, heal our land from the following evils and bring to conversion those who have not come to know the love of the one true God, for a Culture of Life, a Civilization of Love, and the New Era of Peace.

Response: O Jesus King of All Nations, heal our land.

From contraception,
From abortion,
From same-sex sexual acts,
From false "same-sex marriages,"
From false "transgenderism,"
From no-fault divorce and remarriage,
From premarital sexual acts and co-habitation,
From drug, alcohol, pornography, gambling, and all other addictions,
From abuse and neglect of children and the elderly,
From so-called "assisted suicide,"
From all racism,
From political corruption,
From materialism, scientism, and secular humanism,
From violence, terrorism, and war, and
From sacrilegious communions.

The Prayer in Honor of Jesus as True King

O Lord our God, you alone are the Most Holy King and Ruler of all nations. We pray to you, Lord, in the great expectation of receiving from you, O Divine King, mercy, peace, justice, and all good things.

Protect, O Lord our King, our families and the land of our birth. Guard us, we pray, Most Faithful One! Protect us from our enemies and from your just judgment.

Forgive us, O Sovereign King, our sins against you. Jesus, you are a King of Mercy. We have deserved your just judgment. Have mercy on us, Lord, and forgive us. We trust in your Great Mercy.

O most awe-inspiring King, we bow before you and pray; may your Reign, your Kingdom, be recognized on earth! Amen.

D. The I Can Do This! Checklist for the Laity

Many people ask, "What can *I* do?", in the New Evangelization as requested by St. John Paul II.

As a member of the lay faithful, you are called by your Baptism to be an apostle to bring the Gospel message into the real world, such as your family, neighborhood, work, parish, community, the media, politics, sports, etc.

You are part of the priesthood of the laity who offer, by means of the hands of the priest in the Eucharist, Christ's body and blood, Soul and Divinity, with your entire existence, as praise and thanksgiving to God, as intercessors for the needs of the world, and in reparation and atonement for your sins and the sins of the whole world.

The Eucharist must be the source and summit of your Christian life. This leads to what St. Josemaría Escrivá called a "priestly soul and a lay mentality." From this Eucharistic source, you can propose the Gospel message as the best way to solve the personal and social problems of our times, as the best way to seek peace and justice in the family and among peoples, and as the best way to build what St. John Paul II called "a Culture of Life and a Civilization of Love."

As a Lay Apostle, you are special in God's plan for the New Evangelization. Your mission is to allow the Sacred Heart of Jesus to flow through you, as one of his arteries, to bring his grace, mercy, and love to his body, the Church.

You can be a Lay Apostle! You don't need any special education or training. Just be yourself, and practice your faith, hope, and love. But you can do more than you are doing now. You can do this:

1. Be Holy! Be personally holy, according to your state in life as a husband, wife, mother, father, daughter, son, sister, brother, or single person.

2. Love one another and your enemies. Forgive those who have hurt you. Be kind and gentle to others and respectful of them.

3. Pray the Rosary and the Chaplet of Unity, daily.

4. Consecrate yourself to the Immaculate Heart of Mary and wear the Brown Scapular as a sign of your consecration.

5. Wear the medals of protection of Our Lady of America and Jesus King of All Nations.

6. Sacrifice through fasting on bread and water on Wednesdays and Fridays, if you are able, or make other acts of self-denial, such as renouncing addictive behavior of watching television, using computers, smoking, drinking, etc.

7. Practice the First Friday Devotion of attending Mass and receiving Communion on nine First Fridays of the month in reparation for the offenses committed against the Sacred Heart of Jesus.

8. Practice the First Saturday Devotion of praying the Rosary, meditating for fifteen minutes on the mysteries, attending Mass, and receiving Holy Communion, in reparation for the offenses committed against the Immaculate Heart of Mary, on five First Saturdays of the month with confession within eight days of each First Saturday.

9. Practice Holy Hours of Adoration of the Blessed Sacrament and make visits to the Blessed Sacrament.

10. Learn the Catholic Church's teachings on faith and morals by reading the *Catechism of the Catholic Church* and the Scriptures.

11. Practice apostolic action such as:

    ♦ Be a missionary to the culture by speaking and writing seeds of truth in your own environment to family, neighbors, friends, and co-workers. You may be the only Gospel that someone ever sees or hears!

♦ Communicate with your political representatives in favor of good laws and in protest against bad ones.

♦ Communicate with the media or sponsors in protest against any immorality.

♦ Serve in your parish on the parish council; as a lector; usher; sacristan; singer; teacher of CCD, youth, or RCIA; in a prayer group or Scripture study group; or help with maintenance and repairs.

♦ Serve in your community by works of mercy such as visiting the sick, the poor, and the prisoners; feeding the hungry; comforting the sorrowful; and instructing the ignorant.

♦ Use whatever talents that God gave you to bring his Good News to our Culture of Death in the New Evangelization!

E. The Ruini Commission's Report on Medjugorje

In his book, *Medjugorje Dossier*, released in Italian in February 2020, Italian journalist and writer Saverio Gaeta published the findings of the Vatican's International Theological Commission led by Cardinal Camillo Ruini, which judged the first seven Marian apparitions of Medjugorje credible.

In these previously unpublished writings, the members of the Commission explain the reasons why, by an overwhelming majority (13 out of 15 voters,) they considered that the beginnings of the Medjugorje phenomenon have a supernatural origin and cannot be judged a merely human phenomenon. The following are some of the findings of the Ruini Commission as reported by Saverio Gaeta:

The first seven apparitions

In particular, they [The Commission] believe that they "can affirm with reasonable certainty that the first seven apparitions are intrinsically credible, as they were capable of arousing in those who experienced them a reawakening of faith, a conversion of their way of life, and a renewed sense of belonging to the Church." The apparitions took place from June 24 to July 3, 1981, i.e. over a period of 10 days.

Five of the apparitions took place on Podbrdo ("Apparition Hill",) one in the parish facilities of Medjugorje, and another in the village of Cerno, where the then-visionaries, adolescents at the time, were taken by car by police officers.

What happened to the alleged visionaries

In these seven cases, the author [Gaeta] points out, publishing the Commission's conclusions, it is the Mother of Christ who awaits the visionaries; the "phenomenon" (the Gospa, the Figure) [the local people call the Blessed Virgin Mary "the Gospa"] stands before the visionaries, always in the same place (in the first five); the visionaries remember exactly the place and time of the first apparition; the message is not addressed to individuals, but to all those present (visionaries/hearers); the phenomenon occurs "suddenly" and by surprise; and the phenomenon causes fear and disturbance in the souls of the visionaries.

In subsequent apparitions, the apparition causes less and less surprise and is, in some sense, pre-programmed.

No mental alteration

On the basis of these premises, the examination conducted by the International Commission has led to very clear conclusions regarding Medjugorje.

First of all, the visionaries weren't suffering from any psychological disturbances: teens at the time, "they were normal adolescents, not manipulatable and not unduly influenced by others, able to recognize deception and to take a stance in response to it."

With regard to the previous history of the alleged visionaries: "nothing in [their history] prepared them in any sense for the alleged first seven apparitions of the Gospa; the apparitions are something that bursts into their lives and their experiences without having been requested, sought, desired, imagined, willed, or induced."

There are no ulterior motives

The environment in which the visionaries grew up had "the traits of traditional Christian piety, with a significant Marian aspect due in part to the Franciscan charism, but not such as to make them expect, hypothesize, or desire—and much less to invent with malice—a supernatural manifestation of the holy Mother of the Lord."

With regard to the knowledge then available to the presumed visionaries, both on a cultural level and on the level of Christian truths: "at the moment of the first seven presumed apparitions, they appear not to have any special knowledge, inclinations, or interests that set them apart."

They could not know what was going on in the world

Regarding the degree of participation of the presumed visionaries in ecclesial life at that time: "it is not possible to detect, at the time of the first seven alleged apparitions, any particular protagonism or commitment on their part."

Finally, "with regard to information which could be available to the alleged seers concerning the events then taking place outside Yugoslavia, both in Europe and in the world: it's not abundant, given the typical structures of a totalitarian state such as that of Marxist inspiration founded after the Second World War by Tito (†1980)."

The Commission's "judgment"

All these considerations led the Commission to say that "the results of the investigation show in a sufficiently reasonable way that the object of examination, i.e. the first seven alleged apparitions, manifests an essential and structural character of not being deducible from — and, indeed, exceeding — the history, identity, and possibilities of both the alleged seers and their living environment."

In practice, the visionaries, or presumed visionaries, did not have the characteristics to invent such a detailed phenomenon of such magnitude. "At the same time," writes the Commission, "the unpredictable and special religious bond that the event introduces into the experience of its first recipients appears compatible with the supernatural character of the sign."

A "familiar" Gospa

The first seven apparitions aroused in them "a subjectivity, a responsibility, and a protagonism for which the presumed visionaries were neither prepared nor accustomed." The subject of the first seven alleged apparitions, the Gospa, "presents herself with characteristics and familiarity that are unprecedented with regards to what the alleged visionaries might have known about her."

The devil has nothing to do with it

Also, the object of the requests/messages, "namely peace in its essentially theological dimension, acquires an urgency, a dimension, and a meaning that extends well beyond the horizons already possessed, lived, and desired by the presumed visionaries and their living environment."

The report excludes "the hypothesis of a demonic origin for the beginnings of the phenomenon;" such a hypothesis "appears gratuitous and unfounded, being in contrast with what has been observed in the initial profile of the phenomenon, as well as with the positive fruits derived from the phenomenon itself."

Indissoluble link with Christ

The theological elements that unite the first seven apparitions show that "the subject, the Gospa, manifests and maintains an indissoluble bond with the Christ of God, and her person and her actions are incomprehensible outside of this bond."

The requests/messages of the subject, the Gospa, "have a theological structural dimension, both in their cognitive-intellectual dimension and in their practical-operational dimension."

Lastly, the report says that the Gospa's manifestation "revives in the presumed visionaries the sense of their belonging to the Church."

On the basis of these data, the International Commission believes that it can affirm with reasonable certainty that the first seven apparitions are intrinsically credible.

Bibliography

- Connell, Janice, *The Visions of the Children*. New York, New York: St. Martin's Press, 1992, 1997.

- Connell, Janice, *Meetings with Mary*. New York, New York: Ballantine Books. 1995.

- Connell, Janice, *Queen of the Cosmos*. Orleans, Massachusetts: Paraclete Press. 1990.

- Čović-Radojičić, Mirjana Sabrina, *Mirjana Dragičević Soldo, Visionary of Our Lady in Medjugorje*, 2015. A book collection of interviews with Mirjana Soldo available in digital form online from Amazon books.

- de Montfort, St. Louis, *True Devotion to Mary*. Charlotte, North Carolina: TAN Books and Publishers Inc. 2007.

- Fanzaga, Padre Livio, *La Madonna Prepara per il Mondo un futuro di Pace*. Italy: Editrica Shalom. 2002.

- Kraljević, Svetozar, OFM *The Apparitions of Our Lady at Medjugorje*. Medjugorje, Bosnia-Herzegovina: Information Center "Mir" Medjugorje. 2005.

- Laurentin, René, *The Apparitions at Medjugorje Prolonged*. Milford, Ohio: The Riehle Foundation. 1987.

- Laurentin, René, and LeJeune, René, *Messages and Teachings of Mary At Medjugorje, Chronological Corpus of the Messages*. Milford, Ohio: The Riehle Foundation. 1988.

How to Practice the Devotion Through Its Image, Prayers, Medal, Promises, and Graces
www.JKMI.com

READ The Booklet!

THE REMEDY for our times! Newly revised. Read about the origin of the Devotion, the Kingship of Jesus, how *we* can recognize Jesus as King of All Nations, and the promises and prayers of the Devotion. Read about signs, wonders, healings, and conversions!

HEAR
The Story and
PRAY
The Prayers

READ The Journal

The Journal contains all of the visions, revelations, and messages of Jesus in this Devotion.

"One must read the full account of The Journal *to have a comprehensive view and insight concerning the rich spiritual treasures of the Devotion, and the vital apostolate outlined there for our times, NOW TIMES! And get the medal!" Rev. Albert J. Hebert* Granted the *Nihil Obstat* which declares that *The Journal* contains nothing contrary to faith and morals.

Jesus said,
"Enthrone this my image everywhere for I shall be powerfully present there..."

WEAR The
Medal

CARRY
The Package

SPREAD the
Introductory
Pamphlet to
others.

Display and Venerate
The Image

Jesus said,
"This image, my child, must become known. Tremendous will be the miracles of grace that I will work through this image and Devotion of Mine."

Help the Reign of Jesus King of All Nations to be Recognized on Earth by Enthroning His Image!
www.JKMI.com

"Take up my devotion of Jesus King of All Nations for in its practice you shall find for yourselves a haven of Grace, Mercy, and Protection. ***Enthrone this my image everywhere*** *for I shall be powerfully present there and the Power of my Sovereign Kingship shall surely shield you from my just judgment." (Journal 418).*

Honor Jesus by enthroning his Image in your home, parish, or school! Dan Lynch shares with you the Devotion to Jesus King of All Nations and then guides you step-by-step through the process of enthroning and consecrating your home, parish, or school to Jesus King of All Nations. We have everything you will need to make your enthronement. Pass this tradition to the next generation to ensure continued devotion to and trust in Jesus well into the future.

| Beautiful Color Images of Jesus King of All Nations on canvas | 8 x 13 Unframed Jesus King of All Nations Image | Framed Jesus King of All Nations Image | The ONLY medal revealed by Jesus for protection! This unique medal is manufactured exclusively for us. |

**Perhaps Jesus is Calling _You_ to Host a
Visitation of His Image.**

Visitations of the Image of Jesus King of All Nations are for the mission of bringing the recognition of his Reign on Earth. Our apostolate coordinates Visitations of the Image to parishes and homes. We train local Guardian Teams for parish Visitations. These Teams prepare for the Visitations in cooperation with the local pastors.

The Visitations consist of Holy Hours of Prayer for Life, Peace, and Protection from a booklet with the recitation of the prayers of the devotion and veneration of the Image. There is a talk explaining the Image and the messages of Jesus. Religious goods are available for sale to promote the devotion. The Visitations include works of mercy such as visits to hospitals, nursing homes, prisons, and schools.

For more information sign up on our website at www.JKMI.com.

Perhaps Our Lady of Guadalupe is Calling _You_ to Host a Visitation of her Missionary Image.

St. Pope John Paul II said, "May Our Lady of Guadalupe cross this continent bringing it life, sweetness, and hope!"

St. John Paul II prophesied, "Through Our Lady of Guadalupe's powerful intercession, the Gospel will penetrate the hearts of the men and women of America and permeate their cultures, transforming them from within."

You may help fulfill St. John Paul II's prophecy by hosting Visitations of the Missionary Image of Our Lady of Guadalupe and celebrating with Masses, holy hours, processions, and merciful visits to parishes, schools, abortion centers, prisons, convents, hospitals, and nursing homes.

The Image is surrounded by signs, wonders, healings, and conversions.

Commissioned, blessed and certified by the Basilica Shrine of Our Lady of Guadalupe in Mexico City and traveling the world since 1991.

For more information sign up on our website at www.JKMI.com.

More Books by Dan Lynch

Our Lady of America, Our Hope for the States

- The only canonically approved private devotion of Our Lady from the United States.
- Approved messages and requests for Purity and Peace and the promise of Protection.
- The Divine Indwelling of the Most Holy Trinity.

Our Lady of Guadalupe, Hope for the World

"This book will instruct, encourage, and inspire a wide variety of people in the Church and outside the Church. You may be a priest seeking new ways to call your people to a deeper faith.

"Whoever you are, give this book some of your time, and it will repay you abundantly."

Fr. Frank Pavone, National Director, *Priests for Life*

I Will Sing of Mercy: The Journal of the Secretary of the Jesus King of All Nations Devotion

Known as *The Journal*, it contains all of the visions, revelations, and messages of Jesus in the Jesus King of All Nations Devotion.

"One must read the full account of *The Journal* to have a comprehensive view and insight concerning the rich spiritual treasures of the Devotion, and the vital apostolate outlined there for our times, NOW TIMES! And get the medal!"   Rev. Albert J. Hebert

Saints of the States

"This book is a wonderful contribution to appreciate the rich spiritual heritage we possess in the lives of so many heroic men and women of America. Dan Lynch traces the historical development, both secular and religious, through the centuries.

"Dan Lynch has produced a very enjoyable, enriching, and inspiring book. It challenges us to do in our times what these holy men and women did in their own.

Father Andrew Apostoli, CFR

The Gospel of Love

"The *Gospel of Love* is unlike any other book about St. John the Evangelist. It's an accurate, historical fictional autobiography written from John's own point of view. While reading your way through it, you will feel like you are right there with John in 1st century Israel and Ephesus.

"This is a fabulous book! I really hope that it inspires many people who will share it with their friends and relatives.

"When I read my Foreword aloud to my 91-year-old mother, she said, 'I want to read that book just from listening to what you said about it.' Bravo Dan!"

— From the Foreword by Erin von Uffel, DM
(Dame in the Order of Malta)
Vice Postulator of the cause for the canonization of
Sister Marie de Mandat-Grancey

"You will experience John's life as if you were with him nearly 2000 years ago. You will experience John's innermost thoughts and doubts as he struggles to accept Jesus Christ as the Messiah, the Son of Man and the Son of God, and His teachings that constitute the Gospel of Love. You will see John's transformation from tempestuousness to tranquility as he gradually comes to know and believe in the love that God has for all of us.

"More importantly, you will come away with a deeper understanding of how the Gospel of Love taught by Jesus affected John's character and growth in sanctity and how its reading can do the same for you.

"Nothing is so important in life as to grow in holiness by fulfilling the first and second laws of the Gospel: love of God who is love itself and love of neighbor as oneself made in the image and likeness of God. Nothing in life is so sad as not to have become a saint by loving God and neighbor as Jesus does.

"Our thanks to Dan Lynch for this inspiring work!"

— Fr. Peter M. Damian Fehlner, OFM Conv., Author and Theologian

The Coming Great Chastisement and the Great Renewal

We are living in very perilous times. Most people can sense that there is something very wrong with our culture.

Jesus King of All Nations has prophesied a Great Chastisement as an act of his justice and mercy to bring humanity back to a relationship of love with him.

Because of the evils of his secularist enemies, Jesus King of All Nations will intervene in human history. He warned us, *"Awake! Lift up your heads my people! Do you not see the signs all around you?! A great catastrophe is about to befall you! Great is the chastisement that is ready to descend upon this sinful world to correct the consciences of individuals and the conscience of mankind as a whole!"*

However, there is hope for the world. Jesus King of All Nations said, for those who embrace his Devotion, *"I will cover them with my kingly mantle that my perfect justice may not reach them as it will reach those who abandon my law. My children, dear children, do not despair. There is always hope. I have told you of the remedy: the public practice of my Devotion and veneration of my Image.*

"My Kingdom, my Reign is near at hand. My Most Holy Mother is preparing the great triumph. The Triumph of Her Immaculate Heart ushers in the Reign of my love and mercy. My Spirit shall once more descend replete with the cleansing fire of his love. A fire ablaze with the love and justice of God. Let it also be known that a Great Renewal of my Holy Church, of Mankind, and, indeed, of all Creation will follow the cleansing action of my justice."

Learn more from my upcoming book shown on the next page and sign up on our website at www.JKMI.com.

COMING SOON ....

"Dan Lynch has been a zealous promoter of Heaven's causes for many years. In this tremendous magnum opus of his, we find a treasure chest of wisdom for guiding the faithful in these pivotal and perilous times in which we now live (and the unprecedented upheavals of which we stand on the cusp.)

"Indeed, no one who reads this book with an open heart will be able keep his head buried in the sand regarding the Signs of the Times. And, just as importantly, no such reader will either fail to be filled with hope — for what Dan presents to us is not the *Eschatology of Despair* promoted today by a few, but rather he prophetically proclaims the same thing Pope Pius XI did almost 100 years ago in *Quas Primas*: Our Lord Jesus Christ is the King of all the Nations, and we must acknowledge him as such so as to hasten his Reign on earth.

"Do you want that Reign to come soon? Then heed the admonitions presented within these pages. Or, would you prefer that the world continue to limp on in its present agony, mired in evil more than at any point in history, with souls falling into Hell like snowflakes? Then simply ignore these admonitions and pretend that 'ignorance is bliss.'

"I hope that the choice between those two options does not present a difficult decision for anyone. Even if it does, however, it will not remain difficult as you read what Dan has written here. For what is contained within this work is not some rhetorical diatribe like those we are so used to hearing these days; instead, it is meticulously researched and cited throughout, and any reader is bound to derive a veritable education from reading its many quotations from Scripture, Magisterium, Private Revelation, History, and everything in between."

--Daniel O'Connor. Philosophy professor and author of *The Crown of History* and *The Crown of Sanctity*.

255

ABOUT THE AUTHOR

 Dan Lynch is a former judge who is the founder of Dan Lynch Apostolates which promote devotion to Our Lady of Guadalupe, Jesus King of All Nations, Our Lady of America, and St. John Paul II. He coordinates journeys of Missionary Images for veneration and Holy Hours of Prayer for Life, Peace, and Protection. He is an author and a public speaker on radio and television and at conferences, missions, and retreats. He is pictured here with the Missionary Image of Our Lady of Guadalupe.

He produced the video, *Our Lady of Guadalupe, Mother of Hope,* and is also the author of:

Our Lady of Guadalupe, Hope for the World which explains the history of Our Lady of Guadalupe and her modern mission to end abortion and bring a Culture of Life through conversions in the New Evangelization.

Our Lady of America, Our Hope for the States which explains the only canonically approved private devotion from the United States and contains prayers and requests.

Saints of the States which tells the story of the development of Catholicism in the United States through biographies of its saints and blesseds.

*I Will Sing of Mercy: The Journal of the Secretary of the Jesus King of All Nations Devotion (*editor) that contains all of the visions, revelations and the messages of Jesus King of All Nations.

The Gospel of Love, an historical fictional autobiography of St. John, the Beloved Disciple of Jesus King of All Nations.

Dan enjoys hiking, biking, kayaking, boating, and fishing. He and his wife, Sue, live in Vermont. They are the parents of nine children, the grandparents of twenty-five, and the great-grandparents of one.

Made in the USA
Middletown, DE
10 July 2021